Exemplary Public Libraries

Hattiesburg Public Library. See Chapter 9.

Exemplary Public Libraries

Lessons in Leadership, Management, and Service

Joy M. Greiner

Foreword by Bernadette R. Storck

Libraries Unlimited Library Management Collection
Gerard B. McCabe, Series Adviser

A Member of the Greenwood Publishing Group

Westport, Connecticut • London

Library of Congress Cataloging-in-Publication Data

Greiner, Joy Marilyn.
    Exemplary public libraries : lessons in leadership, management, and service /
Joy M. Greiner.
       p. cm.—(Libraries Unlimited library management collection)
    Includes index.
    ISBN 0–313–31069–6 (alk. paper)
    1. Public libraries—United States—Case studies. 2. Public libraries—Great Britain—
Case studies. I. Title. II. Series.
    Z731.G75   2004
    027.473—dc22   2004046516

British Library Cataloguing in Publication Data is available.

Library of Congress Catalog Card Number: 2004046516
ISBN: 0–313–31069–6
ISSN: 0894–2986

First published in 2004

Libraries Unlimited, 88 Post Road West, Westport, CT 06881
A Member of the Greenwood Publishing Group, Inc.
www.lu.com

Printed in the United States of America

The paper used in this book complies with the
Permanent Paper Standard issued by the National
Information Standards Organization (Z39.48–1984).

10 9 8 7 6 5 4 3 2 1

Contents

Part III: Closing

Foreword

Bernadette R. Storck

This book brings together a selection of libraries from a mix of historical backgrounds and diverse locales. Dr. Joy Greiner introduces the reader to two examples of libraries in Great Britain—one in Scotland, one in England. The first is linked to all of modern library history through its founder, Andrew Carnegie. Dunfermline, Scotland, benefited from the largesse of Carnegie in 1879. The second selection is the Croydon Library system, comprised of a central library and twelve branches, which, along with other agencies, provide library service to one of London's boroughs. Both profiles include a mission statement, a historical background, and interviews with local librarians.

The author then moves to the United States, and all of Part II, Section A: From the Heartland—A Midwestern City Library is devoted to an in-depth study of Chicago Public Library. Dr. Greiner provides a thorough review of the history, philosophy, and current practices of this large midwestern library. Through lengthy interviews with prominent leaders the reader learns a great deal about the management of Chicago's libraries. As with the previous entries, as well as all of those that follow, the mission statement is included and becomes the focal point for a test of whether the library actually meets its stated goals.

The author's discussions with commissioner Mary Dempsey, assistant commissioners Barbara Ford, who heads the central library, Charlotte Kim, who guides neighborhood services, and Sheryl Nichen-Keith, who supervises collections, and Kathleen Weibel, the director of staff development, provide the reader with an overview of each function and how they mesh to manage a large system of seventy-eight libraries with a staff of 1,500, serving a population of 2.9 million. No small challenge!

Dr. Greiner moves next to the West Coast, where she gives a full review to the San Francisco, San Diego, and Pierce County, Washington, libraries profiled in her study. San Francisco's role as a very political city is conveyed clearly in both the historical background and the interviews. Another interesting aspect in this review is the discussion of the library in the wake of the 1906 earthquake, in which Dr. Greiner offers a vignette of how individuals and other libraries come forth to help a library in a time of tragedy.

San Diego Public Library dates its history to its founding in May 1882 and its support to a tax levy in October 1882, though there were significant events in the library's history prior to that year. Staff development and training are given special emphasis in this section.

The Pierce County Library System is headquartered in Tacoma. The service population numbers about half a million and is reached via seventeen service outlets. The library, an independent municipal corporation, takes a different approach to staffing by employing people from a variety of educational and experiential backgrounds for various positions.

The libraries of the western states are represented here by the Denver and Fort Worth libraries. Each profile includes a mission statement, historical review, and appropriate interviews. Among Denver's historical notes: Its first director was John Cotton Dana, a luminary in the library world. According to the reference included in the story of Fort Worth Library, one of the women who started the library asked Andrew Carnegie for the donation of a price of a cigar and received a gift of $50,000.

For the southern states, Dr. Greiner selected the Library of Hattiesburg, Petal, and Forrest County, Mississippi, and the DeKalb Library, located in Decatur, Georgia. Some details about a successful bond campaign in Hattiesburg provide a lesson for those who might be planning such an effort. The DeKalb discussion revolves to some extent around the administration philosophy on strengthening the role of middle management. The interviews with the two library directors offer a variety of personal approaches to management.

Dr. Greiner concludes with a summary chapter and a look to the future. A thorough bibliography is included. As an addition to a series on library management, this book offers plenty of material for study, review, and adaptation for public libraries of all sizes.

Bernadette R. Storck is now retired. She was with the Tampa-Hillsborough County Library System for thirty years before moving to Pinellas County. The Pinellas Public Library Cooperative was formed in 1990, and Storck was hired as its first administrator. The headquarters building in Clearwater was named in her honor. Storck also served as an adjunct instructor for the University of South Florida School of Library and Information Science for more than twenty years.

Acknowledgments

I wish to thank the library administrators, their assistants, and the senior library staff for their cooperation in this study. Participants in Great Britain and the United States gave their time to the interview process, read drafts of the interviews, made insightful recommendations, and approved the final submissions.

In Dunfermline, Dorothy Miller, librarian; Chris Neale, information services librarian; David Arnott, Fife councillor, Scotland; and Bill Runciman, secretary of the Carnegie Dunfermline Trust, participated in interviews. Ann Rodwell, the local history librarian at the Dunfermline Carnegie Library, directed me to valuable resources. In Croydon, Adie Scott, head of libraries, and Brenda Constable, central library manager, shared the philosophy of service that guides the successful Croydon Libraries.

Mary Dempsey, Chicago Public Library commissioner, and senior management staff Barbara Ford, Charlotte Kim, Sheryl Nichin-Keith, Kathleen Weibel, Donna Maloney, Karen Lyons, Kathy Biel, Amy Eshleman, and Jamey Lundblad generously shared their time and expertise. Leah Steele, Sulzer Regional Library manager, hosted tours of the Near North Branch library and the Sulzer Regional Library.

Susan Hildreth, city librarian in San Francisco, and Marcia Schneider, director of public affairs of the San Francisco Public Library, participated in interviews. Anna Tatar, current director of the San Diego Public Library, and the former director, William Sannwald, in the San Diego city manager's office, shared information, as did Neel Parikh, director of the Pierce County Library System.

Rich Ashton, city librarian, Denver Public Library; Dr. Gleniece Robinson, director of the Fort Worth Public Library, and her administrative assistant, Tessie Hutson; Pamela Pridgen, director of the Library of Hattiesburg, Petal, and Forrest County; and Darro Willey, director of the DeKalb County Library, also participated in interviews.

Nerida Hague, assistant to Commissioner Dempsey in Chicago; Rachelle Naishut, administrative assistant to Rick Ashton at the Denver Public Library; and Nancy Van Tone in the administrative office at the Decatur Library facilitated communication, arranged interviews, and provided travel and housing information.

I am grateful for the dedication of research assistant Rebecca Campbell during the process of transcribing interviews, and for graduate assistant Lynn Moore, also involved in the transcribing process, and in the organization of information, particularly for the British and United States time lines. Linda Ginn was primarily involved in the final stages of the project. I appreciate her editing and proofreading skills.

Special thanks are due to Gerard McCabe, who was my editorial adviser throughout this process. I am also grateful to Bernadette Storck, retired administrator for the Pinellas Public Library Cooperative in Pinellas County, Florida, who read the manuscript and wrote the foreword.

Introduction

During my experience as a public librarian in the United States, I became increasingly interested in the development, characteristics, and purposes of public libraries. Libraries in Great Britain gained my attention when, as a faculty member in the British Studies Program from the School of Library and Information Science at the University of Southern Mississippi, I guided students through libraries and museums in London and nearby. On a later trip to England and Scotland, I visited Andrew Carnegie's birthplace, in Dunfermline, Scotland. The Dunfermline Carnegie Library was the first public library built with funds donated by Andrew Carnegie.

Questions emerged during visits to historic libraries in Great Britain and the United States. What makes a library successful, what qualities do these libraries share, and what can other libraries learn from these outstanding libraries? The purpose of this research was to find and share the answers to these questions.

Part of my research endeavor was to examine the history and development of selected public libraries in Great Britain and the United States. What were the initial missions of the libraries, and how do they relate to their missions for the new century? The relationship of the current library to the original library, and the unique qualities of the contemporary library were specific areas of interest.

What were the philosophies of library benefactors who were responsible for the earliest public libraries? For example, how does the philosophy of Enoch Pratt, founder and benefactor of Baltimore's public library, relate to that articulated by library leaders in the twenty-first century? In 1882, Enoch Pratt is attributed to have said, "My library shall be for all, rich and poor without distinction of race or color, who, when properly accredited, can take out the books if they will handle them carefully and return them" (Enoch Pratt Free Library 2002).

What are the management philosophies and behaviors of the current library administrators? How do they relate to governance and organizational structure? The role of the library administrator in the political environment was examined. Implementation of technology, budgets, alternative funding, downsizing, partnering with other libraries, community agencies, and other organizations, marketing and public relations, and services to special populations were examined.

My goal was to project administrative philosophies and behaviors as blueprints for public library growth and development in the twenty-first century. Interview questions, designed to gather information about professional philosophies and effective management behaviors, garnered insights on the order of "This worked, but this failed." What primary variables are influencing the library and the management behaviors of the administrators? What are the projections for the future of libraries in general and for the individual institutions? I collected data through observations in libraries and personal and telephone interviews with chief administrators, senior management staff, administrative assistants, and public relations officers. Meetings with appropriate government authorities and a funding organization representative supplemented information about the organizational structures of the libraries and library systems.

Qualitative studies of two public libraries in Great Britain and eight public libraries in the United States were conducted over a period of three years (1999–2002). My communication with the staff of these libraries continued into the year 2003. I collected information about the histories of the original libraries, as well as data about the libraries today. Current data included sizes of populations served, organizational structures, visions and missions, and current activities and achievements.

I chose libraries for the uniqueness of their historical missions and for their current innovative resources and services. This was not a comparative study. My sample did not allow for comparison, nor was this the intent. However, the libraries in Great Britain represent the best in libraries of that country, and the libraries in the United States are indicative of excellence in libraries here.

How does the original mission of a public library in England or Mississippi relate to the perception of that library's responsibility to the citizens in Great Britain or in the southern United States at the beginning of the twenty-first century? How have the architects of public library growth and development anticipated and fashioned the changes that would ensure that public libraries would address the requirements of their citizen clientele?

The Croydon central library manager explained it best when she said, "The public library movement was for the improvement of the working man by access to books—1850s education. Now we think in terms of lifelong learning, equalities, and the delivery of a library service that meets real needs" (see Chap. 2, interview with A. Scott and Constable). In the 1850s, books were the only source of public education.

The libraries in this qualitative study ranged in size of population served from 72,000 to 2.9 million. The dates of the establishment of the libraries are as follows: The Chicago Public Library opened in 1873, two years after the great Chicago fire in 1871; the San Francisco Public Library opened on June 7, 1879; the San Diego Public Library, on May 19, 1882; the Dunfermline Free Library, in 1883; the Denver Public Library, in 1889; the Croydon Public Library, on March 31, 1890; the Fort Worth Public Library, in 1901; the DeKalb Public Library, in 1907; the Hattiesburg Public Library, in 1916; and the Pierce County Library District was established in 1946.

Historical information was available in the local history collections of the libraries. Library minute books provided insight, in their own words and handwriting, of the philosophies and expectations for the public library of the citizens who supported these institutions to serve the common man. Published histories of libraries were valuable resources, as were the current library Web pages.

I initially contacted library administrators by regular mail, e-mail, or telephone. After describing the planned research, I requested the participation of the administrators. I taped some of the interviews and took written notes for others. After compiling the interview transcripts, I submitted the drafts to the participants for their identification of inaccuracies, recommended changes, and approval. After incorporating information from the administrators' responses, I submitted a second draft to them for their approval. The final copy was made from the approved second draft.

Administrators and staff in all of the libraries graciously and willingly talked about their libraries, their concerns, and their creative plans for the future. They provided pertinent information about their libraries and the communities they served and conscientiously reviewed the interview transcripts for accuracy. They continue to share information about awards received, the opening of new branches, and other details on the current status of the libraries in 2003.

I have devoted a significant portion of this book to the Chicago Public Library. There are good reasons why I gave so much coverage to the library system of one of the United States' largest cities.

First, so much is happening in Chicago, a city of great vitality. In his book *Miami and the Siege of Chicago*, novelist Norman Mailer described Chicago as the last of the great American cities (Mailer 1968, 90). This city, celebrated in poetry and song, is a city of great diversity, a melting pot in its own right of many ethnic cultures, from its beginnings as a magnet for immigrants from several different countries, to this day. Like New York in the East, Chicago is a city where the promise of the words emblazoned on the Statue of Liberty can be fulfilled.

The city's cultural diversity with its many ethnic neighborhoods poses a serious challenge to a library system that attempts to fulfill its service obligations to every resident. Public libraries throughout the country face the challenges that today's increasing diversity brings.

Jesse Shera, a highly respected scholar of public libraries in the United States, defined the public library as a social agency rather than a social institution. He did this to help us better understand the relationship of the library to its social environment. Shera distinguished the social agency from the social institution by describing the social institution as primary and basic, and the social agency as secondary and derived. The family and the state, he asserted, are institutions. The school, library, and museum, he said, are agencies. Shera concluded that the agency is the instrument of the institution, and the objectives of the public library are reflections of the transformations in society (Shera 1965, v, vi).

Chicago Public Library fits Shera's description well. Indeed, Chicago is somewhat of a microcosm of the world at large, and the libraries of Chicago give us a path to follow in serving a broad public. Readers of this book working in the smaller cities and towns of this country can find helpful information gleaned from the staff of this library. Students thinking of public library careers will find inspiration in their reading about Chicago Public Library and the other libraries discussed in this book. Chicago is a great city, and its library pursues its obligation with dedication and zeal. With this example, readers can see how the same fervor drives the libraries of the other American cities covered in this book.

Public libraries of the United States, like their British counterparts, have a challenging mission in this modern world, and their competent and well-trained staffs pursue service to their communities with diligence. The libraries examined in this work can be viewed by readers as benchmarks of service to their communities. It is my hope that they will inspire and teach a new generation, showing us the path to our future.

References

Enoch Pratt Free Library. 2002. "Enoch Pratt's Legacy: A History of the Enoch Pratt Free Library, Every Person's Favorite Library." http://www.epfl.net/info/history (accessed November 8, 2003).

Mailer, Norman. 1968. *Miami and the Siege of Chicago*. New York: Signet Books.

Shera, Jesse. 1965. *Foundations of the Public Library*. North Haven, CT: The Shoe String Press. (Orig. pub. 1949.)

Part I

Selected Public Libraries in the British Isles

Section A

Scotland and England

Preview: Selected Public Libraries in the British Isles

In Great Britain, I arranged a series of interviews in Dunfermline, Scotland, and at the Croydon Central Library in London. I conducted interviews with the librarian and the information services librarian at the Dunfermline Carnegie Library, as well as with a Fife councillor, who was vice chairman of Fife Council's Community Services with responsibility for libraries and museums, and with the secretary of the Carnegie Dunfermline Trust. I also met with the head of libraries and the central library manager at the Croydon Central Library in London. Many rewarding hours were spent in the local history rooms of each of the libraries.

W. A. Munford, city librarian, Cambridge, identified similarities in the establishment of town libraries in Great Britain and the United States. "The parallel development of libraries in the United States cannot, however, be entirely overlooked. . . . That upsurge of articulate, near-democratic opinion, which was so marked a feature of the social and political history of the seventeenth century, produced town libraries in Boston, Concord and New Haven just as it produced those of Bristol, Leicester and Manchester. . . . The Reverend Thomas Bray and his associates were active, not only in Britain but also in Maryland. . . . The American Library Association and the Library Association were born within a year of each other. Carnegie benefactions nourished the libraries of both countries" (Munford 1968, v, vi).

The stated purpose of the Library Association in Great Britain, established October 1877, was to provide a stimulus for "a measure of professional expertise" and a "sense of professional solidarity" (Kelly 1977, 100). The American Library Association (ALA) was founded in 1876 (Bobinski 1969, 8). The current mission of the ALA is "to provide leadership for the development, pro-

3

motion and improvement of library and information services and the profession of librarianship in order to enhance learning and ensure access to information for all" (American Library Association 1997, 1).

Jesse Shera identified causal factors in free public library development as "historical scholarship and the urge to preservation, the power of national and local pride, the growing belief in the importance of universal education, the increasing concern with vocational problems, and the contribution of religion" (Shera 1965, 243). More broadly, he considered the example of Europe as a contributing factor in terms of the transfer of organizational patterns and the role of the library in the integration of an emerging culture (Shera 1965, 243).

In Great Britain, individuals who were influential in library development included two members of Parliament, William Ewart and Joseph Brotherton, and librarian Edward Edwards, all strong proponents of the 1850 Library Act (Kelly 1977, 3). J. Stanley Jast was chief librarian of Croydon Libraries from 1898 to 1915 and president of the Library Association from 1905 to 1915 (Roberts 1985). W. C. Berwick Sayers was appointed as Croydon chief librarian in 1915 and remained until 1948. Croydon grew to have the largest library system in the south of England during Sayers's term ("Croydon Public Libraries Facts of 1933–34").

John Shaw Billings, William Howard Brett, Charles A. Cutter, John Cotton Dana, Melvil Dewey, Charles Coffin Jewett, William F. Poole, and Justin Winsor were counterparts in the United States to the library leaders in Great Britain (Bobinski, 1969, 8). John Cotton Dana was the first librarian of the Denver Public Library and William F. Poole of the Chicago Public Library.

Education for librarianship in Great Britain began in 1893 when the Library Association in Great Britain started offering summer schools, classes, and correspondence courses. The Library Assistants' Association (founded in 1895) helped arrange meetings and study circles. In 1919, the first full-time School of Librarianship was established at University College, London (Kelly 1977, 205, 206). The first library school in the United States was authorized by Columbia University in 1884 (Bobinski 1969, 8).

The recognition of the opportunity and responsibility for public libraries to be leaders in technology training for citizens is demonstrated in the United States by private funding and in Great Britain by government funding. Public libraries were able to provide access and training in the effective use of information technology for staff and users by grants in the United States from the Bill and Melinda Gates Foundation in 1997 (Bill and Melinda Gates Foundation 2002, 2) and in Great Britain from the New Opportunities Fund (NOF) in 1998.

The National Lottery Act of 1998 established the NOF as a lottery distributor. This UK wide nondepartmental public body is sponsored by the Department of Culture, Media and Sport. The People's Network is a key government initiative funded by the NOF to install information and communication technology (ICT) learning centres in all 4,300 public libraries in the

United Kingdom and to provide training for public library staff to effectively use the technology and train the public to use the ICT (People's Network 2002).

References

American Library Association. 1997. "About ALA." wysiwyg://52http//www.ala.org/pio/alaid.html (accessed February 2, 2003).

Bill and Melinda Gates Foundation. 2002. "Connections—Progress in Libraries." http://gatesfoundation.org/libraries/relatedinf/connections/connectionsvol11.htm (accessed January 23, 2003).

Bobinski, George S. 1969. *Carnegie Libraries: Their History and Impact on American Public Library Development.* Chicago: American Library Association.

"Croydon Public Libraries Facts of 1933–34." Unpublished History, Local Studies and Archives, Croydon Central Library, Croydon, UK.

Kelly, Thomas. 1977. *A History of Public Libraries in Great Britain, 1845–1975.* London: Library Association.

Munford, W. A. 1968. *Penny Rate.* London: Library Association.

People's Network. 2002. http://www.peoplesnetwork.gov.uk (accessed December 8, 2001).

Roberts, Richard. 1985. "Croydon Public Libraries—A Brief History." Unpublished History, Local Studies and Archives, Croydon Central Library, Croydon, UK.

Shera, Jesse. 1965. *Foundations of the Public Library.* North Haven, CT: The Shoe String Press. (Orig. pub. 1949.)

Dunfermline Carnegie Library, Scotland: "Let There Be Light"

In summer 1997 I visited the Dunfermline Carnegie Library to collect data for an investigation of the effect of technology on collection development of selected public libraries in England and Scotland (Greiner 1998, 73–89).

In fall 1999 I went back to Dunfermline to continue my public library research. The purpose was to examine the management philosophies of library administrators in a sample of public libraries in England, Scotland, and the United States.

As in my earlier visit, I found key people to be available and gracious with their time and information. Dorothy Miller, librarian, Dunfermline Carnegie Library, Chris Neale, information services librarian, with whom I had visited in 1997, Councillor David Arnott, Fife Council, and Bill Runciman, secretary of the Carnegie Dunfermline Trust, provided information critical to this study. Current (summer 2003) information updates were also provided by the participants.

Mission Statement

In response to my question about the Dunfermline Carnegie Library mission statement, Dorothy Miller responded that they did not have a formal mission statement: "The closest is that Fife Council has aims and values to which all services subscribe."

History and Background

In 1880 the Dunfermline Town Council adopted the Free Library Act of 1867 in response to Andrew Carnegie's 1879 offer to finance a library. The

Dunfermline Carnegie Library

Carnegie Library, donated by Carnegie to the town of his birthplace, opened August 29, 1883. This library represented the beginning of Andrew Carnegie's public library philanthropy throughout the English-speaking world. The building included a library room, a gentlemen's reading room, a ladies' reading room, a recreation room, a smoking room, and a librarian's dwelling.

At the focal point of the main entry to the Dunfermline Carnegie Library, a pedestal supports a marble bust of Andrew Carnegie's mother, Margaret, who laid the foundation stone of the library on July 27, 1881. Carnegie wrote about his parents, William and Margaret Carnegie, in his autobiography: ". . . my mother laid the foundation stone there of the first free library building I ever gave. My father was one of five weavers who founded the earliest library in the town by opening their own books to their neighbors. Dunfermline named the building I gave 'Carnegie Library.' The architect asked for my coat of arms. I informed him I had none, but suggested that above the door there might be carved a rising sun shedding its rays with the motto: 'Let there be light.' This he adopted" (Carnegie 1920, 211).

A painting entitled *The Dunfermline Demonstrations,* by Andrew Blair and William Geddes, commissioned by Andrew Carnegie, hangs in the

Carnegie Birthplace Museum. It records the day of the official opening of the library. Andrew Carnegie and his mother, accompanied by national and local dignitaries, arrived by carriage at the St. Margaret's Street entrance of the new library. Margaret Carnegie stands outside the carriage greeting townspeople. Two town councillors stand with their backs to the demonstration, signifying their objections to the gift of the library because it would increase taxes (Derrick Barclay, museum curator, Andrew Carnegie Birthplace Museum, pers. comm., July 1997).

Chris Neale, information services librarian, described the historical relationship of the present library to the founding library. "There is a direct line from the original library gifted to the town in 1883 by Andrew Carnegie and operated by the Town Council as a public library service." He defined the periods of development as follows:

1883, first period	Building construction funded by private donation (Andrew Carnegie); library service funded by rates (local taxes)
	Library service managed by a library committee comprised of 50 percent town councillors and 50 percent householders
	Small branch libraries created in the town (Baldridgeburn, Rosyth); construction funded by Carnegie Dunfermline Trust
1920, second period	Original building extended; extension funded by Carnegie Dunfermline Trust
	1904–1922: Householder places on library committee taken by Carnegie trustees
	1922: Formal connection of Carnegie Dunfermline Trust with library management ends
1974, third period	Local government reorganization in Scotland means end of town councils; Dunfermline and its surrounding area become Dunfermline District
	Dunfermline Library becomes the headquarters of the District Library Service (eighteen libraries)
	Library managed by a committee of district councillors
1996, fourth period	Local government reorganized again; Dunfermline District and two other adjoining districts combined under one authority: Fife Council; the new authority operates *all* local services, including a library service

Dunfermline Library remains the administrative headquarters for its former branch libraries

Fife Council Library Service is managed (politically) by a committee of Fife councillors and (administratively) by four library managers

Fife Council's library service is part of a wider community services division. (For a historical chronology of Dunfermline Carnegie Library, please refer to the general British chronology in the appendix.)

Interviews

I conducted interviews with Dorothy Miller, librarian, Dunfermline Carnegie Library, as well as libraries and learning services coordinator with operational management of West Fife Libraries; Chris Neale, information services librarian; Councillor David Arnott, Fife Council; and Bill Runciman, secretary, Carnegie Dunfermline Trust. A primary issue under discussion was the organizational structure of the government, and its impact on library management.

Organization

Dorothy Miller described the Fife Council structure as it was in fall 2002 (see Figure 1). Fife Council is made up of west, central, and east areas. The council operates on three levels: (a) Fife and strategic, (b) area and operational, and (c) locality. Elected members serve on committees for children's services, adult services, policy and resources, and standards at the Fife strategic level. There are local services committees in each of the three areas: east, west, and central.

Figure 1, an organization chart, shows the structure of Fife Council—Community Services. Each of the four service managers has a strategic, functional role across Fife plus a geographic role for all community services within his or her area. For instance, the service manager for arts, libraries, museums (ALM) has a remit to lead the ALM strategic thrust across the whole of Fife, but also the remit to oversee the operations of sports, parks, amenities, community education, grounds maintenance, arts, libraries, and museums in Central Fife only. Similarly, the service manager for sports, parks, and amenities coordinates the development of these services Fife-wide on a strategic basis, but line manages sports, parks, amenities, community education, grounds maintenance, arts, libraries, and museums in West Fife only.

Figure 1
Fife Council—Community Services

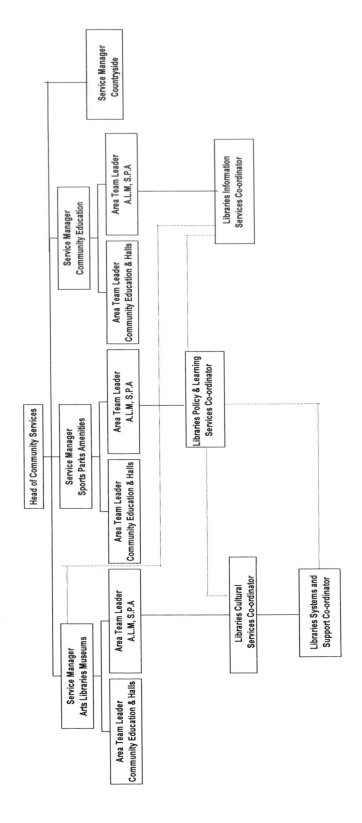

ALM: arts, libraries, and museums; SPA: sports, parks, and amenities

Dorothy Miller explained, "The Library Service also follows a matrix management structure. Thus, the Libraries Coordinators Team leads the libraries. Each of the four team members reports to different people in different areas. I serve as libraries policy and learning services coordinator with operational management of West Fife Libraries (three roles/responsibilities); the information services coordinator with operational management for East Area Libraries (two roles); the cultural services coordinator with operational management for Central Area (two roles); and the coordinator of the support services function of libraries through the area teams has no direct line management responsibilities."

Miller noted, "This structure was introduced in 1996 and was intended to create communicative styles, joined-up, working-together relationships. However, it has drawbacks—it can take too long to get agreement on a course of action and it can be a recipe for muddle—different managers interpreting decisions differently.

"The centre of the organisation that is Fife Council is called Policy and Organisational Development. At the time of our interview in 1999, this section was bombarding the frontline services such as libraries with one changing policy after another. This caused great confusion for a while, constantly changing procedures. This is not quite the same problem as it used to be."

In the 1999 interview, Dorothy Miller had stated, "The government's current agenda will change perception of libraries. The whole library system in Great Britain will be networked (the People's Network). This will give libraries a role nationally in learning and information. The New Opportunities Fund (NOF) will allocate funds to all UK councils to assist with the training of library staff in information and communication technology (ICT) to help their clients make use of the new technology (also being funded by NOF). This will involve partnerships, and the library must be a leader."

In 2002, Miller said that as expected the funding of the People's Network through National Lottery funds had heightened public awareness of libraries and their role in the learning and cultural society. "The full impact has not yet been made on the local politicians, who (mostly) still believe libraries to be only about lending leisure books. But we're getting there with this argument!"

When asked to describe her management style in the current rather complicated government structure, Dorothy Miller responded, "I want to see things happen, keep things moving. We have regular coordinators team meetings on a Fife basis and local management team meetings on an area basis. I want people to participate and take responsibility."

To a question about what drives the library—technology, patron needs, the political environment, the economy—Miller's response was, "The national political environment has been driving libraries within the lifelong learning agenda for the past five years, since the government changed from Conservative to Labour. Prior to that, the emphasis and placing within the political structures leant towards the leisure role."

In 1999, I asked the librarian where she saw the library in ten years, in terms of finances, technology, services, and staffing.

Regarding finances, she replied that a major part of funding would be from trust and charitable status. In terms of services, Miller said she expected that staff would be required to play different roles. "In ten years users will access directly. Libraries will function as centers of learning, reading, information. Libraries will be better recognized. They will play less of the leisure role. Perceptions will change. Procedures, delivery, will change due to technology. How, rather than what. Funding will not be protected."

Dorothy Miller then directed me to the source for Fife Council statistical information. Scottish councils leisure and library services are measured by performance indicators.

They are:

1. average time taken to satisfy library book requests;

2. library stock turnover per 1,000 population;

3. borrowers from public libraries as a percentage of the resident population and the average number of issues per borrower; and

4. target and actual lending stock additions for adults and children and teenagers.

In 2000/2001, Fife Council became one of five councils that exceeded the recommended target additions for children and teenage lending stock (Audit Scotland 2001, 1). For children and teenagers, the recommendation for annual additional stock levels is 100 items per 1,000 population (Convention of Scottish Local Authorities 1995, cited in Audit Scotland 2001, 10). Statistics are not currently available for individual libraries.

Chris Neale, information services librarian, in addition to providing a summary of the library's history, discussed the unique aspects of the Dunfermline Carnegie Library.

Dunfermline Carnegie Library's "uniqueness lies in its historical position as the first Carnegie-funded free library in the world. Other unique aspects are more difficult to pin down. In many ways, because of the national framework of legislation and funding within which local authorities operate their library systems and the standardization of professional training, public libraries are as alike as beehives. In its relationship with its community and its users and in similar, less tangible, ways it is distinctive. Dunfermline people regard the library as *their* library. It is rather a busy library, the second busiest in Scotland by many measures."

Neale noted that Fife Council's policy for all its services is that management should be participative rather than authoritarian. Teamwork is emphasized.

When asked what drives the library—technology, patron needs, the political environment, the economy—Neale's response was "All of these, plus national and local learning/cultural policies."

In 1999, I asked for Neale's projection of the future of the Dunfermline Carnegie Library in ten years regarding finances, technology, services, and staffing. He responded that it was impossible to predict the financial situation. "It is our goal to be part of a network of users of advanced communications technology. Current services will expand. The role as a *leisure* service provider may diminish. Services should relate to making learning, cultural and information resources available to the community at large. Staff *roles* will change and will be related to higher technology provisions. Emphasis on customer service will continue."

When asked how the Unitary Authority—a local government body that forms a single tier of administration—changes had affected the library administration, staffing, and services, Neale deferred to Dorothy Miller, adding "However, one view might be that change itself has had the biggest effect. Adapting to, and responding to, fairly rapid and continuous change is what most affects the work of library managers."

Responding to a request in March 2002 for a summary of changes since the interview in 1999, Chris Neale noted that council libraries had been successful in their application for New Opportunities Funding for information communication technology and that libraries in Fife were going through the process of rewiring, recabling, refurbishing, and installation of public-use PCs. He said that other changes were either newly in place or imminent in 1999.

In October 1999, David Arnott, Fife councillor, vice chairman of Fife Council's community services with special responsibility for sports, recreation, and libraries, discussed changes in governmental structures prior to fall 1990. Dunfermline District Libraries was an independent Department of Libraries and Museums. At this time, Libraries and Museums joined with the Department of Leisure and Recreation to form the Leisure Services Service. All former merging departments were then known as Services. There were thirty-two community centres with four incorporated mini-libraries; when reorganized, administration was reduced from ten to five directors.

In 1996, all local government was reorganized by parliamentary legislation. The Local Government etc. (Scotland) Act 1994 created new authorities, for example, Fife Council (C. Neale, e-mail message to author, November 7, 2002; Local Government etc. [Scotland] Act 1994, 1). Districts were swept away. Elected members set policy, set strategies, set framework for service delivery, set budgets on advice of officers. Service reviews were established to ensure that the objectives that the members set in conjunction with officers were achieved.

David Arnott applied these measures to the library: "We must assure that library service meets the political aims of the administration. Library service is here to deal with educational development of our constituents and at the same time meet social and recreational needs. We must make sure political aspirations relate to the realities of the financial resources available. Adult literacy courses and visual arts are also an important responsibility of Community Services."

Arnott explained, citing this example: "I asked the librarian, Dorothy Miller, to prepare a budget for additional facilities, keeping in mind the council's political ambitions. I will take the budget to the team leader, who will discuss it with the service manager, then with the head of Community Services. The head of Community Services will present it to the Social Strategy Committee, then to Fife Council, and they may make cuts. The primary, majority funding source is from central government. A good librarian must be politically aware."

Arnott added that the New Opportunities Funding for information communication technology is expected to address social inclusion and education for new technology and social skills.

In October 2002 Arnott advised me that the governmental structure had recently been amended and the position of vice chairman of Community Services had been omitted. He had recently been appointed chair of area services. In a private capacity he is executive administrator of the Scottish Association of Local Sports Councils and chairman of the Scottish Football Partnership. The latter is a governmental agency established to provide grant aid to the development of football in Scotland.

Bill Runciman, secretary of the Carnegie Dunfermline Trust, in a November 2002 update to a 1999 interview, described the continuing role of the trust with the Dunfermline Carnegie Library. He said that the library has received many grants from the trust. Since 1999 the principal grant had been the Twentieth-Century Dunfermline project, which cost just over $90,000. Runciman described the project, which is believed to be the most comprehensive public multimedia database in Scotland, as a fully documented and indexed archive of community life over the century. The millennium archive is now in regular use since its presentation to Dunfermline Carnegie Library. National recognition for the Trust's gift to the town of this unique archive of life in the twentieth century was intimated by the gifts inclusion in a short listing (one of only three) in the arts, culture, and heritage category of Charity Awards 2000, the first awards ever to recognize and celebrate excellence in the leadership and management of charities. The nominees in this category of the Charity 2000 Awards were recognized for "significant achievement in charity management practice. The Carnegie Dunfermline Trust has ably demonstrated the high standard that supporters and regulators should look for."

While the Twentieth-Century Dunfermline project is officially closed, some of the large team of volunteers who donated so much time to researching local history continue to unearth interesting data that the trustees hope the local library will add to the archive, thus continuing a true people's project. To complement the Twentieth-Century Dunfermline project, the trust presented photographs and slides of the construction of the Forth Road Bridge, which now form part of the library archives.

Runciman also referred to the International Federation of Library Associations and Institutions (IFLA) Conference in Glasgow in August 2002. Many of the participants came from Carnegie libraries all over the world, and Dunfermline was of special interest to them. Librarians spent a day in Dunfermline, attended workshops, and visited points of interest, learning the local Carnegie history and Andrew Carnegie's influence on the library movement generally. The trust funded leaflets that were distributed by the local library to the international visitors. "We expect that the library will ask for our assistance from time to time and, given its Carnegie origins, the staff know that support from our trustees can usually be relied upon," Runciman said.

Runciman noted some of the activities scheduled in Dunfermline in 2003. The trust will celebrate five centenaries: its own; Pittencrieff Park in Dunfermline, Andrew Carnegie's finest gift to the town; Dunfermline's Old Opera House, the interior of which was moved to the Asolo Theatre in Sarasota, Florida; the Children's Gala, in which all the local schools participate each June; and the founding of the town of Rosyth. While Rosyth did not exist when Andrew Carnegie lived in Dunfermline, it is now included within the trust's catchment area and benefits from trust grants from time to time.

"Let There Be Light"

A primary emphasis in Great Britain and for the libraries that were funded with New Opportunities Funding is implementation of training of library staff to train citizens in the use of the current technology. Dunfermline, as noted by Dorothy Miller and Chris Neale, is one of the libraries that has been awarded funds for this purpose, and the most current information technology is in place throughout the library. Both Miller and Neale anticipated that the emphasis on technology training would change the public's perception of libraries from providers of primarily leisure services to providers of learning, cultural, and information services. Although they expected the roles of staff to shift to higher technology provisions, both concurred the emphasis on customer service would continue.

A vital blend of the culture of centuries in Dunfermline is readily apparent. Dunfermline Abbey (1072), the Carnegie Birthplace Museum, where Andrew Carnegie was born in November 1835 and lived until his family moved to Allegheny, Pennsylvania, in May 1848, and the Carnegie Dunfermline Public Library (1883) reflect the society over the years.

In the Local History Department, the library accommodates priceless historical archives documenting this rich history. The Local History Department houses an extensive collection of original manuscript material and printed volumes, typescript indexes, and notes, all of much value for the genealogist. The collection, which covers the area formerly known as Dunfermline District, includes an international genealogical index (Scotland and Ireland); monumental inscriptions and burial records, directories, almanacs, registers, voters rolls, valuation rolls, lists of ratepayers, burgh and official records, and additional church records (thirteenth to sixteenth century).

I spent many days in the Dunfermline Carnegie Library, often in the Local History Department, reading the handwritten minutes of the library committees, in which donations from Carnegie and other benefactors were conscientiously reported. The local history librarian, Ann Rodwell, not only cheerfully guided me to resources, but also discussed with me the view from the library of the abbey and the cemetery and the magnificent tower honoring Robert the Bruce, national hero of Scotland.

One day as I was on my way out of the library, I met a lady carrying several books who was also leaving the library. On impulse, I asked, "What do you think Mr. Carnegie would think of this library now?" She seemed delighted that a stranger had asked such a question. Then she replied with a smile, "He would be so pleased."

References

Audit Scotland. 2001. "Annual Report 2000–2001." http://www.audit_scotland.gov.uk/annualreport/index.htm. (accessed November 7, 2002).

Carnegie, Andrew. 1920. *Autobiography of Andrew Carnegie.* Boston and New York: Houghton Mifflin.

Convention of Scottish Local Authorities (COSLA). 1995. *Standards for the Public Library Services in Scotland.* Cited in Audit Scotland, "Annual Report 2000–2001" (2001).

Greiner, Joy. 1998. "Collection Development in the Information Age: Great Britain's Public Libraries." In *Public Library Development in the Information Ages,* ed. Annabel K. Stephens, 73–89. Binghamton, NY: Haworth Press.

Local Government etc. (Scotland) Act 1994. 1994. http://www.hmso.gov.uk/acts/acts1994/Ukpga_19940039_en_1.htm (accessed October 23, 2003).

Croydon Libraries, England: Innovative and Inclusive Customer Service

Mission Statement

Croydon Libraries support the social, recreational, educational and economic life of the community by providing materials in printed, audio visual and electronic forms and access to those resources through staff expertise, a network of library buildings and remote access.

History and Background

Croydon, one of the outer London boroughs, has a population of around 340,000. Croydon Libraries comprises the central library, twelve branch libraries, a mobile library, housebound library service, and the tourist information centre.

The new Croydon Central Library was opened officially by Heritage Secretary Peter Brooke on November 5, 1993, during National Library Week. In his remarks, Brooke noted that this was the largest new library that had opened in the United Kingdom in many years ("Broad Brief for Croydon Suppliers" 1993, 9). Its location and appearance are noteworthy. The library is situated in the Clocktower complex adjacent to the Victorian Town Hall, which originally opened in 1896. A statue of Queen Victoria dominates the entrance from the right on Katharine Street, while inside, library users can find state-of-the-art technology. In fact, in 1998 Prime Minister Tony Blair launched the Number 10 Web site in Croydon Central Library. Number 10 Downing Street is the residence of the prime minister. The library's high-technology profile stands in sharp contrast to the historic Victorian Town Hall. A newspaper article described the new library as "Cyberspace in a Victorian Setting" (*News* 1997, 13).

Croydon Central Library

The Clocktower complex includes, in addition to the historic town hall and the library, a museum, exhibition galleries, a cinema, the Tourist Information Centre, and Braithwaite Hall, which is used as a venue for arts events, conferences, and meetings. Braithwaite Hall housed the library's original reference collection, and a historic appearance has been maintained with replicas of leather-bound book jackets lining the walls.

Croydon Libraries are well used. In a message to the council and the public in reference to Croydon Libraries' "Annual Plan 2001," Councillor Raj Chandarana, cabinet member for culture, noted that in 2000–01, 2.7 million people visited the fourteen Croydon Libraries, almost three million books were issued, and 677,000 enquiries were answered (Croydon Council 2001a, 1).

Structure and Organization

Croydon Libraries is one of five service areas that formed the Leisure Services Department. On February 1, 2001, Croydon Leisure Services was renamed Cultural Services, and its chief officer was renamed the director of cultural services. The divisions that comprise the Cultural Services Department are libraries; arts and community development; museum and heritage; sports, parks, and recreation; and policy and support. Adie Scott, assistant director, libraries, has responsibility for the Libraries Division.

Other council departments include planning and development, education, corporate services, environmental services, social services, finance, and information technology. Each of the council departments has a chief officer who reports to the chief executive (Croydon Council 2001a, 8).

> The Borough comprises 24 Electoral Wards and three parliamentary constituencies. It is part of the London Regional Constituency for the European Parliament. The Council's 70 members are elected every four years. Local elections were held in May 2002. Croydon is currently Labour-controlled, with 37 Labour Councillors, 32 Conservatives and one Liberal Democrat. The Council adopted a Cabinet structure in May 2001. The Leader and Cabinet are responsible and accountable for shaping policies, plans and strategies and recommending them to the Council for approval. The Cabinet also gives political direction to service directors on the way in which services are managed and budgets allocated to them. The Cabinet comprises 10 Councillors, including the Leader. (Croydon Council 2002a, 4)

Administration

Croydon Libraries were awarded the Charter Mark for excellence three successive times—in 1993, 1996, and 1999. The winners of "this prestigious Government award were described as 'the cream of public service' by Culture Minister Janet Anderson during an awards ceremony at the Queen Elizabeth II Conference Centre in Westminster on 1 February 2000" (Croydon Council 2000).

All library authorities in England are required to submit an annual library plan at the end of September to the Department of Culture, Media and Sport (DCMS). The plan must be formally approved by the authority's full council meeting. Scores are given to the plans, both for their merit as planning documents and as a reflection of the council's approach to meeting the public library standards, which were introduced in April 2001. Councils have until April 2004 to meet these standards, which include, for example:

- 99 percent of households live within one mile of a static library.

- Every static service point is to provide public Internet access by December 31, 2002. (There is free public Internet access in all Croydon's libraries.)

- 65 percent of adult library users must report success in obtaining a specific book.

- At least one library to be open more than sixty hours per week. (Croydon Council 2001b)

Croydon Libraries "Annual Library Plan 2001," a three-year strategy for Croydon's libraries, was presented to the cabinet as a draft on September 24, 2001, and for approval on October 15, 2001, to the Croydon Council meeting. The DCMS published a report on all the annual library plans—"Appraisal of Annual Library Plans and Approach to the Public Library Standards—2001. Report on Outcomes and Issues." Croydon scored 3, the highest score, for the overall quality of the annual library plan, and 2 for the authority's approach to meeting the standards (Croydon Council DCMS 2001).

The council distributed a consultation leaflet to the public, soliciting comments and input to identify where to focus planning efforts. Key issues and areas of development that were identified through this process are:

- implementing the People's Network and information and communication technology,
- establishing learning centres in libraries,
- developing and sustaining a wide range of lifelong learning activities,
- exploring opportunities for developing library buildings and mobile libraries,
- consulting on charging policies,
- increasing access, and
- seeking views on priorities regarding the public library standards.

The library management addressed social inclusion and equality of access policies by identifying special groups that may have been excluded from library services relevant to their needs. Among the groups requiring specific services are:

- "ethnic minority community groups;
- housebound people;
- children and young people;
- children and young people and their parents and carers in areas of social deprivation in the borough;
- parents and carers;
- residents in parts of the borough distant from static libraries;
- travelers;
- unemployed people;

- people with a visual impairment;

- people with disabilities;

- people with special needs;

- people whose language is not English;

- refugees and asylum seekers;

- lesbians and gay men; and

- people without access to ICT." (Croydon Council 2001a, 54)

Programs, Services, and Initiatives

The installation of Information and Technology Learning Centres in the public libraries demonstrates the government's commitment to re-skilling the workforce; and to economic regeneration. It provides an opportunity for the public to become confident in the use of ICT as well as to provide an access route to information (Croydon Council 2001b, 1). See the People's Network Web site for full details of this groundbreaking project for public libraries in the UK (People's Network 2002).

The UK-wide New Opportunities Fund (NOF) embraces training for public library staff in the effective use of information and communications technology as one of its goals.

Croydon Libraries already provide free public Internet access in all libraries, but the People's Network project greatly increases the number of public access PCs, improves their specification and bandwidth, and enables many more learning opportunities in libraries for all ages. The rollout was scheduled for completion by the end of 2002. It is reported in "Achievement of the Action Plan for 2001/02" in the "Annual Library Plan 2002" that a bid was submitted for the People's Network (Croydon Council 2002a, 97). It is reported in the "Rolling Action Plans and Targets—Action Plan for 2002/2003 and 2004/05" that the 2002/03 objectives identified are to implement People's Network, increase public access to PCs in all libraries, and provide filtered Internet access. In 2003/04, the objective is to promote, monitor, and evaluate the People's Network (Croydon Council 2002a, 118).

The ethnic minorities information officer (EMIO) for Croydon Libraries has the responsibility and the opportunity to work with the 22 percent minority ethnic population in the borough to identify and address their special needs. The EMIO develops links with ethnic groups to make them aware of the services available in the library and in community group meeting places. In addition to dealing with ethnic minority issues enquiries, the EMIO represents Croydon Libraries at meetings with various minority group associations such as the Asian Librarians and Advisors Group (Croydon Council 2001a, 55).

Other recent developments at Croydon Libraries include a new Homework

Help Club in the central library, a joint project with the Education Department, also funded by the New Opportunities Fund. "Homework Help Clubs offer young people friendly one to one help with homework and studying from specially trained staff, books, CD-ROMS, the Internet, word processing, printing and photocopying" (Croydon Council 2002b, 1).

Books on the Move addresses the literacy needs of children in homeless families. This multiagency group project includes Croydon Libraries, Croydon & Surrey Downs Community Trust, the Homeless Health Team, Croydon Education Department, and the Ethnic Minority Achievement Service and is funded by a grant from the Paul Hamlyn Foundation to deliver Books on the Move. The project is designed "to involve parents and carers in their children's learning and break down the families' isolation and lack of access to facilities" (Croydon Council 2002b, 1). In addition to delivering books, this program provides discussion sessions at one of the libraries for parents. Homeless families are encouraged to join the library, which gives them access to a wide array of services (Croydon Council 2002b, 1).

A new mobile van for the Housebound Library Service enables customers to make their own choices from current stock on the vehicle. The service provides reading materials for residential homes and sheltered accommodation in the borough. Previously, customers were limited to the collections in the homes.

In an effort to encourage early love of reading, Croydon Libraries instituted a Baby Book Crawl. Parents or other caregivers shared six books with their babies over the summer. At a special Rhymetime event in September, babies received a certificate and a First-Class Reader badge. The goal is that the hundreds of parents and caretakers of babies who attend the Rhymetime sessions will keep visiting the library and keep sharing books and rhymes with their babies.

Croydon Libraries, in partnership with the Education Department, the Ethnic Minority Achievement Service, and the Refugee Centre, are involved in Refugee Week in June. They developed a new booklist for children: A World of Stories, and a special storyteller visited the central children's library to tell stories to children from schools across the borough (Croydon Council 2002c, 1).

Information for Business in Croydon (IBC) is a comprehensive business information service accessible from the central library. The library provides information about starting a business, business skills, and information for job interviews. There is also a comprehensive CD-ROM network for business use. Experienced staff, with the help of library resources, offer research services to business people (Croydon Council 2002b, 1ff).

Chris Batt, when he was borough libraries and museums officer, London Borough of Croydon, identified the early role of public libraries as "very much the poor man's university, the place where the less fortunate could gain an education on the path to industriousness and betterment" (Batt 1996, 2). Batt describes the Croydon Central Library as "the largest and most technically advanced new central library to be built in the UK since the 1960's. . . . The first public library for the 21st Century, it has become a Mecca for librarians around the world who want to see how technology can be used to better serve customer need" (Batt 1996, 7).

Chris Batt was appointed to be the chief network advisor at the Library and Information Commission (LIC) in August 1999, with the responsibility of implementing the People's Network. In April 2000 the LIC merged with the Museum and Galleries Commission to become Resource: The Council for Museums, Archives and Libraries. Batt is now director of the Libraries and Information Society Team.

Interview

Adie Scott, Head of Croydon Libraries, and Brenda Constable, Central Library Manager, September 1999

Greiner

Does the present library relate historically to the founding library? If so, how? If not, why not?

Adie Scott

Examples of how we relate can be found in our Local Studies Library and Archives. Croydon Libraries aims to be as responsive as possible to community requests, expressed through customers' personal comments, letters, comment forms, surveys, and e mails.

Brenda Constable

The public library movement was for the self-improvement of the working man by access to books—1850s public education. Now we think in terms of lifelong learning, equalities, and the delivery of a library service that meets real needs. Libraries are supporting education, and education is a part of the government's agenda. The emphasis is on information as well as recreation.

Adie Scott

Definitions have broadened. The library provides a neutral environment where learning occurs for all ages from the youngest baby upwards. The library is accessible to deliver important aspects of the government agenda. Libraries are supporting the government's modernization agenda. One of the roles of the library is to provide education for citizenship. The library is recognized as having a key role in reskilling, enabling citizens to be more employable, supporting literacy and the enjoyment of reading for all ages, and promoting reading development.

Greiner

What do you see as unique about this library?

Adie Scott

The building is unique. It is a modern library that integrates the technology with all the library resources. Its popularity is demonstrated by the fact that there are around one million visits to the library each year. It attracts people of all ages; a particular development we have encouraged through promotions and special events is the attractiveness of the children's library to babies and their carers. Young people also find the library an inviting place to study, meet friends, and generally spend time.

Brenda Constable

It has the feel of a modern department store—people can be seen to feel "at home" and relaxed here. There is a good mix of leisure and study seating which encourages customers to sit and browse as well as to study. Users find it a comfortable place to be.

Greiner

What do you perceive as your primary role as a library director? How important is the role of library administrator as politician?

Adie Scott

As politician, the library manager must keep promoting the message of the library's role—which is a changing and developing role. A role for the library manager is keeping councillors informed of customers' requirements, key issues, and developments. Customers have increasing expectations of what their local library service can and should deliver, which they express to library staff. The citizens of the borough vote for a local councillor, who is on different committees that consider and agree on policies. Croydon Council has a cabinet structure, which entails each department having a cabinet member who is responsible for their area of activity. [In the interview, Adie Scott implied by the description of the governing structure the accountability of the library to the customers who elect the councilor.]

Greiner

How would you describe your management style—authoritarian, participative, somewhere in between, pragmatic?

Adie Scott

Participative, delivering objectives through skilled and experienced members of staff, teamwork, sharing tasks and responsibilities, achieving through people. For example, many of the highly successful developments such as Baby Rhymetimes, Sunday opening of the central library, the programmes of community activities at libraries—none of these could be achieved without the commitment of the staff. They are committed to delivering a truly customer-focused service.

Greiner

What drives the library—technology, patron needs, the political environment, the economy?

Adie Scott

All, but the main driver is responding to customer needs.

Greiner

Where do you see this library ten years from now in terms of finances, technology, services, staffing?

Adie Scott

Finances and local government are difficult to predict. Twenty years ago, we would not have known that the new central library as part of the Clocktower cultural complex would be created. For the long term, we must strive to maintain the high quality of customer service. That requires a high level of funding and embracing new ideas. Information and communications technology will be vital in order to keep up with customers' expectations and deliver digital and online services. Staff must be customer-service oriented, with an interest and an enthusiasm in ICT and reader development and in making library services as accessible as possible and as socially inclusive as possible. There will be more working in partnerships.

Brenda Constable

Yes—there will be an increasing number of partnerships to achieve shared objectives and to bid for funding sources, for example, from the DCMS Wolfson Fund and the Heritage Lottery Fund.

Adie Scott

Developing services for potentially excluded groups will continue to be a priority. Twenty-two percent of Croydon's population is from ethnic minority communities.

Innovative and Inclusive Customer Service

The juxtaposition of a high-tech public library and a Victorian Town Hall, with a statue of Queen Victoria that seems to observe the entrance to the library, is a setting that encourages a quest for learning across the boundaries of time.

The "Annual Library Plan 2002" was presented in September 2002 and is available on the library Web page. The 2003 plan was scheduled for presentation to the Cultural Services Department in September 2003. The annual plans project a three-year strategy for achievement of stated objectives. Action plans and targets, assessment against standards, review and progress related to earlier annual plans, and a three-year strategy for the future are included in the annual plan. The planning process begins with documentation of customer responses to questionnaires and surveys, as well as with input in focus groups from users and nonusers.

Social inclusion is a primary objective for Croydon Council and for libraries service. Croydon Libraries provide services to special groups including ethnic minorities, people whose first language is not English, refugees and asylum seekers, lesbians and gay men, people who are housebound, children and young people and parents and carers in areas of social deprivation, unemployed people, people with visual impairment, and people with disabilities.

"Brenda Constable referred to lifelong learning, equalities, and the delivery of a library service that meets real needs."

The vehicle for the delivery of that needed service is likely to be driven by the most current technology, and the identification of the service may be the result of input from customers. In the professionally managed Croydon Libraries, the customer can be confident that the request for service will be addressed promptly.

Chronology

1888, November 21	Croydon Council adopted the Public Libraries Act of 1850 by a majority of 1,746 votes; the move to adopt the act had been defeated in 1886 by 448 votes and in 1887 by 27 votes
1890, March 31	The library opened in two shop premises at 104 and 106 North End
1896, March 14	The library in North End closed and moved to new premises in the new town hall in Katharine Street
1896	The lending library opened, one of the first libraries in the country to allow readers to choose books from the shelves
1898, August 29	L. Stanley Jast appointed chief librarian; during his tenure, 1898 to 1915, Croydon Libraries expanded in size and range of activities
1898	Jast, who realized the importance of communication, established telephone links between the central library and the branches
1899, May 15	The reference collection became "open access"
1905–1915	Jast served as president of the Library Association
1915, November	Jast left Croydon to be chief librarian of the Manchester Public Library
1915, November 22	W. C. Berwick Sayers appointed chief librarian and served in this capacity until 1948; his philosophy of the role of a public library was expressed in his statement "If it is in print, you can get it at the public library" (Sayers 1947, 4)

1917	The National Library for the Blind supplied books in Braille for Croydon Libraries to distribute to local blind readers
1920	The Central Children's Library opened, the first in the country and the first to have a woman in charge, Ethel G. Hayler
1927, August and September	Ethel G. Hayler, Children's librarian, central library, visited children's libraries in the United States and Canada; she also visited the Library of Congress, a business library, a university library, the Hull House Settlement Library in Chicago, the Bowling Green Settlement Library in New York, and the Chicago Art Institute (Hayler 1928)
1933	"Croydon had the largest library system in the South of England with a bookstock of 278,000 and an annual issue in 1932/3 of 2,142,106" (Roberts 1985, 3); it was reported that "70,060 people held readers' tickets, or 33 percent of the town's population over five years of age" ("Croydon Public Libraries Facts of 1933–34")
1936	Hospital library service began with a deposit collection at St. Mary's Maternity Hospital; collections at Warlingham Park Hospital and St. Gile's School for Physically Defective Children followed (Roberts 1985, 3)
1948, January 1	W. C. Berwick Sayers retired; replaced by the deputy librarian, H. A. Sharp (Roberts 1985, 4)
1951, April 2	T. E. Callendar succeeded Henry Sharp as chief librarian (Roberts 1985, 4)
1969, January	A. O. Meakin appointed chief librarian to succeed Callendar, who retired at the end of March (Roberts 1985, 5)
1973	The Local History Collection established; a local history librarian appointed
1978, January 3	First committee meeting of the staff association known as Croydon Public Libraries Staff Associaion (CPLSA) held (Roberts 1985, 5)
1978	Chris Batt came to Croydon Libraries as deputy chief librarian
1979, June 25	Information Bureau relocated in refurbished Study Room; reopened as Croydon Information Centre and included a tourist information centre

1979–1980	Computerization of the library system undertaken
1982	Croydon Libraries acquired their first PC—a Commodore PET
1983	First microcomputer installed in central library
1991	Chris Batt appointed borough libraries and museum officer for Croydon Libraries, Museum and Arts
1993, November 1	New Croydon Central Library opened during National Library Week
1993	Croydon Libraries awarded the Charter Mark for Excellence
1996	Croydon Libraries awarded the Charter Mark for Excellence
1998	Prime Minister Tony Blair launched the Number 10 Web site in Croydon Central Library
1999	Croydon Libraries awarded the Charter Mark for Excellence
1999, August	Chris Batt appointed chief network adviser to the Library and Information Commission (Croydon Council 1999, 5)
1999	Adie Scott became head of libraries in Croydon
2001, February 1	Croydon Leisure Services renamed Cultural Services; department encompasses Croydon's libraries, the museum and arts, recreation and parks and open spaces (Croydon Council 2001c, 1) Adie Scott is assistant director, Libraries, Cultural Services Department, Croydon Council, Croydon Central Library, Croydon Clocktower

References

Batt, Chris. 1996. *The Public Library and the Learning Society*. (Photography of copyrighted document, Local Studies and Archives, Croydon Central Library, Croydon, UK.

"Broad Brief for Croydon Suppliers." 1993. *Library Association Record Trade Supplement* 9 (December).

Croydon Council. 1999. *Croydon Libraries News* 3 (September). http://www.croydon.gov.uk/ledept/libraries/cr-libnews.3.htm (accessed July 7, 2002).

Croydon Council. 2000. *Croydon Libraries News* 5 (March). http://www. croydon.gov.uk/LEDept/libraries/cr-libnews5.htm (accessed March 6, 2001).

Croydon Council. 2001a. "Annual Library Plan 2001." London: Croydon Council. http://www.croydon.gov.uk/LEDept/libraries/cr-libs.htm. (accessed December 8, 2001).

Croydon Council. 2001b. "Annual Library Plan 2001 Consultation." London: Croydon Council. http://www.croydon.gov.uk/LEDept/ libraries/cr-libs.htm (accessed December 8, 2001).

Croydon Council. 2001c. *Croydon Libraries News* 9 (April). http://www.croy-don.gov.uk/ledept/libraries/cr-libnews9.htm (accessed July 7, 2002).

Croydon Council. 2002a. "Annual Library Plan 2002." London: Croydon Council. http://www.croydon.gov.uk/LEDept/libraries/Annual_Library_plan_2002.htm (accessed November 13, 2002).

Croydon Council. 2002b. Croydon Online. http://www.croydononline.org (accessed July 9, 2002).

Croydon Council. 2002c. "Library Developments." http://www.croydon. gov.uk/LEDept/libraries/cr-libs.htm (accessed July 5, 2002).

Croydon Council DCMS (Department of Culture, Media and Sport). 2001. "Appraisal of Annual Library Plans and Approach to the Public Library Standards—2001: Report on Outcomes and Issues." London: Croydon Council. http://www.culture.gov.uk/heritage/index.html (accessed November 28, 2002).

"Croydon Public Libraries Facts of 1933–34." (Photocopy, Local Studies and Archives, Croydon Central Library), Croydon, UK.

Hayler, Ethel G. 1928. "A Report to the Croydon Public Libraries Committee on a Personal Visit to America, August and September, 1927." Children's Library Croydon Central Library, Town Hall, Croydon, UK.

News (Croydon, UK). 1997. "Cyberspace in a Victorian Setting." February 28, 13.

People's Network. 2002. http://www.peoplesnetwork.gov.uk (accessed December 8, 2001).

Roberts, Richard. 1985. "Croydon Public Libraries—A Brief History." Local Studies and Archives, unpublished history, Croydon Central Library, Croydon, UK.

Sayers, W. C. Berwick. 1947. "The Province and Purpose of the Public Library." Croydon Public Libraries, unpublished history, Croydon, UK.

Part II

Selected Public Libraries in the United States

Section A

From the Heartland—A Midwestern City Library

Preview: Chicago Public Library

The modern city of Chicago rose from the ashes of a great fire, and rising with it was one of the United States' finest public libraries. For every visitor from any locale—a small community or a sophisticated American or foreign city—there is an attraction in Chicago, something fascinating about this vibrant city. Its public library reflects its community and revels in serving its people. Other midwestern cities have very fine libraries, too, but the wonderful and magnetic vitality of this city demands attention, and professional curiosity provokes seeking knowledge about its library.

After the great Chicago fire of 1871, as a gesture of friendship and sympathy, the citizens of England presented a Free Library to Chicago. Her Majesty, Queen Victoria; Thomas Carlyle; Benjamin Disraeli; John Ruskin; Robert Browning; John Stuart Mill; Alfred Lord Tennyson; and Matthew Arnold were among the prestigious bestowers of the "English book donation."

Somehow the spirit of the people of this ravaged city captured the hearts of the monarch and these literary giants, prompting this gift. From such munificence a great library had to arise to fulfill the ambitions of its people and the hopes of its benefactors. How and why it did so is the subject of this chapter.

Mary Dempsey, commissioner, Chicago Public Library, and senior management staff participated in interviews over a period of several days in summer 2001. They arranged their very busy schedules to share information about their roles in the continued development of the Chicago Public Library (CPL).

Mary Dempsey graciously participated in a lengthy interview with me. She is enthusiastic about the library, about Chicago, and about her job. Commissioner Dempsey promptly read, suggested revisions to, and approved the final version of our interview. I have maintained contact with Mary Dempsey, who sent me the latest update about new CPL branches in December 2002.

I conducted four separate interviews with senior management staff. One interview was with Barbara Ford, assistant commissioner, central library services; Charlotte Kim, assistant commissioner, neighborhood services; Sheryl Nichin-Keith, assistant commissioner for collections; and Kathleen Weibel, director, staff development. Kathleen Weibel and I continued our interview the next day. Donna Maloney, director, human resources, and Karen D. Lyons, first deputy commissioner, participated in another interview. Kathy Biel, deputy commissioner, administration and finance; Amy Eshleman, director of library development and outreach; and Jamey Lundblad, director of marketing, as a group, discussed their roles in fulfilling the mission of Chicago Public Library. Each participant read the transcripts of the interviews, identified necessary revisions, and returned the transcripts to me. I submitted the revised transcripts for the participants' approval of the final version.

I also had the opportunity to tour the Conrad Sulzer Regional Library and the Near North branch. The Sulzer Library opened in late 1985. The Neighborhood Historical Room houses the Ravenswood-Lake Historical Collection (Chicago Public Library, 2000, 4). The Near North Branch is one of the newer branches and is located on Chicago's Near North Side, one of the oldest and most diverse neighborhoods of the city.

A sense of commitment to the mission of the Chicago Public Library was evident in my conversations with Chicago Public Library staff in every library that I visited. "We believe in the freedom to read, to learn, to discover," part of CPL's mission statement, was demonstrated by the acceptance and celebration of the quest for knowledge characteristic of the diverse society served by the Harold Washington Library Center and by Chicago's "neighborhood libraries."

Reference

Chicago Public Library, 2000. "Serving the Neighborhoods." In "History of the Chicago Public Library: Windows on Our Past." http://www.chipublib.org/ (accessed November 15 2001).

Chicago Public Library, Illinois:
A Library of Neighborhoods

Early Mission of the Chicago Public Library

The founders and early leaders of the Chicago Public Library believed that the Library was an educational institution that should provide an opportunity for "mental improvement" to the citizens of Chicago. In the spirit of democracy, the Library was all-encompassing, providing books and related reading material for popular education, civic awareness and scholarly research. The Board of Directors also saw the Library as a place "where working men and the youth of the city might employ their idle time" profitably in reading instead of wasting it in "haunts of vice and folly and places of ill reputation" that characterized the Chicago of the 1870s. From the beginning, the mandate of the Chicago Public Library was clear—to serve the populace of Chicago. (Chicago Public Library 2000b, 1)

Mission Statement—1995

We welcome and support all people in their enjoyment of reading and pursuit of lifelong learning. Working together, we strive to provide equal access to information, ideas and knowledge through books, programs and other resources. We believe in the freedom to read, to learn, to discover. (Chicago Public Library 2002, 1)

History and Background

At the time of the great fire, October 8, 1871, there were no public libraries in Chicago. Chicago had several private libraries that required fees for services, such as the Mechanic's Institute, but no public library.

Chicago Public Library

As a gesture of friendship and sympathy after the fire, citizens of England presented a "free library to Chicago," eventually totaling over 8,000 titles, which became known as the "English Book Donation." Books were received from Her Majesty, Queen Victoria, and several of the literary giants of the day.

This gift, which was initiated by Thomas Hughes, author of *Tom Brown's School Days* and a member of Parliament, motivated the citizens of Chicago to move toward establishing a public library. Community leaders and prominent citizens, such as Marshall Field, Cyrus McCormick, and Thomas Hoyne, requested a public meeting. This meeting led to the "Illinois Library Act of 1872, authorizing cities to establish tax-supported libraries" in Illinois. "In April 1872, the City Council passed an ordinance proclaiming the establishment of the Chicago Public Library. January 1, 1873, the Chicago Public Library opened in a long-abandoned water tank at LaSalle and Adams, with 3,157 volumes on its shelves." The library was housed in various locations, including the fourth floor of city hall, where it remained for eleven years (Chicago Public Library 2000c 1).

William Frederick Poole, who was active during the planning stages in 1872 and 1873, was appointed head librarian in October 1873. He remained in that position until he resigned to organize the Newberry Library of Chicago in 1887.

Poole projected a public library vision in the *1876 Report* of the United States Bureau of Education: "The 'public library' which we are to consider is established by state laws, is supported by local taxation or voluntary gifts, is managed as a public trust, and every citizen of the city or town which maintains it has equal share in its privileges of reference and circulation" (Shera 1965, 157).

Frederick H. Hild was elected the second librarian on October 15, 1887, and served until 1909, when he was asked to resign by the board of directors due to the failure of the library to expand the extension services system into the neighborhoods. The library moved from quarters in city hall to the new Chicago Public Library on Michigan Avenue, between Washington and Randolph Streets, and the central library opened on October 11, 1897.

Henry E. Legler succeeded Frederick Hild as librarian, and served until 1917. He achieved prominence in library circles for his success in organizing the statewide library extension in Wisconsin. During his tenure, library services were significantly expanded in Chicago's neighborhoods. Branch reading rooms were opened and deposit stations were established in places of business, hospitals, and schools. In 1917 Legler died suddenly, and in 1920 the Henry E. Legler Regional Library, the first regional library in the system, was opened as a memorial to him.

Carl B. Roden came to the library as a clerk during the last year of Poole's tenure in 1886, and in 1909 became assistant to Legler. In 1918 he was unanimously chosen by the board of directors to succeed Legler. During the thirty-two years that Roden directed the Chicago Public Library, the "branch system increased 50 percent; the staff more than doubled; the book stock increased three-fold; circulation doubled; and total expenditures rose more than 400 percent" (Chicago Public Library 2000c, 27).

In 1950 Roden was succeeded by Gertrude E. Gscheidle. Gscheidle had begun her forty-three year career with the Chicago Public Library in 1924 in the branch system, becoming a branch librarian in 1926. She became executive assistant to the librarian in 1942 and in 1944 was promoted to assistant librarian for the Central Library. As librarian of the Chicago Public Library, she adopted the use of "traveling branches," delivering materials and services in the neighborhoods, as supplementary extension agencies.

Gscheidle served until 1967, when Alex Ladenson was appointed chief librarian. Ladenson served until 1974. He was the library administrator during massive street riots and destruction of some of Chicago's neighborhoods. Under Ladenson's direction, the library remained one of the city's most enduring public institutions (Chicago Public Library 2000c, 28).

Ladenson was succeeded by David L. Reich, deputy chief librarian from 1975 to 1978; Donald Sager, commissioner of the Chicago Public Library from 1978 to 1981; Amanda S. Rudd, commissioner of the Chicago Public Library from 1982 to 1985; and Commissioner John B. Duff from 1986 to 1993. Groundbreaking ceremonies for the new central library were held in October 1988, and the library named for the late mayor, Harold Washington, opened October 7, 1991, during John Duff's tenure as commissioner. Karen Danczak

Lyons served as acting commissioner from 1993 to 1994. The current commissioner, Mary Dempsey, was appointed in 1994.

In 1970, after more than seventy years of continuous operation, with only minimal maintenance and repairs, the central library building was showing signs of age. Space was inadequate for the extensive book collection. In 1974, the board of directors authorized a massive renovation of the library building that took three years and $11 million to complete. Meanwhile, in November 1976, the original library building was awarded historic architectural and landmark status. When the Chicago Public Library Cultural Center opened in October 1977, it provided free access not only to books and other materials, but also to a year-round schedule of free programs, lectures, films, plays, concerts, and exhibits.

There were conflicting opinions regarding what would be most appropriate and cost-effective in the long run: adding on to the existing building or constructing an entirely new building. After years of debate and discussion among the library board and the Chicago City Council, Mayor Harold Washington determined that the city should build an entirely new building for the central library. Today, the former Chicago Public Library is known as the Chicago Cultural Center and is home to many arts programs, as well as the offices of the city of Chicago's Department of Cultural Affairs.

The designated site for the new central library was 400 South State Street. Mayor Washington and the city council authorized a design-build competition and approved a bond issue to finance the project on July 29, 1987. The winner of the competition was announced on June 20, 1988, as the SEBUS Group, which included U.S. Equities, developers; Hammond, Beeby & Babka, Inc., design architects; Schal Associates, Inc., general contractors; A. Epstein and Sons, International, architects of record and structural engineer; and Delon Hampton & Associates, architects and engineers.

The library board decided the new central library would be named after the late mayor, Harold Washington, the city's first African American mayor, a great lover of books and advocate of the Chicago Public Library, who had died on November 25, 1987. The mayor at the October 1988 groundbreaking for the new central library was Eugene Sawyer, and the library commissioner was John B. Duff. After nearly three years of construction, the move into the new building was completed August 24, 1991. Mayor Richard M. Daley, Commissioner Duff, and staff joined the public and dignitaries for the dedication on Friday, October 4, 1991. On Monday, October 7, 1991, the Chicago Public Library's Harold Washington Library Center opened to the public.

The Harold Washington Library Center (HWLC) houses its collections in the largest public library building in the world. The center is open seven days a week, welcomes more than six thousand library patrons each day, and collects materials in ninety foreign languages. The library houses special collections such as the Harold Washington Archive, the Chicago Theater Collection, the Civil War Collection, and the Chicago Blues Archive. There are major collections in business, and science and technology, a Teacher Resource Center, and a Talking Book Center. The HWLC also maintains a restaurant, a coffee shop, and a secondhand bookstore.

The Harold Washington Library Center offers a wide variety of free public programs and events, including dance and music performances, author talks, children's programs, and computer workshops. The state-of-the-art program facilities include the Winter Garden, the building's architectural centerpiece, as well as a 385-seat auditorium and many smaller program rooms (Chicago Public Library 2000d, 1).

Organization

The Chicago Public Library has seventy-five branch libraries, two regional libraries, and the central library, a total of seventy-eight locations. The system serves a population of 2.9 million. The library is a department of the city of Chicago, employs approximately 1,500 staff members, and operates under a budget of $80 million annually. Mary Dempsey, commissioner of the Chicago Public Library, appointed in January 1994, is a member of the mayor's cabinet.

Chicago Public Library Five-Year Strategic Plan, 1995–2000

In 1995, under the guidance of Commissioner Dempsey, the library's staff wrote a new mission statement and developed a five-year strategic plan to rebuild the library by improving its infrastructure in five critical areas: staff development and training, technology, funding, capital planning, and materials acquisition.

"Although some of the methods and technologies used to serve library patrons have changed, the goal of the Chicago Public Library remains the same: to inform, educate, delight, entertain, and inspire Chicagoans of all ages, nationalities, ethnic groups, and economic backgrounds. Today more than 80 years after Henry Legler's *Library Plan for the Whole City*, the Chicago Public Library, through its Five-Year Strategic Plan, 1995–2000, continues to meet the challenge of providing free and equal access to library services for all" (Chicago Public Library 2000c, 1).

Finances

The Chicago Public Library runs on a current annual budget of $80 million. These monies are provided by state- and city-appropriated funds. However, the Chicago Public Library also receives funding through other sources, such as grants, partnerships with other Chicago firms and institutions, and the Chicago Public Library Foundation. The foundation, established in 1987, was created to maintain the excellence associated with the library's collections, services, and programs. An independent, nonprofit, tax-exempt, and educational organization, the foundation continuously works with the city of Chicago in a partnership with both the public and private sectors. The foundation's current $8 million campaign, Meeting Information Needs Democratically (MIND), was established to address the city of Chicago's needs via state-of-the-art technology, training—in order to use this technology efficiently—and access to the information superhighway (Chicago Public Library 2000e, 1).

Capital Planning

The Chicago Public Library's services have expanded immensely due to the aggressive capital improvement plan. Through this plan, today's patron can enjoy books at any of the neighborhood libraries, take part in book discussions, participate in workshops, listen to storytellers, and download a myriad of information, including bibliographies, from the library's Web site (Chicago Public Library 2000e, 1).

Programs and Services

Technology: The Library As "Knowledge Navigator"

The Chicago Public Library upgraded its automated public access catalog and circulation system in 1995. This upgrade included the addition of online research databases to all public access catalog terminals in each of the Chicago public libraries. In 1995, the library began offering patrons access to a variety of its information and bibliographies, becoming a gateway to the Internet. In furthering the support of the library's goals, Bill Gates, chairman of Microsoft Corporation, donated $1 million of software and training to the Chicago Public Library.

In a November 27, 2002, update to our May 2001 interview, Mary Dempsey reported that the library has opened one new branch—Austin Irving branch—a 14,000-square-foot branch library building that replaced a small storefront. Library usage in that neighborhood has increased fivefold. Two new branches opened in February 2003—Budlong Woods and West Englewood.

Neither neighborhood had ever had a library. Budlong Woods is a middle-class neighborhood; the West Englewood neighborhood is at the poverty line. It is anticipated that both libraries will be filled to capacity with patrons as soon as they open. The Budlong Woods Branch was dedicated February 8, 2003, and the West Englewood Branch was dedicated August 23, 2003. The projection is that "by the end of the current building campaign in the year 2004, another 14 new projects will have been undertaken and completed." (Chicago Public Library 2003b, 2).

Chicago Public Library launched One Book, One Chicago, a citywide "book club," in September 2001 with *To Kill a Mockingbird*, by Harper Lee. Even the library staff were not prepared for the immediate and enthusiastic reaction to this program citywide from all age groups and economic levels. It went so well that Mayor Daley asked CPL to make this a twice-a-year program instead of an annual program. So, the library selected *Night*, by Elie Wiesel, as the spring 2002 selection and *My Ántonia*, by Willa Cather, for the October 2002 event. One Book, or OBOC as it is called in-house, has garnered so much interest in reading and in the library. Also, the new branches and better marketing of programs have resulted in a 7 percent increase in circulation of library materials over 2001 (Mary Dempsey, e-mail message to author, November 27, 2002).

During the Chicago Book Festival in October 2003, authors including Scott Turow, Maxine Hong Kingston, Frederic Brenner, Sandy Cisneros, and Anne Guyer were welcomed to Chicago Public Library. One Book, One Chicago focused on *The Things They Carried*, by Tim O'Brien, with book discussions and special events. Among other special events at the library are celebrations of Hispanic Heritage Month and Polish American Heritage Month (Chicago Public Library, 2003c).

A Library of Neighborhoods

In 1873 an abandoned water tank housed the first Chicago Public Library's collection of 3,157 volumes. On October 1991, the new 746,640-square foot Harold Washington Library Center opened to the public. The library was named in honor of Chicago's first African American mayor, who was a strong advocate for the library. The collection includes almost 9 million books, microforms, serials, and government documents on more than seventy miles of shelving.

Chicago Public Library serves a "city of neighborhoods" of all nationalities, ethnic groups, economic groups, and ages. Collections include materials in more than 100 languages.

In 1907 Henry E. Legler, the third Chicago public librarian, spoke to the American Library Association about the role of public libraries. "Neither condition nor place of birth, nor age, nor sex, nor social position, serves as a bar of exclusion from this house of the open door, of the cordial welcome, of the sympathetic aid freely rendered" (Chicago Public Library 2003a). Although the means of providing services and access to materials are immensely different from nearly 100 years ago, the philosophy endures and the vision is timeless.

Chronology

1871, October 8	Great Chicago Fire
1872	Illinois Library Act

1872, April	City council passed an ordinance proclaiming the establishment of the Chicago Public Library
1873, January 1	Chicago Public Library opened in an abandoned water tank at LaSalle and Adams
1873, October	William Frederick Poole appointed head librarian
1886	Library moved to city hall
1887	Poole resigned as CPL head librarian to organize the Newberry Library of Chicago
1887–1909	Frederick H. Hild served as head librarian
1897, October 11	Library moved from quarters in city hall to the new Chicago Public Library on Michigan Avenue
1909	Henry E. Legler appointed as librarian and served until 1917, when he died suddenly
1918	Carl B. Roden chosen to succeed Legler
1920	The Henry E. Legler Regional Library, the first regional library, opened as a memorial
1950	Gertrude E. Gsheidle succeeded Carl Roden
1967	Alex Ladenson appointed chief librarian and served until 1974
1974	Board of directors authorized a renovation of the original Chicago Public Library building
1975–1978	David L. Reich served as deputy chief librarian
1976, November	Original library building awarded historic architectural and landmark status
1977, October	Chicago Public Library Cultural Center opened
1978–1981	Donald Sager served as commissioner of Chicago Public Library
1982–1985	Amanda Rudd served as commissioner of Chicago Public Library
1986–1993	John B. Duff served as commissioner of Chicago Public Library
1987	Chicago Public Library Foundation established
1987, July 29	Mayor Harold Washington and the city council authorized a design-build competition and approved a bond issue to finance the new central library

1987, November 25	Harold Washington, the city's first African American mayor, and an advocate of the Chicago Public Library, died; the library board decided that the new central library would be named after the late mayor
1988, June 20	Winner of the design-build competition for the new central library announced
1988, October 13	Chicago Public Library Commissioner John Duff and Mayor Eugene Sawyer participated in the groundbreaking for the new central library
1989	Richard M. Daley elected mayor of Chicago
1991, October 4	Chicago Public Library's Harold Washington Library Center dedicated
1991, October 7	Harold Washington Library Center opened to the public
1993–1994	Karen Danczak Lyons served as acting library commissioner
1994	Mary Dempsey, current commissioner, appointed
1995	Commissioner and library staff developed a five-year strategic plan (1995 2000)
2002	Austin Irving branch, a 14,000-square-foot library, replaced a small storefront library

Chicago Public Library Administrators Speak: Leadership in "A Great American City"

I. The Commissioner

Interview with Mary Dempsey, Commissioner, Chicago Public Library, May 14, 2001

Greiner
What motivates you?

Mary Dempsey
I love a challenge. I love tangible challenges. In this job I have the opportunity to work on entire projects from start to finish. I think it helps enormously to have a great team of people to work with, to have the support of Mayor Daley, our city council, and our board, which is obviously an enormous assistance.

But, think about what we have been able to do here in seven years. Seven years ago we all arrived at a system that had no technology to speak of, very few buildings that were worthy of crowing about, a rather inconsistent budget, and no staff development and/or training. We put together our business plan and we got the wherewithal, funding, and encouragement to go ahead with it, and we did it. It was project by project. Everything that we identified was something that was a priority— and we were able to do it. This is a self-confidence that comes with knowing that your organization is running very smoothly.

This is not about me, it is about everyone here, their enthusiasm, and their pride in the new buildings. Everyone is proud of the new staff development and the way in which the reference committee is coming up with wonderful new ideas and means of doing things.

One of the things I guess I am happiest about is just seeing the creativity blossom within professionals.

44

You know, when I arrived here, I did not see a whole lot of what I would call scholarly work being done within the profession, either writing or speaking, or even a whole lot of "what if we try this, what if we try that" kind of ideas. For whatever reason, people did not bring forward new ideas. It took a couple of years of my saying "Suggest anything, we will try it, and if it does not work—what is the worst that can happen? We just try something else." If we make a mistake, no little children will die, so let's remember that. Nothing is fatal. If it means that you get a funny article in the paper, well, fine, it will be my name on the article, not yours. And, we have really been the beneficiaries of our own hard work and success. I believe that we are all, within and outside of city government, known as a department that is very responsible, responsive, and very solid in doing a credible job.

It is fun to come to work in this kind of environment. It is also extremely helpful to have a board that is completely supportive, such as ours. The board is appointed, not elected, so their only agenda is to come in support of and see to the success of the Chicago Public Library. Our mayor loves the library, understands the mission of the library, and if anything, wants us to do even more because he understands that to Chicago, neighborhood by neighborhood, we are an essential component in the quality of life.

Our mayor frequently comes up with some of our best ideas, such as teen book clubs at every high school in Chicago, facilitated by us. "After School Matters" was the idea of Mayor Daley and his wife. This allowed us to take our cyber-navigators program, which Mayor Daley was very taken with, and extend it to the high school level. Cyber-navigators are college students employed by the Chicago Public Library. Our annual literary book festival, Chicago Book Week, was all Mayor Daley's idea. He will send us little ideas (or "nudges") and ask what we think. If we say, "Mayor, we don't know how we will do this," he will say, "Well, figure it out. Think about it." He is not dictating, but rather consistently providing suggestions. His instincts are incredible. He understands that Chicago Public Library cannot be all things to all people. He knows that we are not capable of being a day-care center, nor does he want us to be. He also understands that we are the public library and not the school library. We have actually had this discussion where he says, "You are right. School libraries need to be strong in order to support the learning environment." We are the public library and have multiple functions, including the needs of preschool students, school students, adults, and seniors. All of the components put together make my job fun. In the beginning it was sort of like, hmm . . . where do we start? There were many daunting challenges. Now, it is—let's see how much fun we can have today.

Kathy Biel came in one day and said, "Let's try e-books." She has a finance background. She is not a librarian. But she hooked up with Sheryl Nichin-Keith, our assistant commissioner for collections, and said, "Let's do e-books." Some of this is based on the fact that she has been doing a great deal of research on e-commerce; she is fascinated by the entire world of the Internet and how it is transforming America. Sheryl is fascinated from the point-of-view of a librarian in acquisitions. These two together asked if we could try this. I say, "Absolutely, why not? What is the worst that can happen?"

I think my job is to help create an environment where people can try out new ideas.

Greiner

It takes a certain talent to create that environment because some people tend to stifle.

Mary Dempsey

I think that it does no good to have really smart people work with you if you don't want to use their minds and be creative. I know where my strengths and weaknesses are, and I like to surround myself with people who are smarter than I am and let them go with their strengths. My background is, I am a librarian who later became an attorney. As a lawyer I did a lot of legislative and lobbying work. So, I am very comfortable working through government, and if there is a difficult issue to sell, that is part of my job. It is also part of my job to find the "big picture" and say to the intelligent and detail-oriented staff, "You do this; you figure this out." I do not know the intimate details of our book acquisitions module and I hope I never do, because I have very incredibly intelligent people who do and can come to me and say we are having a problem with x, y, or z. And, I consider it to be my job to try and help these staff members solve the problems, to break the bottleneck. This might mean that I go to our colleagues in city government and see if we cannot find a smarter way to do these things, to say, "Okay, troops, we are going to change the way that we do some of our ordering." An example of this would be five years ago when our entire acquisition program was not well set up and organized. We had librarians running the acquisition module. I believe that acquisitions is a financial contractual issue. I would rather have finance and contracts people running that aspect of it and have librarians doing the selection. You don't have the same people doing both. So, you have a check and balance, which is appropriate. Secondly, you've got financial staff, whose expertise is contract negotiation. These people are ensuring that your negotiated contracts are being appropriately fulfilled.

Greiner

So actually, you have several staff members who are not librarians, but are specialists in his or her particular area, like Jamey Lundblad, who deals with marketing.

Mary Dempsey

Yes. There are people who might have a library degree who also have those abilities to do other things, which is great. But, if you have these staff working in other areas where they are truly working with their strengths, then bring in someone else where you do not need a librarian to do marketing, press relations, financial compliance issues, and the budget. Again, there are enough of us working in collaboration to put the library pieces into the budget process. And, I also have to say that vice versa, our budget and finance staff have gone out of their way to educate themselves about the mission of this library, the product (if you will) of this library. They are completely committed to this library, what it does, and what it means to the citizens of Chicago. These staff members are not just bean counters or number crunchers. They will research the best way to get the book on the shelf because that is our business, our mission, what we do. For example, they will research the best kind of e-book or bibliographic database to have because this is consistent with our mission. They are very well versed in what we will demand from the vendor to make certain that we achieve our ultimate mission, which is to be a public library.

So, I commend them because they really have gone out of their way to educate themselves in these areas.

Greiner

But they bring a bit of a different perspective. If everyone is a librarian, then you would not have that perspective from the financial community.

Mary Dempsey

I think it is an enormous plus. When you are as big as we are, I think it is almost a necessity. And we have the added advantage that our first deputy and our deputy both came out of the city's budget department.

Karen Lyons [first deputy commissioner] was a budget director for the city of Chicago. Kathy Biel is our deputy commissioner. She began as an analyst and rose through the ranks. Karen has gone on to get a master's degree in library and information science. Kathy already has a master's in public policy. Together they bring a very solid financial understanding. Budget-making ability, understanding not only the city's process, but also understanding how you make budgets work for you as opposed to the other way around, is extremely important.

Greiner

What type of budget do you have, the line item or the program budget, or a combination?

Mary Dempsey

We kind of have a combination budget. It is flexible enough that we are able to do what we want to do. But it is also, in certain areas, detailed enough that we are able to do some kind of cross accounting so that we know where we are going, either up or down. This allows us to know if we budgeted well or not. But a lot of those line items are within our own internal discretion, so that, for example, if the surplus is all under children's or young adults and we have internally devoted a certain amount to this and that, then we are not hamstrung for funds if a golden opportunity comes along midway through the budget year. What we will not do, nor can we do, is transfer funds from operating to capital, or to funds that are set aside for books and equipment. So, we do have those large breakdowns. Generally speaking, our estimates are fairly accurate. What is very useful for me is that every year we prepare our budget by comparing budgets from several other years to see where we have gone in terms of expenditures. This way we are able to use the funds to our best advantage. For example, at one time we were spending enormous sums of money on items that were going to bindery. No one was really taking a look at what was being spent. Many of the items, often paperbacks or dated materials, that we were paying to be bound were not worthy of being sent to bindery. This decision-making process has since been placed under Assistant Commissioner for Collections Sheryl Nichin-Keith. She really clamped down on this problem, and as a result, the things that are important to go to bindery are being sent. We were able to reduce these expenditures a great deal and use the funds for something else that was important. Again, I believe this is a reflection on our understanding that we have this public trust, and at any given time, we want to, because it is the right thing to do, be able to justify our expenditures and justify the faith and trust that the city council and mayor have put in us. Seven years ago we began speaking to the mayor regarding our need to grow and improve in so many areas, and to do this, we needed consistent funding. His idea was that we would be separated as a discrete fund on the property tax bill for the city of Chicago so that the taxpayers could see where their money was going, so that we could have some ability to plan and predict, and so that from year to year we would not be subject to the vagaries of—is it police cars or is it library books this year? As a result of knowing what our portion would be each year, we have seen our portion grow steadily. The second piece of the budget has been the separate bonds, apart from our operating expenses, that have gone into all of the capital that we've got.

Greiner
And they do not require a public referendum?

Mary Dempsey
No. We have the best of both worlds here. We not only have a great mayor, but we are a home-rule entity. And proposed bond issues are not subject to a referendum; they are submitted for a city council vote. The first library bond that passed in 1997 was voted on by the city council, and we sold it to them as the average cost to the average homeowner being about $1.85, less than the cost of a paperback book. So the council voted for it 48 to 2. That really got us going with our building projects. In 1999, when the mayor decided that people were really loving all of the new library buildings and were clamoring for new police stations and fire stations, and they needed to be replaced, he passed an $800 million bond and said it would be used for new police stations, new fire stations, more new libraries, and some park improvements. This passed the city council with a vote of 49 to 1. The mayor's philosophy is that "it is never going to get cheaper, so let's do it now. Let's fund these projects with

capital bonds and go to work on it." So, we are all building as quickly as humanly possible.

Greiner

You are very fortunate to have Mayor Daley. I gather that the previous mayor, Harold Washington, was very pro-library also.

Mary Dempsey

Yes, this building is here as a result of him. I don't think that he had the ability to do what Mayor Daley has done in terms of neighborhood libraries. But he was sort of the impetus for this building before he passed away. So it was Mayor Daley who completed the building and got it going.

Greiner

He grew up with a love for Chicago, his father having been the mayor.

Mary Dempsey

Yes, he did. And I have never known anyone who better understands the importance of paying attention to detail. Whether it is removal of graffiti or removal of garbage, planting of trees and flowers, cleanliness—he understands that it is all of these things that make a city livable. He also understands that if you build a beautiful building people will respect it. This has certainly been the case with our building, the library. This building is ten years old. We maintain it very well. But we have never had a vandalism problem.

We have never had a graffiti problem either. The same is true in our neighborhood libraries. We do not have vandalism problems, and they are beautiful new buildings.

For many of these neighborhoods, there were no neighborhood libraries of any kind, or there were just storefront libraries under Mayor Washington and other mayors. Then, Mayor Daley came in and said, "We are going to spend the money and we are going to build a real library. We are going to respect people's quality of life." People really appreciate that. They are willing to spend their tax dollars this way because they see the tangible benefits to their children. Now that Mayor Daley has made education and reading such an especially huge priority for this city, when summer starts, the schools, parks, and libraries come together to announce what programs we all have planned for the summer. Mayor Daley can say, and does say all the time, "Do not tell me that your child has nothing to do this summer. Schools are in session, the parks have programs, the libraries have programs, and they are in every neighborhood. It is your responsibility as parents to get those kids out to those activities." He says, "I do not want to see these kids hanging around on the street corner." And he is right.

Greiner

He is offering these parents and children an alternative.

Mary Dempsey

He is offering all kinds of alternatives. He spurs us to do more.

Greiner

Students in my management class were very interested in your career ladder; didn't you say that you were a librarian?

Mary Dempsey

Yes. My first job at the age of fourteen was as a page in a library. I come from one of those families where we were the first generation to go to college, and that was the only place that would hire me at fourteen years of age. I have a master's degree from the University of Illinois, School of Library and Information Science. I was a public librarian for two years and, you know, making zero, a little more than zero, but not much more.

Then I went to work for a large law firm here in Chicago. While I was there, the attorneys encouraged me to go to law school. I continued to work there about thirty hours a week, and I went to law school full-time at DePaul University, which is literally right around the corner. I was a lawyer for twelve years in Chicago. The mayor's chief of staff and I coincidentally had offices next to each other. He then left the law firm to be the mayor's chief of staff, and he knew that I had a library degree. He called and began encouraging me to come speak with the mayor. I kept turning him down because I thought, you know, I have a very nice life, very normal, predictable, and I am paid very well. I have a husband who is a well-known trial lawyer, and I've always thought it was very nice that his name is in the papers. Frankly, I did not want my name to be there also. Then, finally, my husband said, "You know, what does it hurt? Go talk to the mayor. They asked you, you did not ask them. You are professionally qualified. You have an MLS. You would do a very good job." You have to be an Irish Catholic from Chicago to understand this, but he said, "Think of the good you could do for the children in the city of Chicago."

Oh, it is like sticking the knife in the back and turning it. I said, "Well, you know, you may regret that." So, I talked to the mayor. I did not know him very well. I believe people assume that I knew him, and I did not. I had only met him maybe twice before. And he just launched in with "Well, now, I think what we need to do is this and this, and the neighborhood libraries are really not in great shape and we need to expand the hours, and do this and that . . ." I walked out of his office and I called my husband. He said, "Did the mayor offer you the job?" I said, "I think he already thinks I work there."

I have never looked back, and that was over seven years ago. It has been the most wonderful experience of my entire life. The first thing that we did was open the libraries on Sunday. We opened the three largest of the libraries on Sunday, which was a $1 million proposition. But it has been incredibly important. Our central library and our two regional libraries open on Sunday, which is the busiest day of the week. The next thing we did was create the strategic plan, then began implementation of it, followed by the building programs, and the addition of more and newer technology. Everything has just fallen into place, one thing after another. So, there you go.

Greiner

That is very interesting that this is the way things happened. Actually, there had been an acting librarian, and she is still here, isn't she?

Mary Dempsey

Karen Lyons was acting librarian for six months. She had been the city budget director, and the mayor suggested that she go and straighten out the finances of the Chicago Public Library. Karen, Kathy Biel, and a team of people came over, including our finance director, and said, "Okay, let's try to figure this whole thing out." She was here for about six months before I was brought in. At the time Karen did not have a library degree.

Greiner

Students also wanted to know about whether or not you do community surveys. What are your data-gathering techniques for the long-range planning?

Mary Dempsey

We do a variety of things. We did not do community surveys for the long-range planning. You have to understand, when we did the plan, my assessment when I walked in the door was, "this is an organization that has zero morale—and for obvious reasons." The buildings were terrible—if there were any, there was no technology, and no staff development. It was an uneven workforce and an uneven budget. There had been a lot of turnover in the leadership. The only way to correct this was for us to decide to work together. We, the management team, were all fairly new to one another. The rest of the team had come over here six months before. So we said the only way to make this work is to put together a business plan and get it out there. We started out by saying "Why don't you tell us, you, the key management people here, tell us what is wrong. Tell us what our weaknesses and our strengths are. Tell us your vision and where you want to be in five years." We made a conscious decision at that point not to do a lot of community surveys, because frankly, there had been a lot of criticism of the system for having short hours, inadequate book collections, etcetera. All of these things were pretty well known. You did not need to hurt people's feelings. You did not need to embarrass them.

So, what we basically decided was, what is said stays in these rooms, so there are no bad ideas. Rank has no privileges. Say what you think. But I did not feel it would have been appropriate or kind or uplifting to say to the community at large, "Tell us how bad we are." It would not bother me because I was brand new. But to the people that had invested a majority of their lives here, could they possibly have felt any lower? I don't think you need to do that. So we pretty much kept these issues internal. I believe that the staff was fairly accurate in their assessment. They knew where the problems were because they had been hearing about them for years. Now that we are up and running, we provide comment cards on a regular basis, and we receive comments by e-mail. The mayor's office has a regular correspondence unit—whenever anyone writes in about any city department, the letter immediately gets routed to the appropriate commissioner for response. We view our neighborhood librarians as our outreach people. We have Friends' groups. And then, we do the traditional thing during National Library Week: "Tell us what we can do better." With the e-books we have been doing surveys. So we use a variety of these type instruments. We do not do any formal "please tell us how bad we are" initiatives. Those never accomplish anything. You always have to count a few of those anyway. I really trust the eyes and ears of the people who work here. They are very good and very smart. They know their communities, and if they don't know their communities, then there is something wrong with the way we are teaching them how to be good managers. So one of the things that we do require is outreach. We do require our librarians to give us a sense of what their community is like. What is so fascinating about Chicago is that we continue to be a city of immigrants, and we always have been. We now have book discussion groups in English, Spanish, Polish, and Russian.

It is wonderful. You know, we have always purchased library materials in over 100 languages. But, I found this interesting today: I had to go from meetings in City Hall to meetings over on the west side of the Loop, and then to meetings on the opposite end of the Loop, and I heard more people speaking foreign languages than I heard people speaking English. It was not just Spanish; there were a lot of eastern European languages spoken as well. So, we continue to see this huge influx of immigrants, and we get that information from our staff, who will say, "You know what? We need to buy more books in Polish as well as the books in Spanish because of this huge population of Polish immigrants." Or, when we did the adult book discussion in Russian, the guy in charge of it came back to me scratching his head and said, "You know, the Dostoevsky is just not moving." I said, "Jim, what makes you think these people want to read Dostoevsky?" He said, "I know, these people want to read John Grisham in Russian." I said, "Very good." So, that is what we bought, and the patrons are absolutely loving it. They want to read Patricia Cornwell in Russian. Nurturing the community-library relationship has to be done using a variety of methods. There is no one perfect way, and I would counsel any of your students that taking the pulse of the community is something you should do every week. Keep your eyes open. Keep your ears open. What are people looking for? What are they asking for?

Greiner

You were saying you started as a page. I had the pages sit in on our staff meetings when I was a branch librarian. Some of the people who had been there for a long time felt that was most unusual. But actually, the pages came up with some really good ideas because they heard the complaints and the wants of the patrons firsthand.

Mary Dempsey

I agree absolutely. When the chips are down and the librarian is helping twenty-five kids with their homework projects, it is the page who is answering the question of the little old lady who lives down the street and cannot find her Agatha Christie.

Greiner

What do you see as unique about this library?

Mary Dempsey

I believe that we are in a golden time. I really do. I believe that there is a renaissance of public libraries in America right now. But I think in Chicago it is an especially golden time. I know I am the most fortunate person in the world to be where I am right now with all of the factors aligned as they are: with the mayor, city council, and board of directors, who are absolutely passionate about what we do and willing to support us in every facet. We have such an incredible management staff, who are imaginative and smart and grounded.

Dynamic Leadership

In her own words, Commissioner Mary Dempsey loves "tangible challenges." She recognizes the value of the great team of people that she has to work with, and she encourages them in their professional development. "One of the things I guess I am happiest about is just seeing the creativity blossom within professionals." She sees her job as creating an environment where "people can try out new ideas."

Several staff members are not librarians but specialists in other areas, for example, a marketing specialist, a former budget director for the city of Chicago, and a former financial analyst who has a master's in public policy. Dempsey described herself as "a librarian who later became an attorney." The commissioner emphasized that the budget and finance staff are committed to the library's mission and understand the value of the library's product.

She emphasized that the Chicago Public Library is very fortunate to have the support of the mayor of Chicago, the city council, and the library board. Mayor Richard Daley acknowledges and values the library's contributions to the people of Chicago. He is involved in the library to the extent that he offers suggestions for programs and participates in library activities. Chicago's mayor "understands that to Chicago, neighborhood by neighborhood, we are an essential component in the quality of life in a neighborhood, to Chicago."

Operations—Unity, Teamwork, Service to the People
II. Senior Management Staff

Interview with Barbara Ford, Assistant Commissioner, Central Library Services; Charlotte Kim, Assistant Commissioner, Neighborhood Services; Sheryl Nichin-Keith, Assistant Commissioner for Collections; and Kathleen Weibel, Director, Staff Development, May 14, 2001

Greiner

Please identify what you do, what your primary role is, how you work with the other members of the management group, and how long you've been here.

Barbara Ford

My name is Barbara Ford. I've been with the Chicago Public Library about two and a half years. I am the assistant commissioner in charge of the Central Library. I work closely with my two colleagues, the other two assistant commissioners, as well as with all of the other managers in the library.

Sheryl Nichin-Keith

My name is Sheryl Nichin-Keith. I've been with the library twenty-eight years. I've been in my current position for about a year and a half now. My official title is assistant commissioner for collections, meaning that I oversee technical services, adult material selection, and also a new position, director of reference. So, my group handles a number of systemwide services, and that means that we work very closely with the other two assistant commissioners.

I was head of technical services for a few years before this. Before that, I was head of cataloging. My side job for about three years, when I was director of technical services, was doing the inventory of the entire book collection at the Chicago Public Library.

Charlotte Kim

My name is Charlotte Kim. I am assistant commissioner of neighborhood services and administer seventy-five branch libraries in three districts, two regional libraries, two bookmobile services, and a new program called the CPL Fellows. The CPL Fellows program is an innovative program that is designed to offer entry-level librarians the opportunity to experience the Chicago Public Library's diverse communities by placing them on a three-month rotating basis at one of the Chicago Public Library's seventy-seven branch and regional libraries. At the same time, the fellows alleviate professional staffing shortages in the branch and regional libraries.

This is my sixteenth year with the Chicago Public Library. Prior to joining CPL, I worked for twenty years at the Carnegie Library of Pittsburgh. I work very closely with my two counterparts, Barbara and Sheryl, as well as with a team of three district chiefs and two regional library directors.

Greiner

Barbara, you said you have been here about two and a half years and came from an academic library?

Barbara Ford

Yes. I had been an academic librarian for over twenty years.

Greiner

It seems that there are several people in this management group who are relatively young in the organization. What do you think is the best thing about being in this group? What do you particularly like best about this organization and about the working environment at Chicago Public Library?

Barbara Ford

Well, it is a large and complex organization. That means there is a lot of diversity and opportunities to learn about and do different kinds of things. I think that is one of the most exciting things. It is also a great time for the system because we have great support from the city. We are opening new branch libraries all the time. This building, our central library, is now ten years old, but it is definitely a destination center and a place that the city takes pride in. Our buildings are mostly in good shape and getting better all the time. We also have support for collections and other kinds of things. It is a very positive time for the Chicago Public Library, with the mayor that can say the "L" word and a city council that supports us. We've built many good partnerships with other cultural and educational institutions as well as the private sector. I think it is just a very good time for this public library. It is a great time to be here in that sense.

Sheryl Nichin-Keith

I think from my viewpoint, as Barbara said, this is a very complex and diverse organization. Even though I have worked here for many, many years I don't feel that my job has been the same for any length of time. I really feel like I have worked for multiple institutions because of the changes that have occurred here on a daily basis.

The emphasis on public service and serving a very diverse population has meant that the role of collections has changed over the years, and the types of collections that we put out for the public are very different from when I started. I believe automation has certainly changed the way we deliver services. The kinds of programming we do have also changed and been greatly enhanced in the last seven years. Now I am going to turn this over to my colleague Charlotte. We are bordering on her area.

Charlotte Kim

We are one of the largest urban library systems in the nation, and third in terms of the number of branch libraries in the nation. In this context, we have a lot of advantages and excitement, as well as many challenges. What I am particularly excited about is that I am part of a very wonderful administrative team with focus, creative energy, direction, as well as a hard-working and devoted staff who really know how to *lead* public service directives. When we go to community meetings or a city budget hearing, we receive many kudos from the public and aldermen for the work that we do. This is a reflection of the job our staff is doing daily and the Chicago Public Library is doing as a whole.

With a sense of direction, vision, and focused energy, we have accomplished a lot and feel much recognition from educational and cultural institutions and from other city departments. They respect the work that we are doing. In turn, when it comes time to cooperate on joint projects, we have much success in building partnerships with them. With philanthropic organizations and businesses, we feel comfortable asking them to "adopt" a branch and/or provide additional resources to their communities. Many of our branches have been adopted by private foundations and companies. Our aggressive capital improvement plan has either renovated or built forty-one new branch libraries during the past eleven years, and about fifteen more are in the second phase of the capital improvement plan. This is an exciting record. Now, in the library community, the Chicago Public Library can hold its head high and say, "We are a darn good library system!" The Neighborhood Services purpose statement, which was developed with input from the entire Neighborhood Services staff, emphasizes that effective public service is dependent upon the collaborative work of each unit within the Chicago Public Library.

In order to build a strong sense of team morale, the Chicago Public Library has been making great strides to pass information down to every single person within the library system. This effort began when we worked on our strategic plan about seven years ago. Everyone recognized the importance of communication. Communication has definitely been a major focus. Chicago Public Library has instituted many means to maintain a spirit of teamwork in this large organization and to promote communication. The senior management team meets every Monday to share information on what is happening in our units and in the system as a whole. I work with the two other assistant commissioners very closely. In addition, Barbara Ford's and my administrative teams have a monthly joint meeting where we discuss library issues and share projects, goals, and accomplishments.

My administrative team is comprised of three district chiefs and two regional library directors. Aside from a constant communication flow on an informal basis, we meet twice a month to develop Neighborhood Services goals, plan public services and programs, share information, and support one another. The district chiefs have monthly meetings with their branch managers. Each branch library and regional library holds its own monthly staff meetings. Chicago Public Library also has an internal newsletter posted on our intranet called *Click This Now*, which has been instrumental in disseminating information to our approximately 1,500 staff members.

Greiner

Your Web site has been very helpful. I would imagine that you all work closely with Amy Eshleman with development and outreach.

Sheryl Nichin-Keith

I want to second what Charlotte just said. The three of us work together very closely. I believe it is facilitated by having offices on the same floor. We frequently appear in one another's office to say something. I meet with my team once a week. My team, the director of reference and the head of technical services, have made a point of going out together to visit various branches and the central library division to meet with people, since they are both fairly new in their jobs. We are all going out to the district meetings this month to meet with the branch heads and let them know what we are doing. That all goes a long way to facilitate communication.

Greiner

You are talking about formal and informal communication, right? If you have an idea, you just get on e-mail or drop by somebody's office.

Barbara Ford

I would say that our communication is both formal and informal. Monday morning is when we let one another know what's going on. I come back and write a brief summary of that, which I share with the unit heads in the Central Library. We meet periodically with one another, the commissioner, and others as needed.

CPL is a very large organization. As a person who is new here, I believe one of the biggest challenges initially is realizing all of the people who have to be involved in things and how far you move to communicate. I also believe that we are constantly working on ways to enhance that because it is such a large organization. Sometimes it reminds me of the elephant and which part you see that day. It is a very different organization. One of my biggest challenges as a fairly new assistant commissioner was, first, to understand and know who the players are. The ongoing challenge is to keep all of those people out at the front lines understanding this, because everyone has lots of work to do regardless of how good our newsletters are, or the e-mail that we send; people are busy.

Charlotte Kim

Neighborhood Services has seventy-five branches assigned to three districts, and each district chief conducts a monthly meeting with his or her branch managers. A forum for cross-district meetings is also provided for managers of branches and regional libraries in order to strengthen team morale. Twice a year each district holds joint meetings with another district or with a regional library. District meetings are also held at the Central Library, where branch managers meet with various division and department heads and share information.

Our children's librarians also have monthly systemwide meetings, as well as children's cluster meetings, where they meet within their districts. In these meetings they are able to get information about systemwide children's services, as well as share information about the many exciting children's programs they are offering in their branch libraries.

Another exciting program has been our leadership seminars, where we encourage professional growth in our next generation of leaders. The sessions are designed in formal as well as informal settings, in which participants exchange many innovative ideas, foster creativity, work on a project together, or network with one another.

Finally, our first assistants' seminars pull together first assistants from units systemwide twice a year. Unit managers are invited to one of these sessions during which first assistants have some much-appreciated uninterrupted time with their unit managers for developing goals for their unit together and for an open discussion of the unit matters. Undoubtedly, these means of communication contribute to build a spirit of teamwork in this large organization.

Greiner

I was thinking that you must have a very complicated organization chart.

Barbara Ford

Well, yes and no. Basically, there are a lot of people in the senior staff, many of whom report directly to Mary. In that sense, the organization is fairly flat at that level. I have six chief positions in the Central Library, plus the head of corporate and private events. It cascades down. It is a complicated chart in that sense. But it is fairly logical and well organized, so that any staff member should know who they need to go to.

Greiner

So everyone knows to whom they are responsible and who the authority is at the next level.

Barbara Ford

Right. Since the authority level does not always go up—sometimes it goes across—that is where our reports work together on a lot of systemwide things. There are some mundane things, like knowing whom to call if somebody does not show up to open the unit that day; and there are the more complex issues of exactly who is responsible if we don't have some key book we need, or if the toilet is not working, or whatever. It runs from the sublime to the absurd. That is all fairly well mapped out so that people know who is responsible. This is part of what we have been working on, for example, with the new position, the director of reference. With Sheryl moving into her new position, my perspective is that there are fairly new comers and this is a very key position. She has a lot of those key but back-room functions that really need to run well. It has really been great to have her in that position because she has a strong library background and understands the issues. In a sense, that is what I see as our role, we are sort of the senior librarians of the organization. We see that the nuts and bolts, day-to-day things run, as well as looking to the future.

I believe I have forty-three service points in this building. Some days just keeping all of the points open and staffed with the basic things such as bookshelves and having reference questions answered is the job.

Greiner

I get the feeling that things seem to be moving so rapidly. There are so many things going on and so much enthusiasm, does anyone ever have a day where they sit down and say they are not going to do anything? If they did, what would happen, as intertwined as the organization is?

Charlotte Kim

Fortunately, we don't have anybody like that. If we did, they would not last very long.

Sheryl Nichin-Keith

I think that learning a great deal is exactly what I have been doing for the last year because I haven't really thought of collections from a public service viewpoint for many years. I worked in the branches early in my career, but I've been in technical services quite a while. At least from our viewpoint, so much is in electronic format. All of the issues of balancing and taking into account print versus nonprint versus electronic, all of those things that everyone is struggling with now make collection development very different from the way it was even five or six years ago.

I still feel like I am learning a lot as we move forward. Fortunately, I have some really great people that report to me and I can rely on them and these two ladies also, Charlotte and Barbara, to make certain that I don't make any tremendous mistakes. Right now, we are struggling to just get a handle on what is in electronic form that we can use most efficiently. I believe that, for a big organization, is a struggle. We have had a number of discussions about what our philosophy is in terms of presenting those collections. Is it something that would be prohibitively expensive to make available systemwide; is it something that we are only willing to make available at Central? That is a philosophical discussion for us because of the way electronic collections have allowed us to equalize services across the system. That is the crux of our discussion. What is appropriate in terms of all of the collections and facilities, from the Web page versus what is appropriate and what depth of subject expertise the individual has at a central library or a regional library has in navigating those electronic databases? I think that is much more complex than what we faced with the print. It was much more clear-cut with the print in terms of where you put it and who then interprets it or helps the patron use that source. It is much more difficult in the electronic format. I don't know yet that we've encountered anything in electronic format that exactly replicates something in print. That is also a big struggle now.

Greiner

Does it depend, in the branches, on the demographics of the community and how much you look at the community market?

Sheryl Nichin-Keith

At least in my viewpoint it does. Now I will look to my colleagues to give you their viewpoints. You hear quite often that Chicago is the city of neighborhoods. People look to their local library facility to be their access point. For us, the real discussion has revolved around the question, Do we provide this reference source for everybody? It does allow us to provide things at the local level that we could not provide before. For the print we definitely look at the neighborhood demographics. It has been different for the electronic formats. I think that is what we are struggling with right now. In some ways it is easier to deliver it to whatever access point we have, but that means that people's expectations are raised. We talk a lot about having equalized access across the city regardless of the size of our branch site. It also then places an additional burden upon the staff to be able to interpret that, or help the patron navigate.

Charlotte Kim

Chicago is a city of neighborhoods, but these neighborhoods are not isolated. People do travel to other parts of the city and use resources at one of our seventy-eight libraries. Many of our patrons regularly visit more than one of our libraries. We do stress equality of access to all our resources through electronic databases, interlibrary loan, and the reserve system. When we make systemwide decisions on the acquisition of resources, there is always branch or regional library representation. Decisions are not made unilaterally, and we try to use our budget as wisely as possible. Because of this, so far, people have been really happy with the electronic as well as print materials acquired through the centralized collection development that we have been providing to all seventy-eight agencies. However, branch libraries do have some autonomy; they have their own materials budget, for example, to build collections that serve their own community's needs.

Barbara Ford

One of the reasons that there are differences is because of the many languages in the neighborhoods. That is where we do make some changes in the collections. We collect in a variety of languages, and of course we have a center here at the Central Library that is a Spanish information center. It also specializes in materials in other languages. The branches, depending on their neighborhood profile, may collect in a variety of languages. We've even had some portable collections that move around the city so that we can meet those changing needs. We try to be flexible as communities and needs change and really address what it is that people need from the library.

Greiner

Everything has been really positive. Is there anything that you would like to do better in this organization?

Barbara Ford

I would just like to say that our size is both our greatest strength and can be our greatest challenge. There are many Chicago Public Libraries, depending on where you are sitting on a particular day. I don't know what we can do about that. That is the way that the library is, and we work on addressing those issues through communication. Of course, I think technology has really helped us there because with Web pages, our internal intranet, and e-mail, we can really get information out more effectively, both to our staff and to our users. A lot of the new tools that we have available are helping us address what I believe to be some of our biggest challenges with such a large system. Again, that is an incredible strength. We are an old library and we do have something for everyone. I am really struck here at the Central Library, which I know best, by the variety of users, clients, and so forth. We are able to have something for everyone. I think our challenge is that ongoing effort to be sure that everyone, our staff and clients, has the information they need.

Charlotte Kim

Well, we all have heard about being a victim of one's own success. We have done a lot of things and done them well. Expectations from our public are continuously expanding. We have very dedicated staff. However, as Barbara said, there are days that we feel we really have to be able to provide that extra effort because of technology and other changes.

[Kathleen Weibel joins the group.]

Kathleen Weibel

Staff development is very important. For my colleagues and I, there are times when we have worked very closely, and in some cases even more than others. As the libraries initiate some new activity, we are involved as part of that planning process. That is one piece. That is an organizational development piece. The other piece is trying to put in place the bits and pieces that would be staff development resources in most organizations for a variety of reasons. In this organization, those things that they had in the past are gone. What we are trying to do is put a sustainable program in place that enables us to have the workforce with the attitude, skills, and knowledge that they need to do their job.

Greiner

Well, I know in the literature you will find that staff don't get the training they need and they generally don't know what the expectations are.

Kathleen Weibel

I don't believe we have all of the bits and pieces in place entirely. Part of it is from the nature of the organization. I can give you the schedule of what we do. Staff development is a very high priority for Commissioner Dempsey and her administration. My department has something that other staff and department areas have not had in the past, which is total administrative support. That comes not only from Mary, but also from other elements of the team. I believe for my predecessors that is a fair thing to say. While there was support, the level was not what it is today. At the time this occurred, it was also when we were switching to automated systems. We had not done anything like this before. We had been on a dead system for quite some time. We didn't build a program separate from the institution's needs. You can look at this as the program that we ought to have, but the reality was that the institution's needs were here, here, and here. So, we put this piece here, that piece there, and that piece in place there. If you look at the program that we ought to have, we have this piece, this piece, and this piece. We are trying to put the connecting pieces in place, so that we have a total program, so someone coming in can move through that program. We are not there yet.

Does that sound like what you are talking about? This is not in a vacuum. It is a team process. It is in partnership with everyone that is here. Chicago Public Library people teach other Chicago Public Library people, so that others who come into this institution don't say, "I got this job and I don't know what I am supposed to do in my job." Is this being reduced? I would hope so. We have really focused more on the people who are here. For example, we had been a mainframe culture with some small bits of PCs out there. We had to move to being a PC culture. For a while we used to run mouse classes. We don't anymore. What we were really focusing on rather than the new people coming in was the people who were already here. I think we now need to make a switch to do both. So, we did what the institution needed.

Sheryl started out as one of our main trainers. From that she developed the idea that the catalog department, when she was head there, whose job it has always been to assist people in interpreting the catalog, should be the source of all the teachers. She has done a program in the Public Library Association (PLA). That is the kind of model that was appropriate to this institution. Staff development is one of the things that makes a difference. It is not just our human resources department. In this institution staff development is not part of human resources. Staff development is part of the services and planning process. That is the big difference.

Staff development is everybody's responsibility. But, we've had to pick and choose in response to the institution's priorities. That is what set our agenda. In the strategic plan there was a priority that staff development would be more prevalent for the staff, and we did need to go beyond the strategic plan. Related to that, it means nothing unless it is connected to what we are doing. Unless it has meaning, in terms of our ability to deliver the services, why invest time and money in it? That is why it is hard when you ask what the role of the management is. I believe all of us come together in various configurations.

Greiner

Do you do any training of middle managers?

Kathleen Weibel

The first assistants do that. The city offers training programs, and we send people to those. In terms of the program and its pieces, I don't think you can really see that from the schedule. I believe the fact that you can't is telling of the way we have put it together. It is really in the next couple of years that you will see the pieces and threads put in. We should, not in three years totally, have the pieces. Since everything is done in partnerships with different programs, some departments of the library more easily or naturally use the training program. I think the catalog is a great example. I think there are others that don't, and we wish they would. We, as coordinators and facilitators, have to work with them. There are times when we are a pain in the neck.

Greiner

I got a lot from the Web page.

Kathleen Weibel

That is a joint effort. There is an area that reports to Barbara—corporate and private events—that is absolutely essential in that process for the logistics. We tend to do the coordination, but the bulk of those programs is done by Chicago Public Library people. Everybody who sits at this table is an essential part of that process. Chicago Public Library people teach Chicago Public Library people. There is nothing like trying to teach someone how to learn something. There is a growing alumni from that program.

[Kathleen Weibel leaves the group.]

Greiner

I saw where Bill Gates had given the equipment and the training, right? Is that separate from what you would have done?

Barbara Ford

There were a couple of staff that were trained. The idea is that they then come back and share appropriate expertise. There was a lot of training to get staff ready for this, which is really part of our ongoing staff development, beginning with how to use the mouse right up through how to search complex databases. We have teams of technical experts that meet periodically and share experiences and so forth. For us, the training from Gates was really trivial. Our situation is very different from that of a small public library. We've had technology a long time. We have some very sophisticated staff members. What Gates really allowed us to do was to roll it out further to more locations and people and give our staff the training and support to make that happen.

Charlotte Kim

The staff came up with a lot of procedures and guidelines for children, parents, and teachers. Other than that, most of the money was for equipment and software.

Greiner

I know in Mississippi, which was one of the first states to get it, our students had the opportunity to be trainers, and that was a scholarship for them.

Charlotte Kim

What kind of perception did you have about Chicago Public Library, and how is it now? How has is changed, if it did?

Greiner

That is a very fair question. The thing that has impressed me most and that I will try to communicate is this strong sense of a team effort.

Sheryl Nichin-Keith

Having been here twenty-eight years, I can say with confidence that this group is remarkably nonterritorial.

Greiner

Right, and that is what you communicated. That is what the group that I met with this morning communicated to me. Jamey was the new kid on the block, with a year here. He is bringing in something different to marketing. Everyone seemed glad that he is here because they were able to get the message out a bit better. Also, it took some of the work off of the others that they had been responsible for. It is an entire library effort. Another thing that impresses me is the level of energy that it must take to be part of such a dynamic organization. No one can drag their feet or they will get lost, or trampled. I see real enthusiasm for what you are doing.

Sheryl Nichin-Keith

Going back to the question about whether there is something that I would like to see done differently. I was just out at one of the suburban libraries on Friday to discuss a little e-book pilot that we've been doing here. I think if there is anything that we don't do, it is get our story out. The e-book is a good example. The Chicago Public Library has done many unique, cutting-edge projects but does not always convey that message to the profession. For example, when I did my e-book presentation at the Oak Park Public Library, I was presenting information that was new to them. I thought of it as a small pilot project and something that was being done at many other public libraries at this time, but to the Oak Park staff, the project was new and unique.

Charlotte Kim

Building on what Sheryl just said, at times because of our success, we feel that we've done it, we've been there, and we've done it better. But we also have the responsibility and obligation to share what we know and what we have done well with other library communities. It is a challenge because we don't always have time to do that.

Chicago Public Library has transformed as a system with a vision and creative energy. It started about eight years ago with the first strategic plan. Through an honest evaluation of our library system and a lot of soul searching, we have learned to see the "big picture" for the future of the Chicago Public Library. We built a consensus on what direction we wanted to go in and what needed to be done to get there. The staff gained confidence with the successful completion of the first phase. We will soon embark on the second phase of the strategic plan with even greater energy and expectations. Chicago Public Library is a very fast moving train; however, we now know who to talk to and work with, and how we can enlist their help. This is a comfort that gives us confidence to go back to the framework of what we are and why we are here.

Greiner

Do you remember anything that you got out of a management class that applies to what you do?

Sheryl Nichin-Keith

I actually took management classes. I believe that I actually do apply elements from those classes quite a bit. If I can look back to one thing that I have applied, it would be evaluating staff. We brought back some ideas and hammered out behaviors that we were looking for.

The other thing I brought with me from those management classes was the quantitative analyzing of workflows, and analysis of other things that we do in technical services.

It helped having group projects. They were the best in helping me with the many different experiences; I had other people helping me analyze the situation. It is harder when you are working for a grade, though. You realize that you might not get the grade that you would have if you worked on the project yourself and perfected it. Whereas, here we are not working for grades; we are working for a common goal.

Charlotte Kim

Library service is a human service. An ability to manage people or a unit requires a lot of personal maturity, experience, compassion, sense of fairness, and good common sense. I took management courses in the library school, but several psychology courses I took while working toward my first master's degree in education were very useful for me in my library work environment.

Sheryl Nichin-Keith

There are some people that are natural catalogers, but I think it is not until you get in the situation and are able to apply it that it truly makes sense because you start to see it in context. You see why certain things work and others do not. I do think that is true for a lot of people. Until you are able to apply things they really don't always make sense.

Update

Barbara Ford left the position as assistant commissioner of Central Library Services to become director and distinguished professor at the Mortenson Center for International Library Programs at the University of Illinois.

Sheryl Nichin-Keith, assistant commissioner for collections, retired in spring 2003.

The Library's Workers—Enhancing Abilities

Interview with Kathleen Weibel, Director of Staff Development, May 16, 2001 (Updated December 15, 2002)

Kathleen Weibel

Let me give you this six-month schedule of CPL staff development activities. I guess any schedule does not include absolutely everything. This is also located on our intranet. You would not be able to get it outside of the Chicago Public Library.

Greiner

Kathleen, how long have you been at Chicago Public Library?

Kathleen Weibel

I have been here probably eight years this time. I was here four years in the 1970s. I was adult specialist for special extension services, the outreach group. Dr. Alex Ladenson was the chief librarian. Mary Dempsey brought me back to Chicago Public Library in 1993.

Greiner

It seems that staff development is very strong and important.

Kathleen Weibel

Yes, staff development is very strong and important at CPL. I believe that Karen Danczak Lyons, our first deputy commissioner, who served as acting commissioner before Mary came, and Mary share that belief. That is one of the reasons that I was interested in coming back to Chicago Public Library.

Greiner

I believe from this schedule that I can tell more about exactly what you do regarding staff development. What is the process for workshops, mentoring, etcetera.

Kathleen Weibel

What we do here at Chicago Public Library is like an elephant dancing on its toes. It may not be the most graceful, the most beautiful, or the best interpretation of the dance. What is remarkable is that the elephant and CPL do it. Our perspective is that there are educational implications in everything that we do. Particularly when we are initiating new undertakings, we need to look at those. Staff development is an integral part of any planning process at CPL.

We are not part of the human resources department. When I first came back, we reported to the commissioner. We currently report to the deputy commissioner, which is unusual. The point I am making is that it does not matter whom we report to as long as it is at the upper levels of the organization. It is unusual to have the staff development function report at the highest level. In our organization it does. That is because of our commitment. Usually the staff development department is buried somewhere in the human resources department. At CPL, staff development is involved with all functions of the library and has the ability to engage with all segments of the organization. In great part this is because of where we are located in the library's hierarchy.

Now, not every problem has an educational solution. Some problems might initially appear to be training issues, but in fact they are system issues. The solution might be to fix the system instead of fixing the people.

We are part of the process when an organizational model is being developed. The best example I can give you is one in which we are currently involved. CPL is about to implement telephone notification of overdue items, where the computer calls patrons with overdue library materials. On one hand we are ready to go, we could just turn this on. But on the other hand, this is a real opportunity to go in and work on this implementation as a service tool. We are meeting next week with a group of people to see how we are going to deal with this. We are not going to drag everyone down here for a class, nor are we going to drag a class out to the branches. We will use this as an opportunity to deliver some customer service messages to the staff and to try and get them thinking about some other things.

Part of what we are doing is hearing the concerns of others on the planning committee, and we need to be able to respond to these concerns in the educational pieces we develop. In our *Holds* classes, which deal with the library's reserve system, we used to talk about the fact that we have fought these battles. Trust us, your perspective was loud and clear but this is where we ended up. By being there and actually having that planning committee do the training, staff realize the trainers were the people who actually spilled their blood on the floor in designing the reserve program, and that the program was designed by people like them. That is our model.

Greiner

The planning committee turned into the training committee?

Kathleen Weibel

Sure. At CPL, the staff development department does not do most of the training. What we do is work with the staff, the people who do the job. For example, the circulation classes are taught by circulation staff, and there are librarians who take the classes as well as pages. When I first came, we were doing some massive training for a new integrated system, and some staff development personnel weren't sure that they were going to let the circulation people teach librarians. If you are doing circulation, you are the only one to teach that class. Our circulation staff have incredible talents and skills, and yet many don't see themselves this way. Some of the things that the circulation trainers have done have changed their lives, people who were leaders but did not perceive themselves as such now do. Now, we have only two outside trainers that we use on a consistent contractual basis. They have been with us for about seven years. They are like staff members. One of the trainers is an absolute ace automation person. She often slips over into consulting and works with computer services.

Most of what we do here, we do in house. The ultimate professional development experience is to actually do the teaching. The real learning process going on is in the people who created the classes. It is not that someone designs the training program and then you go out and speak it. Staff who do the job and will be the trainers design the training program. If we are going to start doing something, we put those who are interested in being trainers or on a planning committee in a room. "You all want to be trainers and we want to know everything someone needs to know in order to do this job." They talk. "Well, that is interesting. How would we teach that?" Someone tries teaching the concept, if someone else wants to try it, then they try it. "What approach do you like best?" When everyone likes an approach, then we put it in the script. The script is not a script that you have to speak; it is an outline, so we have common examples and talking points. Then, trainers are put together in teams, depending upon the trainers' schedules. Chicago Public Library people teach Chicago Public Library people.

There are some specialty trainers, like the reference communication skills trainers, who, when they discuss the several-year design process they went through to produce the training program, will say that the process changed the way they do reference. I have had some of the most intellectual discussions about the nature of reference practice and transactions that involved issues of gender and issues of race during the design of our reference communication skills training. In these meetings one might talk about things such as the impact of the librarian's gender, race, and lightness and darkness of African American skin color on patrons.

Once when I described the kinds of discussions we were having in the reference communications skills design meetings to a colleague who runs a really good continuing education program with lots of member libraries, which is very different than the staff development program, she said, "How did you get a journal club going?" I said, "Journal club; what a joke." Chicago Public Library people would never come to a journal club; they wouldn't perceive that it was important or that they had time. But, if discussion is tied to a task, they will do the task. I have learned a great deal from my colleagues.

When we do something new at CPL, people still ask if they are going to get any training. We tell them that we would not stick them out on that limb. The problem is, it might take us a while, but yes, to everyone.

We took a break this year from massive PCs training, which we out-sourced. You will see in the schedule that there are still quite a few PC and Internet classes. There are still many things that are missing from the schedule as well. This is because we made a major shift from a mainframe-based culture to a PC culture. We desperately needed to do this. We are only now just beginning to play with some PC competencies, where we are actually asking people to check if the staff members have these competencies.

There is not a lot of management training in the catalog. We have begun a leadership seminar; it is in its second year. We have started two biannual seminars for all of the people who are the "number twos." Some people did not know they were number twos until they actually got in the seminar. We have been working with them trying to articulate their roles so they can understand certain aspects of their jobs.

Our children's services has a very high level of training and has for years, when there was nothing available for anyone else. We are trying to integrate this extensive feature into the whole program.

We send an annual letter to every staff member that lists the classes that staff member has taken in the past year. We send out a biannual unit report that lists the classes the staff has taken; this information can be used in job performance appraisals. We are trying to make our tracking system electronic so that it can be accessed through our intranet. We want staff to register online and get the class information they need right away. That is a project we call "the Great Database in the Sky." We keep getting moved back on this one. We really need the management information that such an approach could supply. We need to tie the training closer to the competencies that people do need to have. We need to articulate those competencies. We need to tie the training more with our performance appraisal program.

We've got bits and pieces of the circle and we need to tie that circle up. The main thing is that there is a very strong commitment to staff development on the part of the entire organization. I believe that we see it now as a hallmark of our culture that was not necessarily there in the past. There were always people at CPL trying to develop learning opportunities, but they did not have that overall organizational commitment.

The leadership seminars have been interesting to develop because we made the assumption that to function as a leader in this organization you need to understand the organization. The first one we did I believe had eleven full-day sessions. Each one was created from scratch last year. It was a wild year. We ended up having a real mix of people because all the senior staff attended. You could not really begin this program without the senior staff, but not all of them wanted to be in the seminar. We did not have a planning committee, which was a big mistake on my part. Consequently, each seminar stood on its own, and it was very difficult to get them pulled together. We managed to do that toward the end. We learned a lot from that. We do have a planning committee this year, a wonderful planning committee. We all see things very differently.

We asked for volunteers from the inaugural seminar who wanted to sit in on the planning committee. When we saw who was willing to volunteer, we identified other staff members who were needed to create a representative committee and asked them to join. The committee consists of Karen Danczak Lyons, first deputy commissioner; Carole Medal, who is a division chief in VPA (Visual and Performing Arts) and is fairly new to the system, a perspective we needed; Roberta Webb, who was a division chief but is now south district chief and is a superb manager; Michael Baker, the central district chief, who has been here for a while; Sarah Beasley, a librarian I; and Robin Smith, who is branch manager at Pullman and is also new to the system.

This year we added three circulation staff members to the leadership seminar, which is a big step. We are now acknowledging the different levels in which you can be a leader. We have some associates who are going to library school who are participants. The leadership seminar is not just for the public service people, it also includes other departments. This year we are going to have fourteen activities. We spun off four of the leadership activities, and we started a series called Learn CPL. There is an orientation that HR conducts when new staff members come in—it involves filling out a bunch of forms. Staff Development does a half-day new staff orientation, which includes meeting the commissioner and other senior administration and visits to five departments that provide systemwide service. Unfortunately, it sometimes takes a year before people can get into this class. We really needed something that gives new people a chance to get some idea of the culture. There are the Learn CPL Organization and Vision, which the commissioner conducts, Learn CPL Finances and Funding, and Learn CPL Employees. There will also be a Learn CPL Public Services. We will probably add a fifth one on collections next year. In your first two years here, if you are a librarian, an associate, or a member of a closed department, and your unit head says you need to attend these classes, then you need to take off work for these. The idea is that you get some exposure to the organization.

During the last leadership discussion, we spent an entire day discussing organizational culture. A lot of folks thought we could not spend that long a time on one topic. But, we did, and we did it very successfully, and it was quite interesting. What was really clear from a number of the groups was that informal communication is given much more credence than formal. If it is in writing we ignore it, but you tell me and I know it. I realize this is true anywhere, but we have developed it to a high art. We often need to balance this out. We are trying to incrementally add to our program the pieces that would be part of manager training. I don't know whether it is a mistake not to go outside more for this training. We have gone outside and we have also brought people in to conduct training sessions as part of our program. I may be over-relying on doing all of this ourselves.

My motto is "doable and sustainable." That is where we are going. We are beginning to drop some of the automation basic-skill-related things that we used to have when we were trying to get over the hump of the switch to PCs, and we can begin to address other areas of need.

Greiner

I believe there was a period of time where the technology training was off-set because you got this equipment, but the people did not know how to use it.

Kathleen Weibel

Right. This is very true in any organization. That is what we put in place first. We used to have a thing called Computer Camp, where staff would come in and take apart a PC. We were really trying to demystify, but not so the staff would be techies. It is really mostly air in the PC's. We try and do things with humor when we can.

I should get you an "All Staff Institute Day Catalog." Mary actually wanted to initiate that program, and she made the commitment to do so before I came. Chicago loves being the largest. We are the largest public library that closes for one of these things. There are about 1,200 people that end up coming here. We run approximately eighty-five workshops, some of which are repeated numerous times. There are four sessions and about forty classes to pick from in each session. It used to be run much more like a conference, but it has made more of a shift to a staff development model, where people need to preregister for what they are going to do and they need to talk with their supervisor. I believe this is the eighth year we are doing this. It was kind of a signature event.

Greiner

You mentioned the performance evaluation and staff development. Is there a relationship here?

Kathleen Weibel

Not at this point, but you haven't spoken to Karen and Donna yet. Definitely talk to them about that.

What I would say about that is there are a couple of linking projects. Right now the city is moving to an Oracle-based HR system. Once that is done and we see where we can go with the Great Database in the Sky, I believe that you are going to see a lot more linking. That is what we want. That is what I mean when I say we have parts and pieces of the circle in place. We recently introduced the new performance appraisal form and a new performance appraisal system. We are still looking at what this new form has done and what kind of data we are getting. I believe Donna would probably be a better one to address this. But, is that our vision? Absolutely! This is everyone's vision. This is an administrative tool and we want to be able to make the most use of that tool. We want to put the tool in place, refine the tool, let people know what is available, hold it out there consistently to make it easy for them to get in, and then we need to tie in the concept that this is not for personal growth, but for the ability to do the job. That piece really has to take place at the local level. This is why we try and get out the biannual reports on classes taken in time for people to get the performance appraisals done. Also in terms of the improvement plan, or goals for the next six months, which we do twice a year.

Greiner

You do this twice a year?

Kathleen Weibel

Yes, under the city's requirements. To do this you've got a six-month goal, the time frame is one of the easy things to slot in to the goals. But, we've not really looked at what staff members say they are doing as opposed to what classes they are taking and the impact of those classes.

Greiner

Is there anything else you would like to discuss regarding your role?

Kathleen Weibel

I believe that what is important about my role is that there is an administrative commitment to it. People will look at the staff development department and say "That is all well and good for you. You have a staff of seven or eight people." But, you have to look at the scale. There are 1,500 people who work here. Anyone can do everything that we do if there is the will. We don't have a big budget; we take advantage of whatever opportunities are available. When staff members really want to go to an event in Chicago, like the ALA exhibits or Book Expo, the most who can go while others maintain service is about 100 per day, but we don't set limits on the number who can go. The local unit will let the staff members know if they cannot let them go. With the Book Expo, when it meets in Chicago, staff members can go on library time (except Sunday, when they can go on their own time), and we will pay for registration. We could not get 223 staff members out in one day, but over three days we can. But, to Reaching Forward, which is the Illinois Conference for library clerks and associates, we usually send 100 to 120 staff members every year. People will cover for each other.

One reason you need to get people out to events when you work in a large organization is that otherwise your staff has no context. We really need to get our folks out, but our department has very little travel money. With the little travel money we do have, we provide support if a staff member is giving a talk regarding his or her work at CPL. This year we are sending twelve people to the Springfield conference of the Illinois Library Association, ILA. All twelve are giving presentations. Next year, when ILA is in Chicago, we will send hundreds. CPL staff have not been active in ILA. We are making an effort to increase our activity, hence the number of programs we offer at ILA, which grows each year. We hope that staff will consider joining ILA after making a couple of presentations and get active on committees. What we try and do is maximize the money we have. There are many people here who feel they get the opportunity to participate in many outside conferences, talks, etcetera. The problem for some of the really high-end people who need to go here and there more frequently is that they will typically have to pay the travel expenses themselves.

The other thing that the city has—and it is wonderful—is a tuition reimbursement program that will prepare you for any degree that would be required for any job in the city. You can work at the city library and get a law degree. If you are working for the library and you are getting a library degree, we will also give you some time off to do that.

Internal recruitment, which is part of what my department does, is really important. We grow our own. We have a much higher average of African Americans and Hispanics than libraries have nationally. The major urban libraries have to do this. We have tools that we can use, such as tuition reimbursement. If employees want to take advantage of these opportunities, we can usually find ways to benefit them. I believe it is fair to say that the staff has options. I believe this also creates a positive morale. On the other hand, there are certainly people that I respect that say. Stop doing this because you are denying the public a day of service. You can't please everyone, and I don't try to.

If there is any lesson I can share with any library, it is look at your resources, look at how you are spending your money. Are you really making sure that the investment that you are making in this person is going to come back to your institution? If it benefits them, that is wonderful and nothing makes me happier. It does not always come back to you; people leave the library, but even if the person remains in Chicago, believe me, it will come back to us somehow. Sometimes I have to look at the process and realize that it is the price of doing business. These people also remember the Chicago Public Library. They may end up giving to the foundation.

Greiner

It is wonderful that the library does not have to pay for the tuition, that the city does. Actually, what the library is contributing is that time off.

Kathleen Weibel

Again, we are an unusual model in that we really are a city department. It has good and bad sides. But if you learn how to work that position to everyone's mutual advantage, then it is all the taxpayer's dollars and all to the benefit of the taxpayer.

Greiner

Right. And the taxpayers can actually see what is going for the library.

Kathleen Weibel

We are very fortunate that the people in our upper administration are really very knowledgeable about the city. They are the networks. They communicate the role of the library.

Building Staff—People, Dedication

Interview with Donna Maloney, Director, Human Resources, and Karen D. Lyons, First Deputy Commissioner, May 16, 2001

Donna Maloney described the role of the Department of Human Resources.

Donna Maloney

Human Resources in our organization is responsible for the hiring and terminating of employees. We set policies that have to do with any personnel matters. We handle grievances and union problems. Karen and I are both on different levels of the grievance procedure with our union colleagues.

Greiner

Is this a union operation?

Donna Maloney

It's union, yes. Ninety-nine percent of our positions are unionized. All of our librarian and clerical positions are unionized. Senior administrators are not.

Greiner

The senior administrators, directors, commissioners, and so forth are not unionized?

Karen Lyons

Even though we have 1,500 employees, it's truly only a couple of handfuls of people that are not union.

Greiner

What about your highest level of librarian, isn't it a level five?

Karen Lyons

The Library V title is in the union. We are a city department and are governed by citywide collective bargaining agreements.

Donna Maloney

We do a lot of recruiting, which is one of our biggest responsibilities. We are experiencing, along with most all of the nation, a shortage in children's librarians and minority librarians. We are in a very expansive building and growing period. We just finished one building and we are starting another one. So to staff these new libraries, we need more clerks in clerical areas and librarians, including children's librarians, but it is mostly the librarians that we need when we build in minority neighborhoods. It is sometimes difficult to fill those positions. So, we've got a full-time recruitment coordinator now on the staff and we are trying to get her an assistant. This job has been growing steadily because of the library's needs. The other issue that we are facing is a buyout situation that the city has for people who want to buy out of their employment early. It took us nearly two years to get over the domino effect of filling those positions because we are unionized. Regardless of what position was vacated, we would have to fill, for example, the Librarian II position before we could fill the Librarian III position, no matter which one became vacant first. So the domino effect took us nearly two years to get through.

Karen Lyons

We need to discuss the new performance evaluation process.

Donna Maloney

When I came into the position about six years ago, our strategic plan was already established. One of my responsibilities in Human Resources was performance evaluations. It took us a while, but we did put together a new performance appraisal instrument, which started out as yellow "stickies" on the wall and was completed eighteen months later.

We looked at some of our problems. I think the major problem we were facing was that the scores were not linked to reality. Everybody was excellent; if they weren't excellent, there was a very difficult conversation between the supervisor and the employee that they were trying to evaluate. So, we got rid of that issue by boiling it down to a rating of "meets requirements." Either they were doing their job or they were not.

Another issue was that the appraisal was always linked to the employee step increase, which was pretty automatic. Ninety-nine percent of the time, employees received their increases. It didn't make any sense to have that issue hanging over the performance evaluation. We simply eliminated it by a single question as the last step: "Should this employee have a step increase, yes or no?" We've asked supervisors to change their way of thinking. Supervisors are required to put both good and poor examples into the employee's report. They are required to keep records during the year. One of the problems was that when it came time for performance evaluations, supervisors only remembered what had happened in the past two or three weeks. It's an uphill battle to change this practice, and we are still working on it. We will probably start training our new supervisors again soon. It's been almost a year—more than a year.

Karen Lyons

Yes, more than a year. The result has been to lower the tension surrounding the performance evaluation process. By using this as a mutual goal-setting session, employees bring both what they identify as their accomplishments and their goals for the next six months into the negotiation. We think it is improving the communication and recovering some of the focus.

Donna Maloney

What was not an issue, but is a side benefit for us, for Karen and me, was the role of the performance evaluations in dealing with grievances. If we should end up in arbitration, the new performance evaluations are extremely helpful in supporting our case, which is not what they were intended for.

Greiner

Yes, because any grievance, any warning, has to be documented. Isn't that right? Then you have that documentation when the grievance hearing comes about.

Donna Maloney

More than that, the issues that people were disciplined for were there, in the past, but they were not always well documented. It made it difficult for everybody involved to come to a fair judgment on whether the grievance was legitimate or not. Having these new forms is helpful.

Karen Lyons

When an employee has been with us for more than fifteen years, which isn't that unusual, he or she may have stayed in the same location with the same group of people for that entire time. People want to get along, and they tend to overlook difficult behavior until one day, for example, twenty years later, a supervisor suddenly declares, "I will not and I cannot stand it. I've had it. For twenty years I've put up with your behavior, and it must stop." The whole time they've been an "excellent" employee, and there is no documentation to the contrary. Then suddenly, the supervisor comes to Donna and says, "You must fire her." We've eliminated a lot of this behavior. Some of our employees have bid farewell to us and gone into early retirement. There were other situations that weren't difficult, but employees did not know how to talk to us about their issues or how to communicate with their supervisors. This has really been a positive step in the right direction.

Donna Maloney

Yes, I'm hopeful. It's not perfect yet, but I am hopeful. It really gives employees a chance to shape their future.

Greiner

Do employees have an opportunity to evaluate themselves? I know in a lot of organizations they will do a self-evaluation, the supervisor does an evaluation, and then they meet regarding these evaluations.

Donna Maloney

Employees are expected to bring into the performance evaluation interview, and be ready to discuss, their goals over the last six months and their future goals. They are given their performance evaluations, completed by their supervisor, usually a day or so in advance so they can look at them and be prepared to have a meaningful discussion. So indirectly, they do; but they do not prepare their own evaluations.

Karen Lyons

However, there is an opportunity for them to review their evaluations in advance of the discussion and to comment on their goals.

Donna Maloney

The categories are "meets requirements" or "needs improvement," or "is unsatisfactory." If there is a "needs improvement" or "is unsatisfactory" rating in any category, then there has to be an improvement plan with a deadline for completion. In the employer and employee conference, they need to work out a plan.

Greiner

No one wanted to be in the middle, or satisfactory.

Donna Maloney

If an employee got an "excellent" last time and didn't get it this time for the same criteria, he or she remembers. It then became a very stressful performance evaluation conference. I think we are making strides in the right direction by concentrating on performance rather than rating.

Karen Lyons

The subtexts with our strategic plan have been open communication, fairness, and consistency. Donna and her staff are linking reality-based job descriptions with the bids that come out. Because we are a union environment, there is bid posting. Along with the bid, the interview questions and the requirements are interrelated. This ensures that interview questions are appropriate and job related. This linkage of fairness and open communication is something that Donna has done such a good job on, and is really building a foundation for consistency. We have seventy-eight locations and 1,500 employees. Consistency and uniformity throughout can be a challenge.

Greiner

Yes, I can see it would be. I am having trouble just visualizing it and all of the lines of communication and authority. You seem to have really good communication and you know the person with whom you are working, for example, you and Donna. When I talked with Amy, Jamey, and Kathy, there also seemed to be that excellent line of communication. You also have many meetings, as they do, right?

Karen Lyons

Right, and it is a cooperative team environment. We try and know where the lines of authority are. People that need to be included and are impacted by any decision are consulted. Don't you think that's a fair statement, Donna?

Donna Maloney

I think it's very fair. Mary Dempsey has us together every Monday morning so that we can at least hear what is going on in other areas. Sometimes, and I think this has happened in a lot of organizations, someone will be there telling about something they are doing that might impact what you are doing, or it will provide an idea of how you can contribute. If you don't get together and discuss those things, you may never know, or that great idea may never occur to you, and you might be missing an opportunity.

Greiner

That also causes tension. It is hard to get people to buy into things when they do not feel they are a part of the process.

Karen Lyons

Not all of our senior staff members have MLS degrees, but that doesn't mean that their opinion is not valued or weighed equally with those who do. When I joined this organization I did not have my MLS. I actually went back to graduate school, and I do have an MLS now. My background is psychology and finance. I was a budget director for the city of Chicago before I joined the library. I was coming in from more of a business and management perspective. But a few years ago Rosary College taught some of the graduate-level library classes here in the Harold Washington Library Center. I thought, well if I can't manage to go down two floors in the evening to go to a class, my life is really out of control. I finished my graduate degree in fifteen months.

Greiner

Mary Dempsey was talking about the fact that you had a good system. If you are working here, your tuition is paid and the library will give you time to take courses.

Karen Lyons

I was not eligible for tuition reimbursement. There was some flexibility with my schedule, but I took most of my classes during the evenings and on weekends.

Greiner

This is because you are senior management.

Donna Maloney

Tuition reimbursement is a city benefit through the union.

Greiner

The library's contribution would be flexibility as far as your work sched-ule time.

Donna Maloney

We spent the last year in labor negotiation and we just started our new contract. In fact, we don't even have copies of it yet. This department is very involved in union negotiation. I believe the negotiating committee had about four or five other departments represented that were consistently with us.

Karen Lyons

We worked very hard to establish a good working relationship with the union so that we can agree to disagree, still talk about the issues, and try to identify solutions that benefit management, the union, and certainly the em-ployee. Donna and I have spent a lot of time and energy building up that good working relationship. I've only been here eight years. Donna has been here much longer, so I'm not sure what the history was. Since we have been working on this, everyone recognizes that we have a better working relationship with the union. Compared to other city departments' relationships with the union and the number of cases that proceed to arbitration, I think we are recognized as a model.

Donna Maloney

Karen mentioned earlier that we've been working on job descriptions and interview questions. A major problem when we first began was the number of promotional grievances we were facing. By starting at the very bottom, with the description of the job and questions that linked to that, and worksheets that evaluated the answers, we found that we were able to eliminate many of the grievances. The union often doesn't accept these grievances. Those that they do accept, we have a very good record of winning because of careful documentation. It's really the foundation we needed to avoid some of these bigger problems. The union will look at our paperwork on some of these motions. If they don't see a case, they will tell the grievance presenter, This is not winnable.

That goes back to our relationship we've been building with the union. Karen, in particular, has strengthened this relationship over the last few years. I joined in as a Johnny-come-lately to this. I've been at the library since 1978. I've been in this position for six years now. It doesn't seem that long. It seems like only since yesterday.

Karen Lyons

We don't want to spend all of our time talking about the union. But you should be aware, just to provide context, that our library page positions are the entry level for the entire union. We find really qualified pages, and they will become our clerks. We help them, especially in their automation skills. Then they are promoted; they may leave us to go to the other forty city departments.

Greiner

I see. So you contribute, but then it makes you look good with the city.

Donna Maloney

If that was our wish. We would like to hang on to some of them after we invest in their training.

Greiner

But you have to have a good relationship with the city also.

Karen Lyons

Have the others talked about the relationship with the city?

Greiner

Yes. Everything has been very positive about Mary Dempsey, the relationship with the City, with the mayor, and also with the aldermen. Now, you

have the board of aldermen, which is a pretty complicated situation. I am as-
suming that, maybe you have a Chicago Public Library board of trustees also.

Karen Lyons

Yes, we do.

Greiner

How do the aldermen interact with the city officials?

Karen Lyons

Chicago has fifty aldermen. They are elected by the population at large, along with our mayor and some of the city officials. Our mayor appoints the library board, then the city council has a confirmation hearing. They really are our independent board. They meet with us on a regular basis ten months out of the year. They take two months off, July and August. The board has a facilities committee, which oversees our capital construction, and an administration and finance committee, which oversees our expenditures and budgets. We are a separate line item on the property tax bill. We are a separate fund in the city's funding structure. Our budget is submitted to the mayor's office and the budget office, and then the city council passes our budget with other city departments.

Greiner

When we talk about city council, are we talking about the aldermen?

Karen Lyons

The fifty aldermen love us because everyone wants a library. We are continuing with our aggressive building and expansion program. The aldermen join us as we cut ribbons, and they demonstrate to their communities their effectiveness in bringing library service to the people.

Greiner

The whole life is political, but I think in the library environment, we don't teach enough about how you have to be politically astute. You must think of the ramifications of your decisions.

Donna Maloney

I think every one of our branch managers has positive relationships with their communities, businesses, and community goals—they are all familiar with their aldermen. Our branch managers are very cognizant to the political aspect of their job and know that we are very fortunate that we are funded the way we are. We just don't face some of the problems that other libraries do nationally.

Karen Lyons

Right. Because we are a home-rule unit, and because of the way that the library law was written in the state of Illinois, our bond issues are not passed by referendum. They are presented to the city council with the entire budget and funding package, then approved in that manner. The city sells the bond on our behalf, and the bond has the full faith and credit of the city behind it. Unlike our colleagues in other suburban libraries and throughout the country, our funding is not without issues on the ballot. Have you been out to any of our branch libraries?

Greiner

Yes, I went to Sulzer. Leah Steele took me there and to Near North, which was really interesting, because of its location. It is between two totally different economic areas.

Karen Lyons

Do you want me to talk a little bit about the other areas I work with?

Greiner

Yes.

Karen Lyons

Besides working with Donna on the human resources issue, I work with Kathleen Weibel on staff development. You've met and talked with Kathleen. I am currently directly in charge of automation. We are actually interviewing for a director of library automation now.

[Update: A director of library automation was hired soon after the interview.]

Over the last five years we've really gone from ground zero, in terms of library automation, to a very extensive system with free public Internet access and multiple access points at every location. We have on average, depending on the physical size of the location, a minimum of four to six free public Internet machines in addition to our library catalog and staff computers, all of which are maintained in-house. When we do a major rollout, in terms of a major expansion, for example, the work is performed primarily by our staff. We were the recipients of the Bill and Linda Gates grant, which Mary talked about. That was a major expansion. We also received a second grant. The preparation of the equipment was contracted out, but actual installation is done in-house. We also have a help desk that we staff to assist library personnel in all our locations.

There is a large room called Computer Connection on the fifth floor of the Harold Washington Library Center. There are about thirty computers in that installation. The computer service staff assists patrons and provides free Internet access. Those machines also have spreadsheet and word-processing capabilities for the public, which are also free. We don't have word processing at all of the locations because that is not our mission. We have seven computer centers throughout the city. The largest one is in this building. We are now at the end of our five-year contract with our major library automation vendor, which is CARL. Because of the city requirements, we are required to competitively bid this service.

I also work with the Department of General Services, which is a city department. We fund them to take on the responsibility of security, maintenance, and engineering at all of our locations except this building. For Harold Washington Library Center, we have a private management company. I work with the Department of General Services and their staff on all of those issues. I also work in conjunction with Barbara Ford's office and the management company in the central library on security, custodial, and maintenance issues. I receive security reports on a daily basis. I deal with all building-related issues and occasionally with the Police Department, and the Law Department.

Labor relations in general takes up quite a bit of our time, but not at Donna's level. She is at the negotiating table with the union. Some of our issues with our staff—I am thinking of one in particular right now—really fall into the area of policy and city policy issues that cross many lines. We spent quite a bit of time dealing with the Law Department and the city's Department of Personnel as we work on those issues.

You know that we are a team; I participate in decisions regarding sites for new libraries.

Greiner

It sounds as if you are really very busy. I think the thing that I keep hearing is that all of you work with one another in a team effort.

Donna Maloney

We are really a flat organization and really work at a team approach to management.

Greiner

So the communication is really more flat than vertical.

Karen Lyons

This approach works well for us. I am sure you have been a member of organizations or met people from organizations that say, "Oh, well, we all have an open-door policy," but on a day-to-day basis you never see the person, you never talk to the person, and you had better not knock on the door. But here— don't you agree?—it really is an open communication system. We are constantly busy, but we take the time to touch all of the bases. E-mail has helped, too, and is really changing our culture. Some are more resistant to it than others. Did anyone talk to you about our weekly newsletter, *Read This Now*?

Greiner

Is that the one that Jamey discussed? It's now called Click This Now?

Karen Lyons

It's now *Click This Now*. We just went to the electronic version. Did anyone talk to you about the strategic plan? We have made reference to our five-year plan.

Greiner

Yes, Mary talked about that to an extent, the fact that it started in 1995 and ran until 2000. Is it in the process of evaluation? Are you ready to start another strategic plan? Is there groundwork for another?

Karen Lyons

The whole performance evaluation system arose from our strategic plan The issue is communication. One of our attempts, certainly not the only one, to broaden the communication was through our weekly newsletter. It was a two-sided printed page that everyone received. It was information that was pertinent and time-sensitive. Kathleen Wiebel said, "We'll call this *Read This Now*." That is how we came up with the name. It has been produced for three years now. We just recently shifted this area of responsibility, and it now resides in our marketing and communications area.

With regard to the strategic plan, the last plan was really a nuts-and-bolts, bricks-and-mortar plan. It was a huge undertaking and took us eighteen months. There were thirty-six people on the committee. We had an outside facilitator, but it was not something that a consultant wrote and then dropped off at the library. That has been done in the past, and we didn't want a plan that didn't work. We also wanted a plan that had definite milestones with names associated to tasks and accountability to help the organization. Our goals for the plan included identification of specific tasks and a mechanism to prove to our staff that we could deliver on these tasks. I believe we were very successful. That helped build a level of confidence, a strong foundation, and a desire to be a part of this organization. For probably over a decade, energy was focused on building the central library. This building has been open ten years now. We needed everyone to feel that they were a part of an important organization, that their feelings were important, and that they were cared for.

A year ago, we recognized that we were at the end of that plan, and began discussing the next strategic plan. We are at a different place and want to look at the public library both here in the city, but also as an institution nationally. We want to identify our evolving role. It is going to be a very different type of strategic planning process. We decided to bring in someone to facilitate and to assist in the writing. We had a "beauty contest" with some consultants. The results of that process were surprising in their proposed approaches to the process, the ultimate product, and the associated costs. The proposals did not provide any fresh ideas.

An important aspect of the last plan was our communication with staff. Twice each year we reported on the plan and the progress made in the last six months. Every single staff member reviewed this information. Between the disappointment in the consultants' proposals a year ago and hosting the American Library Association's annual conference and the Urban Library Council's Economic Development Conference here, and all of the capital construction we were doing, we were pretty sure that we could not take this on internally. We still needed some assistance from a consultant in some capacity. We've not gone back out yet to try and find new consultants with a different perspective. We haven't abandoned it, but we were really stalled last year. I believe now, as an organization, we've got to get our focus back on track. We are committed to the planning process, the importance of the strategic plan, and have identified some benchmarks through thoughtful input, but we need to move with it.

Donna Maloney

I think we are also pretty much a victim of our own ambitions and what we want to accomplish. There are so many things that we want to do that we have a tendency to start them, commit ourselves to them. It takes up all of our energy, but it is basic to our success.

Karen Lyons

Earlier this year, the mayor became very public in his unhappiness with the reading scores in the public schools. He believes this is not only a local problem, but also a national problem. We needed to focus on the issue, and he asked the Chicago Public Library to convene a reading roundtable.

This was a one-day event with leaders in the education fields and literacy fields that we identified and assembled. Efforts continue as we seek effective ways to improve literacy levels.

Our children's services department is nationally recognized. We are so proud of them because of their excellent work. But they are victims of their success. A few years ago, the mayor wanted book clubs in all of the high schools. Our children's services staff took on the program. Then he said, "We need after-school programs for teens." I don't know what the situation is with your public library and your public schools in Mississippi, but for many years we really were by default both the public library and the school library.

So, with our assistance and support, the board of education has reinstituted its Bureau of School Libraries. In fact, one of our former district chiefs is heading the bureau. She went over there sixty days ago. They are trying to hold up their end of the bargain, while still working closely with us. In the meantime, there are tens of thousands of schoolchildren that need libraries.

Greiner

Actually, the mayor's initiative became a part of your strategic plan then, right?

Donna Maloney

One of the things that did come out of that situation was the fact that when we were done and we added up the results, almost every department had added responsibilities to their lists. They did not have all of their wish list on the strategic plan, but they went ahead and implemented it anyway. They did more than they had planned to do—much more. Seeing the completed list was very positive reinforcement too. It really gives you a feeling of accomplishment. We were held to our dates, and we met all our goals.

I think our libraries are very proactive. They are very concerned about their communities' needs and take part in community activities. They reach out to their communities through business and school units.

Karen Lyons

One of the major issues, I think, in the profession is our reluctance to market library services and share our success stories.

Greiner

I don't think we are selling ourselves as well as we should.

Karen Lyons

No, we're not. We're trying now, recognizing now the shortage of children's librarians, as are libraries nationally. We are doing a lot of growing our own. Did anyone talk to you about that program? Not only do we actively recruit from our colleagues in other libraries and from the library school, but we also focus internally.

[Update: Donna Maloney, director of human resources, retired in spring 2003.]

Money, Infrastructure, Publicity, Teamwork

Interview with Kathy Biel, Deputy Commissioner, Administration and Finance; Amy Eshleman, Director of Library Development and Outreach; and Jamey Lundblad, Director of Marketing, May 14, 2001

Greiner

Where does each of you fit in this management team? What are your specific roles?

Kathy Biel

As deputy commissioner of finance and administration, I am kind of in a varied role, although finance is the major part of what I seem to focus on through grants, finance, and the contracts departments. The business portion of the acquisitions group reports directly to me, as well as the building program units, interagency department, and the transportation department; basically everyone from accounting to truck drivers. It is a varied group—most of the backroom kinds of operations for the library.

Greiner

How many people do you supervise directly and to whom do you report?

Kathy Biel

I report to the commissioner and also to the first deputy commissioner. But there are formal lines of authority, obviously. What is critical here is that none of us can do anything without the other senior team members' input, as well as the division or unit heads that report to them. We are not really too hung up on titles and direct areas of responsibility because we believe the only way we can be successful is to really cut across all that and have a big systemwide perspective. If we were all locked into our own unit or focused specifically and only on our direct areas of responsibility, we would certainly forget some critical input that is necessary. We got past that a long time ago, I think.

Greiner

So, you have good communication—formal and informal.

Kathy Biel

Absolutely. Jamey will talk a little bit about how we try to maintain communication and accurate up-to-date information with our internal staff. We were just talking with senior staff members this morning about *Click This Now*. Jamey, do you want to tell her a little bit about what this is?

Jamey Lundblad

I am not sure how many years that *Read This Now* has been in place. There was a paper format of a weekly staff newsletter called *Read This Now* that was straightforward and direct, but included staff announcements, congratulations to staff that have gone above and beyond their specific duties, and other items like meeting dates. We decided we would save some paper and move this paper publication into an electronic format. It will be published twice a month on our intranet site, which is called "Cooper's Town." We are asking that all staff and unit managers access this before staff meetings in order to get new information and announcements. I think we just did a demo of that this morning at our senior staff meeting. It will change and evolve as time goes on. I believe that will be a very critical place to share systemwide information with everyone who needs to know what is going on.

Greiner

I am assuming there is a lot of informal communication going on also.

Kathy Biel

Yes. When the team first came on board—the commissioner came seven years ago; I came slightly before that as first deputy commissioner—we developed the strategic plan, and communication is one of the critical elements of that. Communication and timely information universally available to seventy-eight locations and 1,500 employees were two areas greatly missing and were heavily focused on within our strategic plan.

Greiner

That must be a tremendous task, getting that information out. Of course, the technology does make it easier, such as e-mail. No one sits down and writes anymore, or at least very rarely. What about when you have a budget crunch, as I think most libraries are experiencing? I know your strategic plan was set from 1995 to 2000. How are things financially now?

Kathy Biel

We are very fortunate in the city of Chicago. Most of our support is from city resources. We get very little state, and even less federal, financial support. Our current budget is about $89.1 million, and that is just the operating budget. In addition to that, we had a $65 million library bond, and then subsequently, we will also receive over the course of four years another $44 million for capital construction, specifically directed to the branches. So, we've been in a really fortunate area. However, if there was a budget crunch, you can be assured the things that would not go—and we would fight tooth and nail—are the kinds of resources in the areas that we believe are fundamental, such as staff development and training. Again, that is one component of the strategic plan, and we have seen such a tremendous benefit from it. *Click This Now* or *Read This Now* and the other kinds of ways that we have to try and provide information, such as staff development—training for the staff in the resources that we implement. If we put a new database out there, we want the staff to be trained to use it. We don't want to stick the new technology out there where folks have to figure it out on their own. We need to train staff in how to appropriately use and market it. So, we have been using staff development to try and drive down some of the changes and provide information for people.

Amy Eshleman

As Kathy said, the great thing here is that we all work as a team. I get to work with so many people because my job is broadly defined because of the ways it has evolved.

I report to the commissioner, but on different projects. I (and others) end up reporting to other people, and we are always including other people to add content to what you are doing. Development and outreach (at the Chicago Public Library anyway) is bringing in resources above and beyond what the city, state, or federal grants are able to provide. We are in collaborative partnerships and other things of that nature. Some of these partnerships are to provide funds to the library and some are to provide services and programs or other things of this nature. We have a 501C3 foundation that was formed about ten years ago. This is a separate entity from the library, with a separate staff and office. My department really works with the foundation to raise funds for the library for projects that we feel are important, that we might not be able to do with our corporate budget. Oftentimes it is a pilot project—a crazy idea that we want to try—that we think will work, but we want to begin small and maybe expand. We go to our foundation with an idea, a proposal, and they find funding to implement it. A lot of what I do here is work with the foundation staff to help them set priorities for the library in finding sponsors, partners, and others who are able to fund projects. Once we get the funding, then the library upholds its end of the bargain. We do the projects that we say we are going to. Because we are so large and have so many grant-funded projects going on simultaneously, we need a central clearinghouse department to keep an eye on things, make sure that our summer reading program, for example, which is funded with a number of grants from corporations and other foundations, is falling into place. For example, we make sure that the Bank of America gets the recognition it deserves. We compile statistics and submit written reports. We do have one sort of central place here at the library where that happens, and that is usually my department. Other things included in this department are accountability, facilitation, setting priorities, and going out and actually talking with potential partners. We work with a number of museums on many different projects, such as our summer reading program. We have a free museum pass program which is also facilitated in my department. The foundation has always been very supportive of our staff development initiative, which Kathy was talking about. We have spent approximately $4 million of private funds for staff training, mainly in the area of technology. Not only are there projects we do that involve other partners, more visible projects, but we also have grant-funded projects that happen internally, such as staff development initiative. It has been great since Jamey has been here, because many of these programs were really lacking a marketing perspective. We tried to do a little of the marketing aspect before, but Jamey has really taken control of projects such as the summer reading program and other technology projects. We can add a really big marketing portion to that whole project, and it is nice because our partners love getting the extra exposure.

Greiner

How do you come up with all of these ideas? Do you brainstorm, or do you think of something and then run it by several people?

Amy Eshleman

I think we do sort of brainstorm, or often the need is pretty obvious or critical.

Kathy Biel

One thing I want to mention is, it is not just Jamey, Amy, or a bunch of senior administrators. There are people who are out there trying to direct public service and have an "aha" moment and say, "This would be great, but if we did *x, y,* or *z,* it would be even better." Our people have the kinds of relationships where they feel no hesitation in calling up someone like Amy, Jamey, or any other staff member to say "It would be great if we could do this." Then, we kind of develop this pool of ideas. That is one of the fun things. Amy, Jamey, and the rest of us know that we can come up with a lot of ideas that we should implement, but what about the people who execute the ideas? So, we have to make certain that we have "buy in," and that people feel they have the resources and the ability to do whatever the implementation entails, in addition to their normal duties, so they can successfully carry this out. I think what Amy was saying is, we are very particular. If we commit to something, our name is the one on there, not just those providing funds. We care very much, as they do, that whatever the program, it is very successful.

Amy Eshleman

As Kathy was saying, before we roll something out, there should be numerous discussions, not only with senior staff, but also with all of these various groups. There is a whole team of people that we call the "neighborhood services team." They are people who work out in the neighborhood and in the branches, our district chiefs and other things. We will go to their meeting and say "Listen, we've got an idea, what do you think?" We often begin the dialogue that way. They may speak with a couple of their branch heads and managers, and we will start getting feedback that way. There are also the children's and young adult service's librarians that all get together at various times for discussion. I think we all know that the first step, once you have a kernel of an idea, is taking it out and seeing how people feel about it and tweaking it. That is the nice thing about doing projects in a small way. We find out what works and what does not. We really do work as a team, and we all understand that we need one another to make a project successful.

Kathy Biel

We really drive it down extremely far. We will get truck drivers to understand what their role is in the summer reading game. It might be that these drivers are just transporting to each location all of the brochures or posters. The people in the city's interagency group do all of the mail sorting and distribution, but we want them all to understand. The accountants need to understand that the requisition that they see, which is the hundredth one they've seen today, is not meaningless. We get pretty crazy in some ways about this. But we believe it is critical that people truly understand that they are a cog in the wheel here and they are really important. We want everyone to know that if they do not do their jobs with some enthusiasm and understanding, then somewhere down the line we do not provide the service. For example, the summer reading program marketing campaign is of no use to us if we cannot get the purchase order for the poster. If we cannot get those posters on the truck and out, then it is not helping us. It is really important to us all that everyone understands. It makes everyone's job more enjoyable, and we all appreciate what everyone else does and what he or she brings to the project. We know that finance is their job, for example, but they have an understanding of what it means to our projects overall. We try and get this message out to everyone.

Amy Eshleman

It really creates 1,500 advocates for the library. Someone might ask staff members a question about the library that perhaps they should not really be expected to know the answer to, but now they may know that answer. They can talk about the summer reading game even if they are an accountant. They are not providing direct services. They will never provide direct service, but if they know about the library's programs, that creates more knowledge and more advocates out there for us.

Jamey Lundblad

Also, though, in talking about where ideas come from, especially over the past few months, I asked my staff to look inside at the library. Obviously, that is the biggest part of their job—to understand what programs and services we offer, because that is what we are promoting. I think in terms of where our ideas come from, I am constantly asking my staff to look at other models, too, such as corporate models, what the museums are doing, what the Gap is doing. I see what I am doing as very competitive, trying to clamor for the public's attention, gain a new audience, while keeping the audience that we have. That is really important for me, too, to get my staff to bring a fresh approach to what they are doing. We have an integrated creative team that includes public relations—media relations, people on my staff, and designers who are meeting every other week to come up with marketing plans for each of our programs, and also contribute outside ideas into the pot and see how we might apply these ideas to our marketing program.

Greiner

How much time do you spend in scheduled meetings on an average?

Jamey Lundblad

I believe we meet a lot. I have four meetings today. That is fairly typical, especially for managers. Often that is because we want to make certain we are communicating effectively with other departments. It is also the staff development part: I have meetings internally within different units of my department every week—all of the departments. All of these meetings are to constantly try and build my staff's skills and get them thinking in a new way. This is really important.

Greiner

Does anything ever not *work? We are all reluctant to say what did not work. But it looks like everything is working very well here.*

Kathy Biel

I believe you succeed when your strategy is "We're going to try something and pile it in, then we are going to tweak it, and fix it," or when you are flexible enough going into a project, like we did with our strategic plan. We spent a lot of time modifying the strategic plan. If there was a deadline and it did not seem appropriate anymore, we extended the deadline. I believe we dropped one item from the strategic plan. It was not that the dropped item was no longer relevant, but it was no longer a priority for us. When you go in with this mind-set, where nothing is hard and fast—it must be this way or that—then you have more success. We would have many more failures if we were not, as Amy said, willing to change things as we go along. To some degree we have some failures, but we do not see them as failures. We simply see them as modifications of our plan.

Greiner

I believe the most impressive thing to me is that you do see changes not as failures, but as modifications. I see the evidence of how intertwined all of you are, yet how open you are.

Amy Eshleman

I believe a lot of this is the environment. It trickles from the mayor down. The mayor hires very good staff members and lets them do their jobs. I believe the staff that have come in the last ten years are people that work this way. Of course, people have to be at least somewhat territorial in particular areas. But we all look to each other and realize that we cannot succeed without one another. There really is this feeling of camaraderie and teamwork among ourselves, the mayor, the commissioner, other city commissioners, and city departments we work with. We all realize we are in this together. I believe this is why we work the way we do, very successfully.

Kathy Biel

You are right. There is this expectation on the mayor's part that all of his units will work together. You have to. Much that we do impacts others, especially in the capital area. We are really good about working with the planning department, schools, and parks so that we understand what kind of development is going on, what they will be doing, how we can leverage resources, stimulate economic development by placing a library there, including other public use functions, and what kind of environment all of this combined will create. When you are used to working in this kind of environment, those practices trickle down through the entire staff.

There are times when I will be working on something and will have forgotten someone, and they will let me know; as I will let someone else know when a member from my group should have been at a particular meeting. We keep each other honest in terms of making sure we are involved.

Greiner

Rather than simply harboring resentment because you were not included, you are able to discuss inclusion with other staff and staff groups.

Kathy Biel

Yes, I am able to say to other groups, "You know, I should have been there." Or, you get an e-mail, someone from your staff reports something to you, and you think, "Next time I need to be at this meeting."

Greiner

In the other city departments the library is an organization that is going to help them rather than hinder their work, or work in competition with them for funding. In some cases when funding is tight you see that people believe the library is a nonessential organization that is taking money away from those essential services.

Jamey Lundblad

I know that the mayor has a cabinet for his commissioners. There are others farther down in the ranks, public information officers, and these media relations persons meet on a somewhat regular basis and have a central office in the mayor's office. They collaborate and share information. For the last several months, all of the marketing directors at all of the city agencies have gotten together every two weeks or once a month to share ideas, information, and resources. I feel that also contributes to the whole collaborative idea. I also think that being part of those groups, the marketing directors, helps other city agencies see the library as an agency that does bring in other partners. We are a natural gathering place for people, as well as a distribution system for the city.

Amy Eshleman

Because we have built so many new buildings in the past ten years and because we are having to work so closely with the planning department, public building commission, and the mayor's budget office, I believe we've started forming these partnerships that extended out into other areas. We were working with city departments five years ago to build a new branch. Doing a number of new and different programs allows others to become aware of what the library can offer, what the library means in the neighborhood, and what services we provide. I believe Barbara Ford, the assistant commissioner for this building, and her team are meeting with every city department over the next few months to speak with each of them regarding what the Chicago Public Library can do for each city department, such as: how we can help each department with research, or if a department has a special collection—maybe it should be housed here in the library. There is a lot of outreach happening that will create many new projects for us. It is a natural way that we see our mission, and that is the way we work around here.

Kathy Biel

To go along with that, I believe that we always look for opportunities where we can have a transference of information. We heard that the telephone operators that receive the nonemergency calls, or calls for service, would be meeting with city departments so they would know how to direct calls. In this case, we reached out to them and said, "What about the library?" We certainly wanted to make sure that they understood exactly what services we provide. We do not want them to think that we simply give out library cards and loan books. There is so much more to it than that. We look for every opportunity available to inform people about us. Then, they become our advocates. We have a very good relationship with the city's budget office, and that usually translates into resources. A few of us actually came from there. We have deep roots and a level of comfort with that office because they know we can handle our finances here at Chicago Public Library.

Teamwork

A prevailing sense of energy was communicated by each of the participants in the senior management staff interviews. I asked, "Does anyone ever have a day where they sit down and say they are not going to do anything? If they did, what would happen, as intertwined as the organization is?" Charlotte Kim responded, "Fortunately, we don't have anybody like that. If we did, they would not last very long."

Communication and teamwork, numerous meetings representing different management levels, and ongoing staff development were issues that surfaced in the discussions in each of the interview groups. The participants described instant communication on an informal basis—meeting a staff member in the hall or dropping in an office for a quick discussion. The library also has an internal newsletter posted on the intranet: *Click This Now*.

The organization chart enables everyone to know the person to whom they are responsible and who the authority is at the next level. The library has a strong staff development program that is an integral part of the planning process at CPL. The director of staff development said that their department is located in the library's hierarchy, and as such is part of the process of the organization's development. As a part of their involvement in the planning process they hear the concerns of others on the planning committee and can develop educational pieces to respond to those concerns.

Chicago Public Library is a union operation, and the department is very involved in union negotiation. The library is a city department and governed by citywide collective bargaining agreements. The director of human resources and first deputy commissioner credited the new performance evaluation process as contributing to a better working relationship with the union. The process was simplified by reducing performance evaluation categories to "meets requirements," "needs improvement" or "unsatisfactory." The appraisal was separated from the employee step increase and has now become a mutual goal-setting process. Supervisors have kept employee records over the entire evaluation period, and employees have the opportunity to identify and discuss their accomplishments and goals.

The deputy commissioner of administration and finance spoke about the interaction of senior team members and the division or unit heads. She emphasized the importance of a big systemwide perspective. The director of library development and outreach talked about resources above and beyond what the city, state, or federal grants provide. She mentioned collaborative partnerships with private foundations and companies. The director of marketing discussed the advantages of meeting and sharing ideas, information, and resources with all of the marketing directors at all of the city agencies.

The assistant commissioner of neighborhood services summarized the responsibilities of library managers: "Library service is a human service. An ability to manage people or a unit requires a lot of personal maturity, experience, compassion, sense of fairness, and good common sense."

References

Chicago Public Library. 2000a. "Appendix: The Librarians." In "History of the Chicago Public Library: Windows on Our Past." http://www.chipublib.org/003cpl/003cpl.html (accessed November 15, 2001).

Chicago Public Library. 2000b. "Early Development of the Chicago Public Library." In "History of the Chicago Public Library: Windows on Our Past." http://www.chipublib.org/003cpl/003cpl.html (accessed November 15, 2001).

Chicago Public Library. 2000c. "A Free Public Library for Chicago." In "History of the Chicago Public Library: Windows on Our Past." http://www.chipublib.org/003cpl/003cpl.html (accessed November 15, 2001).

Chicago Public Library. 2000d. "A New Central Library." In "History of the Chicago Public Library: Windows on Our Past." http://www.chipublib.org/003cpl/003cpl.html (accessed November 15, 2001).

Chicago Public Library. 2000e. "A New Kind of Library: Looking Toward the 21st Century." In "History of the Chicago Public Library: Windows on Our Past." http://www.chipublib.org/003cpl/003cpl.html (accessed November 15, 2001).

Chicago Public Library. 2000f. "Serving the Neighborhoods." In "History of the Chicago Public Library: Windows on Our Past." http://www.chipublib.org/003cpl/cpl125/neighborhoods.html (accessed October 10, 2003).

Chicago Public Library. "Chicago Public Library Mission." 2002. http://www.chipublib.org/003cpl/003cpl.html (accessed November 15, 2001).

Chicago Public Library. 2003a. "Serving the Neighborhoods." In "History of the Chicago Public Library: Windows on Our Past." http://www.chipublib.org/003cpl/cpl/125/neighborhoods.html (accessed May 5, 2004.

Chicago Public Library. 2003b. "New Branch Construction. http://www.chipublib.org/002branches/construction.html (accessed May 4, 2004).

Chicago Public Library. 2003c. "This Month at CPL What's New?" http://www.chipublib.org/003cpl/003whatsnew.html (accessed October 15, 2003).

Shera, Jesse E. 1965. *Foundations of the Public Library*. North Haven, CT: The Shoe String Press. (Orig. pub. 1949.)

Section B

Public Libraries on the West Coast

Preview

The West Coast libraries that participated in this study include the San Francisco Public Library, the San Diego Public Library, and the Pierce County Library System. I conducted face-to-face interviews at the American Library Association conferences in San Francisco and Chicago, and subsequently with participants via e-mail.

In summer 2001, while attending the American Library Association conference, the director of public affairs of the San Francisco Public Library participated in a personal interview. I spent productive hours in the San Francisco History Center and toured the library. The city librarian responded to questions sent to her by e-mail in September 2002.

The history of the city of San Francisco dominates the history of the San Francisco Public Library. The destruction caused by the earthquake of 1906, the role of citizen activists in rebuilding the library, and the intense political climate shaped the public library. San Franciscans responded to the earthquake much as Chicagoans responded to the accidental fire of 1873.

The current director and the former library director of the San Diego Public Library participated in an interview during the ALA conference in San Francisco. The former director is now assistant to the city manager, library design and development, city of San Diego. Both the current and former directors are masters of initiating public relations campaigns that earn community support. They exemplify a commitment to the community and demonstrate that political skills are indeed a part of their management profiles.

The director of the Pierce County Library System in Washington and I met in Chicago in June 2000 at the American Library Association conference for an initial interview. She forwarded information and suggestions throughout the time of the study, the most recent in early 2003. A primary strength of the system is the interaction of the community and the library. Community leaders are active participants in the strategic planning process. They attend retreats where they are involved in the identification of priorities, in planning strategies to implement activities to achieve objectives, and in the evaluation of outcomes.

"Libraries Build Community" was Sarah Long's theme for her year as American Library Association president (1999–2000) (McCook 2000, vii–ix). Kathleen McCook urges library administrators to recognize a compelling commitment to building communities and to authorize staff to represent the library in community activities (McCook 2000, 100, 101). San Francisco Public Library, San Diego Public Library, and the Pierce County Library System are excellent examples of cooperative community and library achievements.

Reference

McCook, Kathleen de la Pena. 2000. *A Place at the Table*. Chicago and London: American Library Association.

4

San Francisco Public Library, California: Citizen Activism, Cooperation, Realization of a Dream

Mission Statement

The San Francisco Public Library is dedicated to free and equal access to information, knowledge, independent learning, and the joys of reading for our diverse community.

History and Background

San Francisco has been characterized as the literary mecca of the West. It has been home to major writers such as Mark Twain, Bret Harte, Robert Frost, Ambrose Bierce, Kathleen Norris, and Jack London (Ferguson 1985, 2).

As was typical in many cities, private libraries preceded the opening of the first San Francisco Public Library. In 1852 Robert Woodward opened a library to guests and the public in the What Cheer House, a men's temperance hotel. The Mercantile Association formed the city's first subscription library in 1853. The association raised funds by the sale of shares at $25 each. Edward Everett, who was a key figure in the founding of the Boston Public Library, was an honorary member. In 1854 the Mechanic's Institute Library was formed. Other libraries were opened by the International Order of Odd Fellows, the Society of California Pioneers, the Young Men's Christian Association, and La Ligue Nationale Française. In 1870, a group of San Francisco lawyers established a law library, and several personal libraries were also in place (Wiley 1996, 94, 95).

On March 18, 1878, Governor William Irwin signed the Rogers Act, which authorized any incorporated city or town to levy a tax not exceeding one mill on the dollar of assessed property to raise library funds and create a board of trustees (Wiley 1996, 10). The public library would be governed by a self-

Main San Francisco Public Library

perpetuating board of trustees which was meant to keep the library free from the "general corruption of city politics" (Wiley 1996, 98, 99).

San Francisco's first free public library opened on the second floor of Pacific Hall on Bush Street June 7, 1879, with a collection of 6,000 books. The board of supervisors appropriated $24,000 of the $75,000 promised to the citizens who campaigned for the new library (Ferguson 1985, 3, 4). Andrew S. Hallidie, inventor of the cable car, and Denis Kearney, drayman and union leader, along with other concerned citizens of San Francisco led the campaign for a public library. Hallidie labeled $24,000 as "a miserable appropriation" (Ferguson 1985, 4).

In 1888 the library moved to the Larkin Street wing of city hall, then in 1893 relocated in city hall to the third floor of the McAllister Street wing.

In 1901, about twenty-two years after the first free library opened, the foundation funded by Andrew Carnegie gave $750,000 to the city to help fund a new library and several branches. In 1903, San Francisco voters passed a bond issue to supplement the Carnegie bequest. The money accepted in 1901 had not been received from Carnegie because the city had not met Carnegie's stipulation for receiving the gift ("The San Francisco Public Library", 7).

On April 17, 1906, Daniel Burnham, Chicago architect and leader of the City Beautiful Movement in San Francisco, presented his plan for a new civic center that would include a new public library, among other public buildings. The next day the city was devastated by a giant earthquake. City hall and the main library, as well as its collection, were destroyed. Two of the six branches that opened before the earthquake were ruined (Wiley 1996, 17, 18). After the earthquake, temporary library headquarters were established in the Sacramento Street Branch. It later moved to the McCreery Branch at Sixteenth Street ("San Francisco Public Library", 7). In 1907 a temporary main library was built at Hayes and Franklin Street (Wiley 1996, 10).

Private individuals, businesses, libraries, and educational institutions throughout this country and abroad contributed to the library's rebuilding efforts.

"Mme. Emilia Tojetti of the prominent San Francisco family of painters, herself a singer and the first president of the California Club, donated her operatic collection of 700 scores so that a music library could be started. The Boston Athenaeum and the Library of the New England Historic Genealogical Society sent four cases of books, the Brooklyn Public Library sent six cases, and a sympathetic woman from New York forwarded 150 volumes relating to the Civil War" (Ferguson 1985, 8). The Cleveland Public Library, Dartmouth College, Harvard and Princeton universities, the Smithsonian Institution, and His Majesty's Controller's Stationery Office in London also made contributions. Other benefactors of the library included Tiffany and Co., the American Baking Powder Association, the *Pittsburgh Daily Live Stock Journal*, the Santa Fe Railroad, and the Weather Bureau (Ferguson 1985, 9).

The issue of the Carnegie gift offered in 1901, but not received because the city had not met Carnegie's specifications, surfaced again in November 1912. There was disagreement among trustees and supervisors about accepting the $750,000 gift. The former mayor, Edward Robeson Taylor, a library trustee, had always been against the Carnegie gift. He felt that the great city of San Francisco should not beg Carnegie for what he described as "tainted money." The library's trustees voted eight to one to accept the money, and the supervisors voted thirteen to three in agreement. In a general election in November 1912, citizens voted to accept the money (Wiley 1996, 126–128).

Ground was broken for the new main library in 1915. The civic center location for the library was the block bound by Larkin, McAllister, Hyde, and Fulton Streets. The cornerstone was laid in 1916 and the main library was dedicated and opened to the public in 1917 (Wiley 1996, 10).

In 1921 Carnegie Foundation funds were used to finance branches in North Beach and on Sacramento Street, and in 1929 a business branch opened in the Russ Building in the financial district. Although the main library reached capacity in 1943, the voters turned down a bond issue to fund eighteen branches and an addition to the main library in 1948.

Citizen groups, such as the Committee of Fifty, created by Mayor George Christopher and a group of prominent cultural and business leaders in 1959, formed to build support for the library. In 1962 the San Franciscans for a Better Library and the San Francisco Library League joined with the Committee of Fifty under the new name, Friends of the San Francisco Public Library. Keep Libraries Alive! was created in 1972 to protest the closing of branches to meet the cuts in the city's budget for the library system. The Library Commission, the Friends of the Library, Keep Libraries Alive!, and other citizen groups were successful in

retaining Marshall Square as the site of a new main library. In 1986 the Library
Foundation of San Francisco was established to support the building of a new
main library. In the same year, the Friends of the Library inaugurated a private
fund-raising campaign for the new main library (Wiley 1996, 10–11).

After years of citizen activism, successful and failed bond issues, generous
contributions of money and collections, the vagaries of a highly political environment, and economic growth and decline, the goal was achieved. The new San
Francisco Public Library located in Marshall Square opened April 1996. Frank
Jordan served as mayor of San Francisco, and the city librarian was Ken Dowlin.

Isabel Allende in "Where Spirits Dwell," the foreword to *A Free Library
in This City* by Peter Booth Wiley, celebrates the sense of the history of San
Francisco that lives in the San Francisco Public Library. She pays "homage to
the spirits that live in the public library. . . . It is full of presences; the air vi-
brates with memories, secret voices, and stories. . . . Everything that has ever
happened, is happening, or will happen in this city and its surroundings is con-
tained between these walls, as if the library was a vault where the essence of
San Francisco is preserved forever from the erosion of time and the dust of
oblivion" (Wiley 1996, 8).

Organization

The San Francisco Public Library operates as a department of the city of
San Francisco. The library commission acts as the board of trustees of the library. Susan Hildreth is the city librarian, appointed March 2001. Paul Underwood was appointed deputy city librarian November 2001 and will serve as
chief operating officer and oversee all public services in the main and branch
libraries (San Francisco Public Library 2001).

Information about the San Francisco Public Library was provided in an
interview with Marcia Schneider, director of public affairs, and in later cor-
respondence with Susan Hildreth, city librarian. Materials in the San Francisco
History Center in the San Francisco Public Library, particularly the *Revised
History of the San Francisco Public Library,* by Jane Ferguson, and *The San
Francisco Public Library* were very helpful. *A Free Library in this City,* by
Peter Booth Wiley, released on the same date that the new main library of San
Francisco opened, was a valuable resource and a joy to read.

Interviews

Marcia Schneider, Director of Public Affairs of the San Francisco Public Library, June 2001

Marcia Schneider, director of public affairs of the San Francisco Public
Library, described the library of the city and county of San Francisco as "a

Mayoral Department." The library commission, the policy-setting body of the library, is appointed by the mayor of San Francisco, and the city librarian of the San Francisco Public Library is appointed by the mayor. The library commission forwards three recommendations for city librarian to the mayor prior to the appointment.

Schneider explained that the city charter changed in 1996. The new version of the charter gives more power to the board of supervisors. Before the city charter was rewritten, the commissions, the mayor, and the chief administrative officer of the city held most of the power. Under the new charter, the chief administrative officer has become part of the mayor's office.

The board of supervisors has gained a great deal of authority over departments that it did not have in the past. It used to be that the board of supervisors could add money to a budget once the mayor had submitted it, but they could not take away from the budget. The board of supervisors now has the authority to move things around in the budget. The balance of power has shifted away from the city commissions. The city commissions are the policy-setting bodies, but they do not have final approval of the library budget. They review and approve the library budget, but the mayor and board of supervisors can still change the budget.

The mayor revises and approves the library's budget before it goes to the board of supervisors. The board of supervisors can recommend that the library spend the money in a different manner. In the past, the commission would have made that decision. "The library commission ultimately has the role of being the policy-setting body, but under the new charter they can be overridden by the board of supervisors. The board does not have a role in appointing the department head, but they do have a role in shaping the direction of the institution," Schneider explained.

In response to a question about the political role of the library administrator, Schneider stated, "San Francisco is a very political city. City politics affect people in many different ways. It affects the department head in that you can have conflicting opinions about what role the library should be taking in the community." She went on to explain that the department head must stay on friendly terms with the library commission, the board of supervisors, and the mayor. The library commission acts as the board of trustees. The library commission may have one set of opinions and each member of the board of supervisors may have a different opinion. The city department head reports to the mayor, whose opinion is very important. "When the mayor and the board of supervisors are not of the same opinion, it can be very complicated."

Schneider explained that the library's organizational design was based on how the library was structured in the city budget. The library had gone through reorganization recently. "When Ken Dowlin left the library, his interim successor was Regina Minudri, who was the former library director of Berkeley. She did some reorganization of the management structure, much of which was based on an audit that Mayor Willie Brown had commissioned of the library.

The audit was commissioned to ascertain the underlying causes for the library's running over the budget." A Washington, D.C., audit firm recommended an internal reorganization system that would allow more accountability when it came to expenditures. The recommendations, which were accepted, were hiring a chief operating officer, a chief financial officer, and a city librarian.

Schneider said the advantages of the current budget are "that it is understandable to the division heads" and "there is greater accountability. You know how many full-time equivalent employees (FTEs) are authorized in the budget. You get ongoing reports that tell you how you are doing in terms of those expenditures. So, you know how you are doing in terms of your operational and personnel expenditures, as well as other items you might have in your budget."

Susan Hildreth, who had been deputy city librarian, then acting city librarian, was appointed city librarian. The deputy city librarian, Paul Underwood, is chief operating officer. George Nichols is the finance officer, and there are eight division chiefs. The divisions are children and youth services; main library; branch libraries; information and resource management, collection development and reference, including electronic databases and e-books; public affairs; operations and maintenance; technical services and automation; and human resources.

Marcia Schneider, director of public affairs, started as a branch librarian with the San Francisco Public Library in 1974. She came into the administration in 1989 as the community relations librarian, and then was promoted to chief of branches. Schneider was chief of branches at the time of the implementation of Proposition E, the Library Preservation Fund. Proposition E allowed a 47 percent expansion of library hours, as well as a significant increase in the book budget and improved funding for facility maintenance.

As division chief, Schneider was also in charge of collection management for the branches. According to Schneider, "This involved allocating a fourfold increase in the materials budget, putting greater emphasis on materials in alternate formats and other languages.

"When it came close to time for opening the new library, I worked with the consultants who did the publicity and management for the opening of this library. Public relations then became part of the branch division. When Regina Minudri came as acting director she reorganized the divisions and split the responsibilities of the chief of branches. She said the library needed a full-time public affairs representative and a full-time chief of branches."

Schneider noted the increase of public affairs and public relations offices or divisions in public libraries since she started as head of community relations in 1989. Only the larger libraries had public affairs offices or divisions: the New York Public Library, the Queens Borough Public Library, and Denver Public Library, which "always had quite extensive communications and marketing programs. Los Angeles and King County, Washington, also had excellent public affairs divisions." She said that, depending on a library's particular needs, there is some function for publicity, public affairs, marketing, or communications in most major urban and other libraries.

Schneider described the public affairs office of the San Francisco Public Library. It is responsible for exhibitions and public programs. The public information and communications functions, including media relations and reproduction and graphics, are handled by another unit. A third unit is responsible for meeting room and event management, as well as media production and audiovisual services.

Schneider explained that media and audiovisual services fit into public affairs because of the close relation to meeting room management, as well as public programming, which are both in public affairs. It was previously in the automation department, which was appropriate because of the changing technology. "As computers change, so do audiovisual systems. They have to be compatible with one another. You have to have a familiarity with both. There are interesting ways of regarding this particular service and where it is placed organizationally within the library, but it is currently in this division and working nicely."

Management

I asked Schneider to discuss the management environment of the San Francisco Public Library. She described Susan Hildreth as "a very hard working, hands-on city librarian. Her management style is participatory in that she has working groups and committees that complete assignments and report back to their division chiefs.

"Recommendations are made by staff at all levels and, for the most part, are implemented. But, in my opinion, administration does not take every suggestion." Schneider said that Hildreth had an open door and made people comfortable about coming to speak with her.

The library is unionized, and both librarians and technical staff are represented. The library has a labor management team. Hildreth meets regularly with labor and their field representative to talk about their concerns and work with them. Schneider emphasized that Hildreth was "very active in working with city government. She visits all members of the board of supervisors regularly. She works closely with the mayor's office on policies, budgets, and all other major and important aspects of running the department."

Finances

Schneider said that Hildreth had taken a strong leadership role in the branch library bond measure, which in November 2000 passed by nearly 75 percent. "It was a great show of support. I credit this support largely to Susan."

Schneider talked about the library's situation at the time of the bond issue. "San Francisco has always been supportive of library measures. However, we were in an unusual position with this bond because there was so much criticism about the main library. This put a lot of distrust in people's minds. I believe that Susan's very straightforward and hands-on style of speaking with the press, community groups, and going out and working and campaigning made a significant difference."

Schneider credited Hildreth's experience as one of the reasons that the statewide bond measure for library renovation (Proposition 14) passed. When Hildreth was hired by the San Francisco Public Library she was the volunteer statewide library coordinator for the bond measure, and treasurer of the California Library Association (CLA). "Her job at the state library was as a consultant to other libraries, and not about Proposition 14. But as a volunteer with CLA and the treasurer of CLA, she was involved in the statewide bond measure and the development of that bond, both politically as well as regarding the substance of the bond."

When Regina Minudri, the interim city librarian, suffered a massive stroke in May 1999 and Hildreth was appointed acting city librarian, she relinquished her role as chair of the California Library Association Bond Act Task Force but continued to be involved in the implementation of Proposition 14. The bond passed with the highest rate of approval in the city and county of San Francisco. "When Susan was speaking to our own Proposition A bond that passed in November 2000, of course she had that statewide experience as well, which was quite an asset to us," Schneider commented.

Schneider said that the $106 million branch bond would allow the renovation of nineteen branch libraries, which will include "seismic interior renovation for infrastructure upgrades, wiring, technology, improvements to both the interiors and exteriors, and ADA access." Most of the small branches are not going to be enlarged, and use of space will be a great challenge. The bond will also cover the replacement of "four rented branch facilities with permanent city-owned facilities.

"We are building a new library in the emerging South of Market waterfront district called Mission Bay. There will be a significant increase in housing and commercial development in that area in the next decade. These projects are decades in the making, but we are seeing the beginning." Schneider added that they hoped to expand at least two other branches with state library bond funds. She mentioned bringing in people with fresh ideas and perspectives, and having a combination of city and private architects involved in the projects' design. "There is just a lot of work that needs to be done," she said.

I commented about the controversy in the late 1980s between the branches regarding funding for the branch libraries and funding for the main library. I had read that the mayor, at one time, had requested that some of the branches be closed. Also, I wanted to know whether Ken Dowlin's emphasis on technology, and the cost of technology, were the reasons the library was over budget.

Schneider replied, "There were a lot of things that happened during that administration that changed the face of this library system. Clearly the emphasis on technology was an important one. Although, when you look back on it, the San Francisco Public Library was by no means the first to implement the kind of technology that is so prevalent in libraries today. The things that were controversial then, today what libraries don't have them? The smallest libraries have these technologies today. Perhaps the vision was a little ahead of the reality, but there were accomplishments during that period."

Passing Proposition E was a significant achievement for the library. It allowed increased branch hours, provided a dedicated source of funding, and implemented the computer system that had not existed before the online catalog and community databases. Proposition E was credited as challenging the budget the most. One of the reasons was not having a strong central grasp on the position count—the number of city-approved position slots. "There was no official roster that actually matched what was in the city's annual salary ordinance (ASO). It took years to get this to match up, which it does today."

Schneider went on to say that although Proposition E provided an enormous increase in the library budget, there were not resources to manage it properly. The legislation required that the library implement a minimum of 1,028 service hours weekly. The library commission, under Mayor Jordan, who was anxious to please the community, asked that 1,172 hours be implemented, more than the legislation required.

"I believe that was when we began running into budget difficulties. At the same time, we were also bringing a new main library online. A building of this size and magnitude of course costs quite a bit more than the old library. The building systems and infrastructure alone cost much more. San Francisco as a city, during those years of difficult budget times in the late 1980s and early 1990s, had ignored infrastructure issues in its buildings. That is something that we have really tried to take a look at—improving the infrastructure of our buildings."

To obtain community input for the current branch renovation program (Proposition A 2000), the library held five focus groups and a series of six community meetings and distributed a communitywide written survey. The focus groups included a group of nonusers, teenagers, people in their twenties, and two groups of seniors and parents. Some members of the nonuser focus group said they bought their books and accessed information online, or they were businesspeople who used business resources that they got at work or in trade journals. Other nonusers cited service issues and mentioned issues with the facilities, which had already been remedied. Schneider also commented that some people want changes and some want their old libraries to remain as they are. A unanimous opinion will not be achieved. The main concern of the administration, Schneider said, is to make the libraries safe and able to "withhold a seismic event, or earthquake, and to make them accessible to all of our citizens."

Focus group participants were asked about features they would like to see, and were asked for opinions about possible new features, such as self-checking and self sorting, or one service desk rather than the current model to address space limitations. One change they did not want was having the children's and adults' nonfiction integrated, except in a small library.

"The emphasis is definitely branches now," Schneider stated. The bond measure included $10 million to move the technical services department out of the main library. There is separate funding to renovate the main library. Although the bond measure does not include money for the main library, moving technical services will free up a significant amount of space on the first floor, which will lead to future improvements in terms of having more of the collection accessible to the public. Schneider identified money available for the main library renovations as money remaining from the 1988 measure that built the building, interest from the 1988 bond, and money that the city received in a settlement from the architects.

Money from the 1988 bond was used to seismically renovate five branches. Three of those branches will not need a lot of new work under this new bond, but will see some infrastructure improvement. Two of the branches, which are basically finished, will not be touched.

Susan Hildreth, City Librarian, September 2002 (via E-mail)

Susan Hildreth, city librarian of the San Francisco Public Library, discussed the manner in which the present library relates to the historical founding library. "The founding library certainly laid the groundwork for the present system and provided a main facility and branches early in the existence of the system."

When I asked Hildreth what she would describe as unique about the San Francisco Public Library, her response was "The library has several unique collections, particularly the San Francisco history collection, Hormel Gay and Lesbian collection, and special language collections, among others. The main library is a landmark building with an outstanding array of services for the disabled as well as other users. The system has an interesting array of small branches that serve the wide diversity of neighborhoods in San Francisco."

When asked about her role as politician, Susan replied, "I don't see myself as a politician, but my job is a political one. I need to communicate well with all elected officials, making sure that they know the value of the library. I need to be politically sensitive as many of the service and facility issues that we are involved with can become politicized."

Marcia Schneider had described Susan's management style as participatory. I asked Susan whether she would like to add to that statement. Her answer was "I feel strongly that everyone should participate in managing the institution. I appreciate input from all levels of staff. Yet I am willing to make hard decisions that may not please everyone. But I will not do so until I have considered all points of view."

I asked, "What drives the library—technology, patron needs, the political environment, the economy?" Susan responded, "All of those issues are important factors in defining a service plan. I believe that the needs of our users drive the service plan. Technology is a method of delivering those services. The community environment really helps to shape the service plan, and the economy is a factor that we deal with in terms of how extensive the service mix can be."

I asked Susan where she saw the San Francisco Public Library ten years from now in terms of finance, technology, services, staffing. She replied, "The library has dedicated property tax funding, which will need to be reauthorized in about 2008. We will mount a strong campaign for reauthorization, which I hope will be successful, as the library receives a share of tax collected, not additional tax above what is required for other services. Technology will continue to be a service methodology, and I would anticipate increased virtual use—visitors coming into our system from their PCs, obtaining information but not always visiting the physical library. We will offer the services our community needs in any year and try to make sure those services are relevant to the changing demands of our residents. Staffing will continue to be a critical element of service provision because the human 'touch' that our staff adds is one of the most valuable services the library offers."

I asked Susan to describe significant steps in her career progression to the position of the San Francisco city librarian. She responded, "I have had a varied career and worked in a variety of sizes of libraries in different roles. I have been a director in a small city library with one facility and in a suburban county library with ten facilities, and a deputy director in a fairly large system (Sacramento Public Library), among other positions. All my experience has prepared me for this job, but my experience at Sacramento, which is a system with a central library and twenty-four branches in a somewhat less urban setting, prepared me well for San Francisco. There is little that occurs in the San Francisco Library that I have not seen in some form in Sacramento. *But*—I have not experienced anything similar to the local politics in San Francisco. It is a good learning experience."

Citizen Activism, Cooperation, Realization of a Dream

Private libraries, personal libraries, and subscription libraries were forerunners of the public library in San Francisco as in other cities in the United States. The Rogers Act (1878), signed by Governor William Irwin, which authorized any incorporated city or town to levy a tax to raise library funds and to establish a library board, allowed San Francisco to establish their first public library in 1879.

When I visited the new San Francisco Public Library, which opened in Marshall Square in 1996, the city librarian and director of public affairs, as well as the staff in the San Francisco History Center, exemplified profession-alism. A "Friend of the Library" who guided me to the best current source about the library was friendly, enthusiastic, and very knowledgeable.

Marcia Schneider, public services director, has a successful history with the library. She imparts a sense of competence and understanding about the li-brary and how it deserves to be presented. The city librarian, Susan Hildreth, brings a wealth of public library experience to San Francisco Public Library. She demonstrates political astuteness, and a strong sense of her responsibility to seek and heed recommendations from external and internal sources, to eval-uate all points of view, and after careful consideration to make the final hard decisions. She described her job as political with a responsibility to make sure elected officials understand the value of the library.

The San Francisco Public Library has experienced a turbulent past, and will no doubt face challenges in the future. But with determination, political astuteness, proactive citizens, supportive elected officials, and competent and enthusiastic library administrators and staff, the San Francisco Public Library will continue to prevail.

Chronology

(Compiled from Wiley 1996, 10, 11; Ferguson 1985, 13; and Schneider interview [this chapter].)

1878, March 18 Governor William Irwin signed the Rogers Act authorizing any incorporated city or town to levy a property tax to raise library funds

1879, June 7 San Francisco's first free library opened on the second floor of Pacific Hall on Bush Street

1888 Library moved to the Larkin Street wing of city hall

1893 Library relocated in city hall to the third floor of the McAl-lister Street wing

1901 The foundation funded by Andrew Carnegie gave $750,000 to the city to help fund a new library and several branches

1903 San Francisco voters passed a bond issue to supplement the Carnegie bequest

1906, April 17 Daniel Burnham, Chicago architect, presented a plan for a new civic center that would include a new public library

1906, April 18 San Francisco earthquake and fires destroyed city hall and the main library and its collection; two of the six branches opened earlier were destroyed

1906	Temporary library headquarters established in the Sacramento Street Branch and later moved to the McCreery Branch at Sixteenth Street
1907	Temporary main library built at Hayes and Franklin Street
1912	Gift from Andrew Carnegie accepted in 1901 but not received because city had not met Carnegie's stipulation for receiving the gift; in November 1912 general election, citizens voted to accept the money
1914	Carnegie Foundation funds earmarked for building branch libraries in the Richmond, the Mission, the Sunset, Noe Valley, and Golden Gate Valley
1917	Main library dedicated and opened to the public; the library stood on the east side of City Hall Plaza, at the Southeast corner of McAllister and Larkin Streets; total cost was $1,153,000: $778,720 from the city and the balance from the Carnegie Foundation (Ferguson 1985, 13)
1921	Carnegie Foundation funds used to finance branches in North Beach and on Sacramento Street
1940	Library Staff Association campaigned to secure civil service status through a ballot measure; the measure won by a margin of two to one
1948	Voters turned down a bond issue to fund eighteen branches and an addition to the main library
1949	The first, short-lived Friends of San Francisco Library formed
1959	Mayor George Christopher created the Committee of Fifty, a group of prominent cultural and business leaders, to build support for the library
1960	San Franciscans for a Better Library—a citizen's group—formed
1961	San Francisco Library League formed
1962	Committee of Fifty, San Francisco for a Better Library, and the San Francisco Library League joined under the name of Friends of the San Francisco Public Library
1969	Librarians formed the Librarians Guild, replacing the Library Staff Association

1970	Librarian Guild supported the four-day citywide strike of public employees
1972	Keep Libraries Alive! formed to protest the closing of branches to meet the cuts in the city's budget for the library system
1974	Library Commission, the Friends of the Library, Keep Libraries Alive!, and other citizen groups fought successfully to retain Marshall Square as the site of a new main library
1978	Proposition 13 decreased property taxes, which negatively affected the city's ability to fund libraries and other public institutions
1985	Friends of the Library offered to work with Mayor Dianne Feinstein on the completion of the civic center, including use of Marshall Square for a new library
1986	Library Foundation of San Francisco established to support new main library
1986	Friends of the Library inaugurated a private fund-raising campaign for the new main library
1987–1989 (probable but no specific date given)	To prevent antagonism between supporters of the new main libraries and the branches, Ken Dowlin founded the Council of Neighborhood Libraries (Wiley 1996, 216)
1988	Proposition A—city bond measure—provided $109.5 million to build new 376,000-square-foot library and renovate branch libraries; a state bond was the source of additional funds
1991	Library Foundation officially announced Campaign for the New Main
1992	Special Gifts Campaign was launched to solicit funds from various constituencies (affinity groups) for particular collections and capital gifts
1994	Library reached $30 million fund-raising goal and continued the drive
1994	Proposition E—the Library Preservation Fund—provided the library with a substantial base of funding through a local tax set-aside that enabled expansion of branch library hours by 47 percent, significantly improved book budget, and im-

	proved funding for facility maintenance (see Schneider interview, this chapter)
1995	New main library completed; by the end of the year, the Library Foundation had raised $35 million
1996	New San Francisco Public Library opened
2000	Proposition A—Branch Library Improvement Program—provided $106 million (see Schneider interview, this chapter)
2000	Proposition 14—statewide bond measure for library renovation—approved (see Schneider interview, this chapter)

References

Ferguson, Jane. 1985. "Revised History of the San Francisco Public Library." San Francisco History Center, San Francisco Public Library, San Francisco, CA, January 9.

San Francisco Public Library. 2001. "News Release: Paul Underwood Appointed San Francisco Deputy City Librarian." News Release Archives, November 13. http://sfpl4.sfpl.org/news/news_releases.html (accessed November 15, 2001).

"The San Francisco Public Library." *n.d.* San Francisco History Center, San Francisco Public Library, San Francisco, CA.

Wiley, Peter Booth. 1996. *A Free Library in This City*. San Francisco: Weldon Owen.

San Diego Public Library System, California: The Library's Image—Staff, Buildings, and Collections

Mission Statement

The Mission of the San Diego Public Library is to:

- *Respond to the information needs of San Diego's diverse communities.*
- *Ensure equal access to local, national, and global resources.*
- *Anticipate and address the educational, cultural, business, and recreational interests of the public.*
- *Develop and provide welcoming environments. (City of San Diego 2002, 1)*

History and Background

In her chronology of the development of library services to the citizens of San Diego, Clara Breed identified the following periods.

The first books were brought to California when Father Junipero Serra founded the San Diego Mission in 1769. The years 1769–1852 comprise the Mission Period.

In 1870, subscription libraries, beginning with the Horton Library Association and the San Diego Library Association, were established, followed by the San Diego Free Reading Association in 1872.

On April 28, 1880, the California State Legislature approved an act to establish free public libraries and reading rooms. This act gave cities the authority to levy taxes. The possibility of establishing a free public library was discussed in a meeting in Judge M. A. Luce's office in 1881 (Breed 1983, 179). On May

Mission Valley Branch, City of San Diego Public Library System

19, 1882, five men met at the home of Bryant Howard to found San Diego Public Library (Breed 1983, 12). In October 1882, the city first levied a tax for library support (Breed 1983, 179, 180). The first library opened on the second floor of the Commercial Bank, featuring a small reading room for ladies. It appears that Archie Hooker, the library's janitor, acted as librarian from June 1882, when the library opened, until the first San Diego city librarian, Augustus Wooster, was hired. Wooster served from 1884 to 1887 (Breed 1983, 17, 187). Wooster was suceeded by Lulu Younkin, who served from 1887 to 1895 (Breed 1983, 187).

San Diego became the recipient in 1899 of Andrew Carnegie's first gift to any library west of the Mississippi. Carnegie's initial gift was $50,000, later increased to $60,000. The library's cornerstone was laid March 19, 1901, and the Carnegie Library opened its doors to the public on April 23, 1902. Mary Walker was the city librarian (1895–1903) during this period of growth (Breed 1983, 187).

Early library leaders had a vision, which is demonstrated by their list of firsts. Books were first let out for home reading in September 1883. In 1901, a program called Traveling Libraries initiated the first service to rural areas. Hannah Davison (1903–1916) replaced Mary Walker. In 1903 the library hired a boy to put away books and in 1904 purchased the first typewriter. In the following year, 1905, an art gallery opened on the second floor of the Carnegie Library (Breed 1983, 180–83). In 1916, Althea Warren, the first professional librarian, was hired to replace Hannah Davison, and served until 1926 when Cornelia D. Plaister was appointed.

The city of San Diego experienced many changes between 1926 and 1945 when Cornelia D. Plaister was city librarian. The Great Depression and the Second World War were events that impacted San Diego and the library as well.

The economic downturn resulted in reduction of library funding, lost positions, and reduced hours. In spite of the dismal situation, Plaister's priority was a new main library building for San Diego, and she actively campaigned to achieve that goal. She increased publicity about the library with news releases, speaking engagements, and involvement in clubs, educational organizations, and civic groups (Breed 1983, 59).

On March 23, 1937, a $250,000 bond issue to be matched with a W.P.A. grant failed by 900 votes. In 1945, the city council appropriated $500,000 in a pay-as-you-go plan to build a new library.

Cornelia D. Plaister became ill and was replaced by Clara E. Breed in 1945. Breed wrote of her predecessor, "Although she didn't build the new main library she dreamed of, she laid the groundwork for it" (Breed 1983, 79).

In 1949, a bond issue for $2 million passed by a 70 percent majority. Architects for the new central library were hired in the same year. In 1952 a contract for construction of the central library was awarded. The main library moved to Balboa Park, the annex was closed, and the Carnegie Building was demolished. A new central library opened on June 28, 1954 (Breed 1983, 183).

Marco G. Thorne (1970–1978) followed Breed as city librarian, and during his administration, the Friends of the Library started in 1973, and the Master Plan was published in 1977 (Breed 1983, 185). L. Kenneth Wilson (1978–1979) followed Thorne, and William Sannwald was appointed to replace Wilson. Sannwald was appointed city librarian in 1979 (Breed 1983, 187). Sannwald served as city librarian until 1997. Sannwald left the city librarian position after Breed's book was published. The current city librarian, Anna Tatar, was appointed to replace Sannwald.

Organization

San Diego Public Library system is a large urban library system consisting of a main library and thirty-three branches serving diverse populations. The library's service area covers 331 square miles. (City of San Diego 2001). The system serves a population of 1,197,700 (R. R. Bowker 2001–2002, 189).

Interviews

Anna Tatar, San Diego Public Library Director, and William Sannwald, Assistant to the City Manager, Library Design and Development Manager, June 15, 2001

I met with Anna Tatar and William Sannwald in San Francisco during the American Library Association conference. Anna Tatar was appointed as library director in 1997. She had joined the San Diego Public Library system in 1972 and was the assistant director before she was appointed director. Sannwald had been the director of the San Diego Public Library for eighteen years (1979–1997). He is past president of the Library Administration and Management Association (LAMA). Sannwald said he works in the city manager's office and is out of the city library chain of command, although he continues to play a major role with the library.

The San Diego Public Library is a department of the city of San Diego. The library commission is an advisory committee, but it is very influential and powerful, although it does not control the library budget. While there is not an administrative library board of trustees, the library commission represents the library to the mayor and city council as well as the general public. The library director reports to the city manager's office, as does the assistant to the city manager. Both Tatar and Sannwald were hired by the city manager.

Tatar said that she learned from Sannwald: "He challenges you and gives you the opportunity to make a difference." Tatar credited Sannwald with bringing to the San Diego Public Library a vision about revitalizing the system through enhancing its facilities. "In 1979, the library was approximately 5,000 square feet. The system has changed drastically because of the new libraries that we have built, with the minimum size for a branch at 15,000 square feet, and many in the area of 20,000–25,000 square feet. As a matter of fact, Bill was the first recipient of the Irving Gill award from the San Diego chapter of the American Institute of Architects, which is their highest award, for his work in developing branch libraries."

Tatar identified the three critical elements of library services as staff, service portals or buildings, and collections. She emphasized that Sannwald had transformed the buildings and physical facilities, all of which had really made a difference for the library system by making the libraries significant centers for the communities they serve. She went on to describe how this growth has brought excitement to the community about the library and what it has to offer because when one area of the city sees the great buildings going up, the other areas of the city want the same thing. She noted the emphasis, when she was in library school, on staff, personnel, collections, and issues such as how to be a good reference librarian, rather than on library buildings.

She talked about the significant donations for San Diego libraries, saying that the library is on its fourth or fifth $5 million gift for building new branch libraries. Neither Sannwald nor Tatar know of any other public library in the country that has had major donations such as these for its branch libraries.

Sannwald said, "I believe that it is more than just the buildings, it is the image that is created for the library. People like to be associated with a winner. They like to have a facility that has a "wow" factor, and that is why when Vartan Gregorian became president of the New York Public Library, the first thing he did was restore the Forty-second Street Library, to enhance the library's image."

Tatar added that libraries now hold a very important place in the community. They are a gathering area for people from all kinds of socioeconomic backgrounds, which is significant in San Diego because of the diversity of the citizens in the city. The library buildings themselves have become rather complex because they must be equipped to serve all of the different groups, both ethnically and intellectually. The libraries now serve as places where everyone in a community can come together.

Sannwald discussed the history of the Friends of the Library and the library commission. He said the Friends organization had grown from ten or twelve people when he came to San Diego to approximately 5,000 members. There is now a Friends group at every branch, and these groups make a difference in the support the library receives. He referred to a budget hearing attended by approximately fifty members of the Friends of the Library, who reinforced to the city council that libraries are a vital public service.

The library commission has progressed from being an organization having no apparent influence and wanting to disband when Sannwald came to the library to become an incredibly powerful organization. The people involved in the library commission are people who make a difference. The current president, Mary Lindenstein Walshok, is a vice chancellor at the University of California at San Diego, and very influential in the community. According to Sannwald, one of the most effective and politically savvy commissioners was James R. Dawe, who served as president of the commission for ten years, and was voted "Trustee of the Year" by both ALA and the California Library Association, elected president of the Urban Libraries Council during its major period of growth, and served as president of the California Libraries Services.

Tatar emphasized the funding that the library is beginning to receive. The Friends of the Library had considered a ballot measure to increase the library's funding, but the city council instead has adopted a policy to increase the percentage of the city general fund that goes to the library. Tatar noted an increase in the library's budget of approximately $5 million each of the last two years. Sannwald attributed the unprecedented budget increase of 18 percent to an alignment including the support of the Friends of the Library and the mayor having chosen library improvement as one of his ten main goals for his term of office.

Tatar credited the San Diego Public Library's being ranked by the Public Library Policy Institute as number one in a category for efficiency, in comparison to forty-four other urban libraries over a seven-year period, to a "staff that makes a difference." There were only two other libraries that ranked in this category. She said that the very dedicated, hardworking, and knowledgeable staff also helped the library get the greatly needed increase in its budget.

She emphasized that today's library buildings require an increase in staff with expertise in technical and subject areas, as well as more electronic workstations to access information available electronically. Electronic resources are very staff-intensive, and also require the materials budget to be stretched to accommodate both paper and electronic media. Tatar recommended listening to and relying on other professionals for their expertise. In addition to staff with technological expertise, she emphasized the importance of public relations professionals. She gave an example of having traded a budget analyst position for a public information officer position.

Tatar described the role of the San Diego Public Library in a Library Awareness Campaign, funded by the California State Library. When the state asked for a volunteer library to do an experimental campaign, Tartar volunteered the San Diego Public Library. The library was given approximately $70,000 to hire a media consultant. The library became television partners with KGTV, Channel 10/ABC, Cox Cable of San Diego, Time Warner Cable of San Diego, and the Hispanic television station Univision. The stations presented public service announcements (PSAs) for the library, but not necessarily in prime time. Some money was given to each of these stations by the campaign, and the stations aired the public service announcements during prime time and pre–prime time, allowing the library to leverage the $70,000 to a value of $500,000. Many of these public service announcements aired in January, February, and March 2001.

The director described some of the library's media releases during National Library Week in April. One release described a teacher who has been bringing his classes down to the central library for twenty-five years. He takes the students into different sections and teaches them about the collections.

Spokespersons for the library who are very well known in the community include "Bill Walton, a great basketball player for UCLA, whose mother and grandmother both worked for the library, the artistic director from the Old Globe Theatre, and a prominent San Diegan who does PSAs for the chamber of commerce, who did very effective fifteen-second spots for the library."

After the campaign was over, the library conducted a survey to see whether people remembered the PSAs, and approximately 60 percent of respondents recalled the campaign, which is very good for any type of promotional message. The state library asked the library to participate in the campaign again for the months of July, August, and September 2001. Tatar said that in this campaign Audrey Geisel, Dr. Seuss's wife, appears in a spot, as does Joan Embery, the spokeswoman for the San Diego Zoo. San Diego Padres player Trevor Hoffman and an Asian family discuss how important reading and the library are to them.

Tatar added, "The myriad of people that we are including in the campaign is incredible. The library is also trying to appeal to teenagers through advertising spots with the Nissan Design Center in San Diego and one of the soccer players from the San Diego Spirit, Shannon MacMillan, who is doing a spot for the library in the computer lab."

In a discussion about the political role of library administrators, Sannwald said, "I believe this role is very important, which is why we have spent so much time developing the Friends of the Library, and a strong relationship with the library commission, to get this grassroots community support, and build these libraries in the communities so people have a place in the community that they truly admire. I spend a good portion of my time speaking with community groups. This helps people identify and feel an affinity with the library."

Tatar said that having the Friends and other groups, rather than library staff, acting as spokespersons for the library is important. The more nonstaff library advocates that can be recruited, the better, because politicians listen to an outsider more than they would the staff.

Tatar described the library's partnerships with the Society for American Baseball Research (SABR), the San Diego Museum of Art in Balboa Park, and the Museum of Contemporary Art San Diego. The president of SABR is head of the Metropolitan Transit Board. SABR approached the library, asked for assistance to "build a great research collection," and gave the library a check for $4,000. The library continues to develop the collection and maintain the partnership. The city matches donations for books, dollar for dollar, and in this way the library was able to double SABR's initial donation. Tatar said that some members of the society are interested in having bus billboards advertising the public library.

When the San Diego Museum of Art has an exhibition, the public library's art librarians put together a bibliography of books about that exhibition that are available at the public library, along with the books' central library call numbers.

Tatar described a special library exhibit on display at the Museum of Contemporary Art San Diego unveiling the design for the new main library. "The exhibit also emphasized the city's new view of libraries taking a systems approach by including four branches that are in various stages of design. On opening night of that exhibition, the museum had 800 visitors, which was the largest number of people ever to attend an opening there. People came from the outlying areas of the city, and some of them came to the downtown area from their neighborhoods for the first time. As a result of the exhibit, new library buildings became the talk of the community, building enthusiasm for the library."

Sannwald has been an adjunct professor in the business school at San Diego State University for more than twenty years, teaching a variety of marketing and management courses. I asked him how different it was to teach about business as opposed to libraries. He responded, "I believe that it is different, but I also believe that many of the techniques you have in library school transfer over to business and management techniques. One of the things that I spoke about in a workshop that I did today was conflict; the different roles that people carry in a building process; why that might lead to conflict; why conflict is not necessarily bad if you turn it into a positive matter for a more positive project; and how to get people to buy into that project. Applying a lot of the techniques and skills that you learn in business, such as benchmarking and best practices, really helps in the library. I do not see anything wrong with applying business skills to libraries, but I am opposed to some of the private companies taking over the operations of libraries, and I believe that in most cases this method does not work."

Tatar also discussed benchmarking, saying that one of the reasons the library received such positive ratings from the community was because "we actually had quantified some of this information so the citizens could understand what our products are, what our outcomes are—given the dollars that are put into the library department. For example, conducting surveys of customers, holding focus groups—these practices are very important, because they provide us with feedback. If it is good news that we are getting back, then we want to share that with the staff, and also recognize the staff for their efforts. If there are some things that need correcting, then the patrons' feedback gives us something concrete to work with. Using those kinds of tools is a very positive thing."

Sannwald mentioned as an example an annual city survey of all the public services during the last year that he was director. "The library rated the highest in the minds of the citizens on public service. It ranked higher than the police and fire departments. It was considered the service that citizens received the most benefits from."

Sannwald responded to a question I posed about communication: "I believe there is good communication among all of our branch managers. We have section meetings. Anna usually attends these meetings and speaks with the managers. I always did when I was director of the library, and I still talk with them. When I first came to San Diego there were quite a few problems in the library. Both staff and patrons were unhappy."

He described an organizational effectiveness intervention that he established just after he became director of the San Diego Public Library. The purpose of the program was to improve communication among the library's different groups. Trainers, a communications specialist, and a master's student in public administration, among others, worked with the library staff for two years and set up an employee advisory group that made procedural and programmatic suggestions. Every employee in the library was surveyed. Sannwald had been at the library only a month when the survey took place. One of the questions was "What is the biggest problem in the library?" One respondent wrote, "The new director." That was in 1978 with a very unhappy library staff after the passage of Proposition 13. Proposition 13 was a tax cutting measure approved by California voters that reduced local tax revenues—a significant source of revenue for public libraries.

Anna added how critical communication is. She does not think that administrations will ever have time to do enough regarding communication with staff. "Employee e-mail has enabled staff to communicate fairly easily among themselves, and the library has a newsletter that goes to the public, which helps with fund-raising, and a second that is distributed to the staff, which keeps staff informed of ongoing activities. The internal newsletter, published periodically, reports kudos that the staff receives. The library strategic plan, which took about a year to create, is at the point where it is ready to be published. It will be shared with all library stakeholders, including the library commission, elected officials, and the community at large. When published, the plan will help everyone see the direction in which the library is going."

Training and employee recognition are important to the San Diego Public Library. In the early 1990s, Sannwald "cut a deal" with the San Jose State University library school to offer classes in San Diego. The public library provided classrooms in branch meeting rooms, and the university gave a scholarship for each room being used. The result is that library paraprofessionals from San Diego no longer have to travel the ninety miles to Los Angeles to attend library school. Many of the professionals on the staff today have benefited from the program.

Staff receives training through many city-run and external training opportunities. Staff members who are promoted to supervisory positions are sent to a two-week training session run by the city. Staff members being developed for administrative positions are sent to the city's management academy for cross-disciplinary training in management.

Sannwald described the employee recognition plan in the city, which began about ten years ago. "The city manager identifies employees in each department, and each department nominates employees for awards. The library usually has anywhere from two to four people win awards, and the recipients get to meet with the other nominees or award winners from the other departments, such as the police and fire departments. Each department director talks about the person receiving the award. The person who receives the award is generally decided upon by the staff. The staff not only hears about the people in the library who receive the award, but also the police officers, firefighters, and others that receive awards, and what exactly they did to earn the award. All of the recipients get a day off to go to a baseball game. They sit up in the city box, and the city manager staff serves them hot dogs and other refreshments. It makes them feel more a part of the city team." In addition, library employees are acknowledged for their work during the year through recognition ceremonies, cash bonuses, and days off.

Tatar described the city's performance evaluation system, which was "revamped" a few years ago. This evaluation is separate from a salary increase. Employees were involved in the planning and development of measurable and quantifiable evaluation documents. Tatar believes the new format is much more functional than the previous single page of short-answer, fill-in-the-blank, and multiple choice questions. More narrative is required, which, combined with short-answer questions, allows for more feedback, "which is exactly what we are looking for." Employees have the opportunity to assess their own work performance. They create a list of their accomplishments, including job responsibilities that they need to improve. "One of the things that I have asked the supervisors to do is ask the employees where they want to go with their careers, and how they can, as supervisors, help them achieve their goals. I believe it is very important for management to provide that kind of leadership so the employees feel as though they are valued, nurtured, and supported."

The Library's Image—Staff, Buildings, and Collections

Father Junipero Serra founded the San Diego Mission in 1769. He understood the need for available reading materials and brought the first books to California. The first public library was in rent-free rooms on the second floor of the Commercial Bank, and the first main library opened on April 23, 1902. The city council appropriated $500,000 in 1945 of a pay-as-you-go plan to build a new main library, and that dream was realized when the new central library opened on June 28, 1954. The history of the development of the San Diego Public Library system chronicles the influence of proactive citizens, cooperative city officials, and responsive, creative library administrations.

The San Diego Public Library system in the twenty-first century continues to anticipate and to respond to the expectations of the diverse population it serves. Although information access may be provided through implementation of the latest technology, the philosophies of Father Junipero Serra, city librarians Hannah Davison, Althea Warren, Cornelia D. Plaister, Clara E. Breed, and many other library pioneers prevail.

The current library director, Anna Tatar, seeks input from and is responsive to the expectations of the citizens of San Diego. The former director, William Sannwald, currently in the city manager's office, plays a major role with the library. Tatar and Sannwald emphasized administrative philosophies and strengths in our interview in 2001. Tatar credited Sannwald with bringing a vision of revitalization of the system through enhancement of facilities. She stressed the importance of the library as a place where a diverse citizenry can come together. Both stressed the importance of employee training and recognition.

Citizen involvement and support are critical to the success of the library in terms of daily operations and long-term major achievements. Tatar emphasized the value of customer input through surveys and focus groups. Communication and cooperation have been major success factors in the growth of the San Diego Public Library system. The library commission and Friends of the Library are influential supporters of the library.

The current library project is the San Diego Public Library's new main library, to be located downtown, between Eleventh and Twelfth avenues and J and K streets. The completion of the 495,942-square-foot building at a cost of $149.5 million is scheduled for spring 2007 (City of San Diego n.d., 1).

Chronology

1769–1852   Mission Period

1870   Subscription libraries opened

1872	San Diego Free Reading Association established
1880, April 28	California State Legislature approved the act to establish free public libraries and reading rooms
1882, May 19	Five elected trustees founded San Diego Public Library
1882, June 15	Library opened in rent-free rooms on the second floor of Commercial Bank
1882, October 10	City of San Diego first levied tax for library support
1883, September	Books first let out
1884	Augustus Hooker hired as librarian
1887	Lulu Younkin hired as librarian
1893	Library moved to second floor of St. James building, over the post office
1895	Mary Walker hired as librarian
1898	Library moved to fifth floor of Keating building
1899	Andrew Carnegie gave $50,000 for a library building to San Diego, the first to any library west of the Mississippi; he later increased his gift to $60,000
1901, March 19	Library cornerstone laid
1901	Traveling libraries initiated first service to rural areas
1902, April 23	Main library opened
1903	Hannah Davison hired as librarian
1904	Library purchased its first typewriter
1905	Art gallery opened on second floor of Carnegie Library
1915	Althea Warren hired as "trained organizer," the first professionally trained librarian
1916	Hannah Davison named "librarian emeritus," Althea Warren librarian
1917	First World War; books sent to army, navy, marines
1925	Bond issue for $60,000 failed
1936	Althea Warren resigned; Cornelia D. Plaister hired as librarian
1945	City council appropriated $500,000 in a pay-as-you-go plan to build new main library; Cornelia D. Plaister became ill and was replaced by Clara E. Breed, librarian

1949	Bond issue for $2 million passed by 70 percent; Johnson, Hatch and Wulff hired as architects of new central library
1950	Githens and Wheeler hired as consultants for new central building
1952	F. E. Young awarded contract for new central building construction; main Library moved to Balboa Park; annex closed; Carnegie building demolished
1954, June 27	Central library dedicated; opened June 28
1970	Clara E. Breed retired. Marco Thorne appointed
1973	Friends of the Library established
1978	Marco Thorne retired; Kenneth Wilson appointed
1979	Kenneth Wilson resigned; William W. Sannwald appointed
1980	Robert Rolfe studied consolidation of city and county libraries
1981	Microfilm readers installed for use with first installment of computer-output catalog of books
1982	Centennial celebration
1997	William Sannwald resigned to join San Diego city manager's office
1997	Anna Tatar, former assistant director, appointed director

References

Breed, Clara E. 1983. *Turning the Pages: San Diego Public Library History 1882–1982*. Kingsport, TN: Kingsport Press.

City of San Diego. n.d. "Library Building Projects: New Main Library." http://www.sannet.gov/public-library/about-the-library/newmain. shtml (accessed October 12, 2003).

City of San Diego. 2001. Manager's Report. San Diego, CA (February 22).

City of San Diego. 2002. San Diego Public Library Mission Statement. http://www.sannet.gov/public-library/about-the-library/mission. shtml (accessed June 30, 2002).

R. R. Bowker. 2001–2002. American Library Directory. 54th ed., Vol. 1. New Providence, NJ: R. R. Bowker.

6

Pierce County Library System, Washington: Outstanding Community Involvement

The Pierce County Library System (PCLS) is guided by a mission statement, a vision statement, and values.

Mission Statement

To connect the people of our communities to a world of information and imagination through:

- Skilled staff;
- Diverse resources;
- Response to community needs;
- Excellent customer service;
- Community involvement.

Vision Statement

The library will enrich lives and strengthen communities by creating opportunities for the discovery and exchange of information and ideas.

Values

At Pierce County Library System we value

- *The public;*
- *Service;*

Steilacoom Branch, Pierce County Library System

- *Equitable access;*
- *Freedom of access;*
- *Resources;*
- *Staff;*
- *Accountability* (PCLS 2002a, 1).

History and Background

The Pierce County Library System (Pierce County Rural Library District) was established as a public library district in 1946. In June 1945, the county commissioners appointed the first board of trustees of the Pierce County Rural Library District. The early PCLS operated as a department within the Tacoma Public Library. Marian Cromwell, librarian, and Margaret Bixby, assistant in charge of work with children, began work on January 2, 1946, in a room in the Tacoma Public Library, an old Carnegie building. Six weeks later they moved to an old store building, which they leased for $75 per month. The new rural library and the Tacoma Public Library negotiated a contract that allowed county borrowers to use the books and facilities of the established Tacoma Public Library. During the first quarter of 1946, PCLS circulated 34 of their own books and 1,206 of Tacoma Public Library's books.

Although PCLS was established when times were hard and supplies scarce, primarily due to World War II, the system experienced great progress in the first year of operation, with requests for service before the system was organized. The stations of Gig Harbor, Longbranch, American Lake Gardens, and Parkland were established by June 1946. Each opened with only 200 volumes on its shelves, which quickly emptied (PCLS Administration 2002b 1).

In 2002 the system had more than 1,258,888 items for loan, including books, videotapes, compact discs, DVDs, cassettes, talking books, and periodicals, plus access to powerful databases (PCLS 2002a, 1).

Organization

The Pierce County Library System in Washington State is an independent municipal corporation established under the Revised Code of Washington 27.12. The library is a junior taxing district funded from a separate property tax levy. Ninety-five percent of the 2001 total estimated $14,046,698 general fund revenue is derived from a property tax levy at a maximum of $.50 per $1,000 assessed valuation (Pierce County Library System 2001).

The county library district serves by contract all of unincorporated Pierce County and the annexed cities and towns of Bonney Lake, Buckley, Dupont, Eatonville, Edgewood, Gig Harbor, Lakewood, Milton, Orting, South Prairie, Steilacoom, Sumner, University Place, and Wilkeson. The population of the service area in 2002 was 468,693, covering an area of 1,600 square miles. Service outlets include seventeen branches, consisting of two system-level branches, four regional branches, and eleven community branches. Additional service outlets are 2 bookmobiles, 1 nursing-home van, twenty-six nursing and retirement homes, 106 daycare programs, and 61 individualized visits to homebound residents. The staff size is 314 employees, full-time and part-time—the equivalent of 208.9 full-time employees. Pierce County Library System ranks fourth in total circulation, fourth in population served, and fifth in operating budget in Washington State (PCLS 2002a, 1).

Public Library Districts

"Special library districts are most common in suburban areas, where they may encompass parts of townships, villages or unincorporated areas of the county. . . . Almost always their creation is subject to referendum by those who would be included in the district" (Sagar 1984, 34, 35).

Lee Brawner identified public library districts as the transfer of public library financing directly to the citizens rather than going through the traditional channels to municipal councils and county officials. To replace local property tax income, special taxing districts are voted on and approved by the taxpayers. "Only about eight percent or 758 of the 9,019 public libraries are organized as independent taxing districts. Municipal libraries represent more than 55% of the total. Next county libraries and nonprofit corporations, each representing about one-eighth of the total" (Brawner 1993, 59–62).

John N. Berry III, editor in chief of *Library Journal,* referred to the Brawner article in his editorial of June 15, 2002, titled "More Successful Than Begging." He recommended independent library districts as an alternative to traditional funding from local property tax, and from state and federal sources. Berry acknowledged that although fund-raising from private sources had been successful for some libraries it was not the answer in all situations.

Berry reported that in 1993 library districts were allowed in sixteen states and noted that a few have been added since then. He cited Kentucky, with 88 percent of the libraries governed by independent library districts; Delaware, with more than half of the libraries as library districts; Colorado, with nearly 40 percent; and Idaho and Illinois, each with about 48 percent. Michigan has 33 percent library districts, Arizona, 25 percent; Nevada, nearly 40 percent; and Washington, 31 percent.

The advantage of the independent library district is that it gives the library the authority and power to go directly to the voters for library support (Berry 2002, 8). Brawner (1993) referred to the Kalamazoo Public Library, later to be designated as the Gale *Library Journal* Library of the Year 2002. Berry attributed the key to the Kalamazoo Public Library funding stability and success to the move from a school district library to a library district in 1990. He also refers to the Ann Arbor District Library in Michigan, winner of the Gale *Library Journal* Library of the Year 1997, and to the success of bringing several very small community libraries into a strong district system in Delta County, Colorado.

Berry advocated independent library districts as a national lobbying priority. "Nearly every time libraries can get on the ballot and go directly to the voters, they win support. It is a proven strategy, particularly in a downward economy, that must be made available to all libraries" (Berry 2002, 8).

Administration

Pierce County Library System Director

Neel Parikh, the third director of the library system, became the director of the Pierce County Library System in October 1994. Formerly the chief of branch services in the San Francisco Public Library, her career in librarianship extends over a twenty-five-year period. Parikh began working in libraries in high school at the Los Angeles Public Library, and worked her way through college (University of California, Berkeley) at the Berkeley Public Library. She received her master's in library science from the University of California, Berkeley in 1971.

Parikh spent her first ten postgraduate years with the Alameda County Library System, except for two years, in the middle of the ten, in Peekskill, New York. Parikh then moved to the San Francisco Public Library as head of children's services (1984–1990), and subsequently became chief of branches there until 1994.

Parikh is currently the chief administrator of the library system and reports to a five-member board of trustees. The trustees are volunteers appointed by the county executive and confirmed by the county council. The trustees act as the governing board for the library, setting policies, determining the library levy, approving the budget, and overseeing labor-relations matters. The system is a union operation, AFSCME (Washington State Council of County and City Employees) Local 3787.

"The Director develops, implements, and administers library services to meet the cultural, informational, and educational needs of the library system, develops and maintains productive working relationships with Pierce County communities and library support groups; directs and manages the ongoing human resources and operational programs for the District's 314 employees; develops strategies and long-term plans for the System; develops and oversees administration of district budgeting; and oversees the administration of 17 branch libraries, bookmobile, daycare and senior outreach" (PCLS 2002a, 1).

Interview

Director Neel Parikh described the Pierce County Library District in an initial interview, in June 2000, at the American Library Association conference in Chicago. We maintained contact through early 2003. Parikh continued to provide me with information updates through the completion and approval of the strategic plan 2002–2007.

Neel Parikh

The establishment of the Pierce County Library District results from an approval vote by the citizens of the unincorporated areas of Pierce County. The library is then mandated to serve unincorporated areas. Cities or towns may choose to be served by the library by contract or annex by voting to join the library system and to be taxed to support that system. Thirteen cities and towns have annexed to the library; one town contracts for service. In 2000, two cities previously not served by the library voted to join the system; one resulted in adding a branch to the system. The cities can also vote to de-annex. The state law provides for an organized property tax structure, based on a millage rate and a taxing limit based on 101 percent of property tax collections for the previous year plus the amount resulting from new construction, or inflation, whichever is lower. By law the maximum millage rate is $.50 for each $1,000 property evaluation. There is no way to increase the legal millage rate; however, there is a method to allow taxation at the maximum millage rate in the instance where the rate has fallen below $.50. This "lid lift" is an election to allow the rate to go up to the maximum levy.

Greiner

How does the present library relate historically to the founding library, or does it?

Neel Parikh

History shows who we are. The system is changing from rural to suburban or urban. At the beginning, the library system was centralized. Services were coordinated from an administration building where the only system librarians were employed. Direct library services operated from small buildings throughout the county. Most of the buildings were rentals or temporary facilities. There was only one permanent separate facility. From 1988 to 1996, ten new buildings were built, establishing two new branches, and the library took ownership of three buildings and renovated and expanded those facilities. With the construction of new and larger facilities and growth of the service area, the management structure of the library changed.

There are two large regional reference centers located in two major regions (there is no main library). Because of the complicated geography of the county (the service area includes four islands and two peninsulas on the other side of a busy bridge), a third library is being slowly upgraded to act as a regional reference center. Three other libraries (for a total of six) are designated as regional libraries and also provide the full range of library services. Currently, these six branches are the only branches with professional staff.

Twelve and one half percent of the staff are professional librarians as compared to 60 percent of the staff being library professionals in San Francisco, when I was there as head of branch services. At Pierce County Library System, the managing librarian in each of the six large sites also supervises the smaller branches. At least one youth services librarian is assigned to the larger sites and also provides services for smaller branches. Recently, a youth services librarian has been assigned to serve three sites where there is no professional staff. Story times are provided by paraprofessional storytellers at every site. Masters of Library Science (MLS) reference staff provide reference at the six larger branches.

For smaller sites, information services are provided by paraprofessional staff, and more complicated reference services are provided by calling one of two reference centers. The youth services librarians and reference librarians throughout the system are supervised by the youth services or reference coordinators, not by the branch managing librarian. Smaller sites are expertly managed by paraprofessionals who also effectively represent the library in the community. However, over the next few years, the library will be evaluating methods to provide more librarians, reference, and youth services, particularly at the smaller sites. Communities are growing rapidly. The issue is where and how to expand the physical organization.

The system is hiring staff from other professions for specialized positions: professional facilities manager, finance director, development director, communications coordinator, human resources director, and information technology (IT) manager. Nonlibrarian staff members with different specialities, for example, a person who manages information technology, enrich and diversify management.

For example, the facilities manager comes from Nordstrom department stores and brings a strong customer service orientation. The IT coordinator comes from state government and brings extensive project management skills. The finance director comes from a neighboring city, bringing valuable expertise and experience in municipal finance. Communication across different professions can be challenging. But the blend of skills, values, and experiences enriches library decision making and helps make for a stronger library focused on customer and community needs. The staff prides itself on good customer service and provides exemplary responsiveness to all the library's patrons.

Greiner
What is unique about the Pierce County Library System?

Neel Parikh
Unique facets of the system include

- Outstanding community involvement. Library staff participates on community boards, in planning groups, and in service organizations. We exhibit at community fairs, and even have a book cart drill team made up mostly of staff who march in parades (about six a year) on their own time!

- Extensive community involvement in planning processes, such as the last two strategic plans.

- Community involvement demonstrated by public surveys that help determine budget priorities and open hours.

- Outstanding public/customer service.

- Innovative outreach programs—to the elderly, and for our child-care programs, but most recently to low-income youth isolated by poverty, and to at-risk families, educating them about the importance of reading.

Greiner
What do you perceive as your primary role as a library director? How important is the role of library administrator as politician?

Neel Parikh
I strongly believe that it is essential for the library to be relevant to the community it serves. This means that we must stay alert to community needs and offer services that the community needs and values. The library director sets the stage for this to happen, but the director must also utilize any resources available, empowering staff to support reaching this goal. The library director stays alert to the community trends and needs, and plays a visible leadership role with community leaders and the public, promoting the services and value of the library. Citizens know they are paying for the services. The library staff has a responsibility to design services to meet their needs. The library staff must be sure that the branch programs match the character and special needs of the community.

The director and the staff must be visible and active. This is especially important because the county is so large and serves such a wide variety of communities. I encourage and support staff at all levels to represent the library in the community: on community coalitions, on planning boards, at resource fairs, through public speaking, and through community organization activities. Staff need to be out in their communities to develop credibility with local leaders. The community needs to look around and see that the library is "at the table," that we care about the community we serve, we listen, and we are responsive. In the small town of Orting, the branch supervisor is the face of Pierce County Library. She lives in the town, everyone knows and respects her. The director does not have the same credibility or even appeal to the local community. One example is the experience we had of working with the new editor of a local newspaper for a small city. The newspaper's publisher met with the director and the communications coordinator at the library administration building. Then, the newspaper's editor met with the communications coordinator and the managing librarian at the city's library. The librarian successfully engaged the editor's interest in the library's programs and services. The result was that the newspaper provided free advertising for local library programs.

I also encourage and support staff in developing services that are responsive. A recent successful example is the expansion of service to the Spanish-speaking patrons at the Sumner branch. Staff created a major outreach initiative to the local Spanish-speaking community, developing effective connections with key aspects of the community. The Spanish-language collection has been increased. On their own time, staff learned Spanish. And, working with the community, the staff recently presented the second highly successful Posada program for 300 people. Posada is a traditional celebration of the Christmas season in the Hispanic community.

Our recent planning process showed another important role for the library. The public sees the library as a focal point or center for the community. They embraced the Public Library Association concept of "commons." This was particularly clear in libraries in unincorporated areas or rapidly growing communities. For many communities, the library may be the only public building in the community. This allows the library a powerful role as a community center, which the public defined as a public facility to gather and exchange ideas. But people also understood that a commons can also gather information about the local area and help people learn about the community, not only in the building, but also through the Web.

My background is in political science, and I always tell people that this was outstanding preparation for being a librarian. Everything in my role involves political awareness and the ability to position the library and work effectively with leaders and decision makers. This is the largest and most important role for the director. However, it cannot be done alone. The understanding of local issues and credibility of the local staff are important for developing good political relations. For example, I learned through working with the Chinatown

Branch manager in San Francisco to carefully navigate the issues and concerns of a very tight-knit and unique cultural community. This is all still true in the larger cities as well as the smaller towns within Pierce County.

Greiner

Where do you see this library ten years from now in terms of finances, technology, services, and staff?

Neel Parikh

A recent initiative passed by the voters has limited our revenue growth. It has affected our ability to expand and grow in the system. However, I believe the system will continue to be healthy because the community is growing and supports the library. We have increased the number of hours the library is open, increased the book budget, enhanced the depth of service, and added staff. The system is most advanced for outreach activities, for example, day-care centers and teaching parents/teaching kids programs. In ten years, I expect we would have two, three, or even more new branches, and add one or two cities. We would continue to be politically active. Washington is a high-tech state, enhancing the virtual library. The library will continue to be at the table as a community center. There is an outstanding staff working effectively to improve our services.

Community Support Groups

The Pierce County Library Foundation is a group of community volunteers who raise funds to expand library services, purchase books, and purchase other resources beyond the limits of the library's operating budget. Foundation donations provide books and audiovisual materials for the library's day-care service, funds to augment the summer reading program for school age children, created the "Our Own Words" poetry and writing contest for teens twelve to eighteen years of age, and purchased a step van to serve homebound residents in nursing, retirement, and family group homes in Pierce County. Recently the foundation raised funds to create a collection for book clubs and the purchase of a kids' bookmobile.

Friends of the Libraries groups in many Pierce County Library System branches sponsor special events and donate books, furnishings, and other items, which the library's budget cannot provide.

Pierce County Library System Volunteers are valuable members of the library's workforce who share their time and talents and make a difference in their communities.

Grants Awarded to the Pierce County Library System for New Projects in 2001

The Discuren Foundation gave $100,000 for staff to plan and implement a new kids' bookmobile to visit low-income neighborhoods and school sites.

The library foundation agreed to raise approximately $150,000 for the purchase of the bookmobile (Parikh 2001).

Pierce County Library System also received $50,000 from the Cheney Foundation and $50,000 from the Russell Family Foundation to purchase the new kids' bookmobile.

A Library Services and Technology Act provided funds for library staff to work in partnership with the Tacoma/Pierce County Department of Public Health to support instruction to parents on the importance of reading to their preschool children. Library staff will train public health nurses who visit at-risk parents. Public health nurses will train library staff to work with this at-risk population (Parikh 2001).

The Gates Foundation awarded Pierce County Public Library System a grant to provide Internet access for low-income communities. This grant project was particularly focused on access for the Spanish- and Korean-speaking patrons, as well as patrons who are visually impaired (Tacoma Rotary 2001).

Two additional Library Services and Technology Act grants were received for the conversion and addition of the Milton collection to the Pierce County Library System database, and for providing bookmobile customers with access to the library database holdings (Tacoma Rotary #8 2001).

Activities and Awards

Carol Bell, managing librarian in charge of the Sumner Branch of Pierce County Library, won the Washington Library Association Merit Award for Advances in Library Services for her outstanding efforts to reach out to the Hispanic community in the Sumner area.

Neel Parikh and Pierce County Library System were named "Employer of the Year" by Tacoma Rotary #8.

Cindy Bonaro, managing librarian in charge of the University Place Branch of the Pierce County Library System, won an Emerging Leader Award from the City Club of Tacoma for her work in the University Place community.

Strategic Planning Processes

Where Knowledge Grows—A Strategic Plan for Pierce County Library System 1996–2001 was completed and evaluated by the library board. One of the activities of the planning process was a retreat attended by community team members and staff. Participants agreed that their vision was that the "Pierce County Library District will be recognized as the leader in Pierce County in connecting people to the communicated resources of the world" (Tacoma Rotary #8 2001).

The system's strategic planning process was a focus of a program at the Public Library Association conference in Kansas City in spring 1998. Participants reported on the innovative and productive community–library planning process.

The strategic plan for 2002–2007 has been completed. Roughly based on the Public Library Association planning process, the Pierce County Library System strategic planning process included an intense community outreach phase. A twenty-two-member community planning team, consisting of key community leaders, helped guide the process. The library staff interviewed twenty-nine key community leaders and held eleven public meetings throughout its service area, asking for community input.

Orientation for library staff and board of trustees members was held in February 2001, and a series of three community planning team meetings convened through June 2001. The completed plan was presented to the library board for approval and distributed to the community planning team and library staff. In September, the plan was approved, and implementation began in early 2002.

The community planning team identified their expectations of the library's roles in meeting community needs as:

- Library as the center of the community
- Collaboration and partnership
- Hosting a center for learning
- Children
- Low-income
- ESL
- Outreach
- Marketing

The top six service directions for the library are lifelong learning, commons, current topics and titles, basic literacy, general information, and outreach.

Outstanding Community Involvement

A major initiative of the library system is community involvement. As Parikh said in the June 2000 interview, "The managing librarian is the face of the library. Everybody plays a role. Staff are expected to participate in countywide meetings and activities. For example, librarians attend city council meetings and chamber of commerce meetings, are involved with United Way, Goodwill, Business and Professional Women, Family Support Groups, Literacy Coalition, Adult Basic Education, Kiwanas, Statewide Database Licensing Coalition, Cultural Arts Commission, Rotary, Ministries Clergy and Church Staff Orientation, and Youth Forums. The staff cooperates with elementary, middle, junior high, and high schools, and is involved as well in after-school projects and adult basic education." Director Parikh stresses that the community library must be "a presence in the community."

Chronology

1945, June	County commissioners appointed the first board of trustees of the Pierce County Rural Library District
1946	Pierce County Library System (Pierce County Rural Library District) established as a public library district
1946, January 2	Marian Cromwell, librarian, and Margaret Bixby, assistant in charge of work with children, began work in a room in the Tacoma Public Library
1946, February	Library moved to an old store building, leased for $75 per month
1946, June	four library stations established in Pierce County; each opened with 200 volumes on the shelves
1970	Pierce County Library System Foundation established (Pierce County Library System, *n.d.*, 1)
1988–1996	Ten new library buildings built, establishing two new branches; library took ownership of, renovated, and expanded three buildings
1994, October	Neel Parikh became the third director of the Pierce County Library System
1995	Strategic planning process for "Where Knowledge Grows—A Strategic Plan for PCLS 1996–2001" began early in the year
1996	Strategic plan completed
1998, Spring	Community and library staff participants in the strategic planning process (1996–2001) reported on the successful community–library planning process at the Public Library Association conference in Kansas City
2001, February 14	Strategic planning process 2001–2006 to update the 1996–2001 plan discussed at the board of trustees meeting (PCLS Administration 2001, 2)
2001, March 29	First meeting of the community planning group for the strategic planning process scheduled (PCLS Administration 2001, 2)
2001, September	Strategic Plan 2002–2007 approved by the library board

References

Berry, John N. 2002. "More Successful Than Begging." *Library Journal* 127, no. 11 (June 15): 8.

Brawner, Lee B. 1993. "The People's Choice: Public Library Districts." *Library Journal* 118, no. 1 (January): 59–62.

Parikh, Neel. 2001. "Grants Awarded for New Projects." Pierce County Library System. July 23.

PCLS Administration. 2001. "Board Meeting Minutes." February 14. http://www.pcl.lib.wa.us/BoardMinutes/BMFeb_14_2001.htm (accessed November 10, 2003).

Pierce County Library System. 2001. *Overview*. March.

Pierce County Library System. 2002a. "Pierce County Library System Administration." http://www.pcl.lib.wa.us/pcl_info.htm. (accessed September 14–19, 2002).

Pierce County Library System. 2002b. "PCLS Administration: A Short History of Our Library System." http://www.pcl.lib.wa.us/pclhistory.htm (accessed September 19, 2002).

Pierce County Library System. n.d. "About the Pierce County Library Foundation." http://www.pcl.lib.wa.us/foundation/about.html (accessed November 15, 2003).

Sagar, Donald. 1984. *Managing the Public Library*. White Plains, NY, and London: Knowledge Industry Publications.

Tacoma Rotary #8. 2001. Tacoma, Washington. February.

Section C

Public Libraries in Western States

Preview

At the ALA conference in San Francisco in July 2001, I made arrangements for a telephone interview with Rick Ashton, the director and city librarian of the Denver Public Library. His dynamic approach to leadership particularly impressed me. During our interview, he emphasized that service to the community was the driving force for the library.

The Denver Public Library is an award winner. It was designated in 2001 and again in 2002 as the number one public library in the United States serving a population of over 500,000 by Hennen's American Public Library Ratings Index. The Denver Public Library was one of eight recipients of the 2001 Award of Excellence for Library Architecture.

One of the library's important assets is the Western History Collection. It is unique to the library and demonstrates the Library's relationship to the history of Colorado. The director described the collection as one of "a research library in a public library environment."

In July 2001, I made a site visit to the Fort Worth Public Library in Texas. I interviewed the administrative assistant to the library director, and subsequently found valuable information in the Local History Room about the beginning and development of the library. In August 2001, the library director participated in a telephone interview. Since that time, I have maintained contact with the director and administrative assistant.

After the librarian in the Fort Worth Library introduced me to the Local History Room, I planned to spend a brief amount of time gathering pertinent facts. As I looked through the minutes of the meetings of the early library and began to read accounts of the development of the library and the individuals who were major contributors to the survival and growth of the library, time became irrelevant.

In the late nineteenth century, the ladies of the Woman's Wednesday Club were proactive in their endeavors for a library. One granted a plot of land for the library and another wrote to Andrew Carnegie asking for a donation. The drama of the development of the library and of the individuals who played prominent roles lends a sense of intrigue and excitement to the library's history. The sense of commitment to the establishment of a free library for the citizens of the community was evident both in Denver and in Fort Worth in the late 1800s. The first librarians of both the Denver and Fort Worth libraries demonstrated a belief in their institutions' opportunity to provide a variety of cultural experiences to their patrons. John Cotton Dana, an early leader for the profession of library science, was the first librarian in the Denver Public Library and also a leader in the museum world. Denver's Western History collection, built by Malcolm Wyer, city librarian from 1924 to 1951, is a distinguished research collection that documents the history of the West through extraordinary works of art, along with a variety of other materials.

Fort Worth's first librarian, Jennie Scheuber, took an active role in the cultural affairs of Fort Worth, including the library and the art museum. The Fort Worth Museum of Art was housed in the library, and Mrs. Scheuber was director of the museum and of the library from 1910 to 1937 (Texas State Historical Association 2002, 1).

The philosophies of the first librarians, John Cotton Dana in Denver and Jennie Scheuber in Fort Worth, are alive and well today as demonstrated in the interviews in the next two chapters with the current library administrators. They define public library roles as providing information services as well as access to cultural resources. Library administrators must communicate and promote the worth of the library to the political community. Current library leaders emphasized the responsibility to seek input from the citizens and respond to needs and wants of diverse communities.

Reference

Texas State Historical Association. 2002. "Jennie Scott Scheuber." The Handbook of Texas Online. http://www.tsha.utexas.edu/handbook/online/articles/view/SS/fsc39.html (accessed July 18, 2002).

Denver Public Library, Colorado: Legacy of Access and Service

Mission Statement

The mission of the Denver Public Library is to help the people of our community to achieve their full potential.

- Actions: *Inform, educate, inspire, entertain*
- Means: *The printed page, electronic resources, expertise, programs, facilities*
- Values: *Service, communication, diversity, teamwork, safety, free and equal access to information*
- Style: *Open, inclusive, friendly, respectful, responsive, confident, innovative, nimble.* (Denver Public Library 2002b, 1)

History and Background

The first Denver Public Library (DPL) was established in a wing of Denver High School in June 1889. John Cotton Dana was the first city librarian, and he referred to the library as a "'center of public happiness.' Dana left Denver in 1895 or 1896 to go to Springfield, Massachusetts where he was responsible for the public library and the museum" (see Ashton interview, this chapter).

In 1910 Andrew Carnegie funded a central library building, located in downtown's Civic Center Park. Carnegie's philanthropy also included underwriting construction of Denver's first eight branch libraries.

The central library served downtown Denver for forty-five years until the city commissioned the firm of Fisher and Fisher/Burnham Hoyt to design a new central library (Denver Public Library 2002a, 1). A new central library at the

Denver Public Library

corner of Broadway and Fourteenth Avenue opened in 1956 to replace the main library in Civic Center Park. The new library provided more than twice the space of the Carnegie building. However, the population continued to grow, and by the late 1980s the central library and the new branch libraries did not have adequate space to house the collections, nor were the buildings adaptable to the rapid growth of technology in the information age.

In 1990, a $91.6 million bond issue to build a new central library, and to renovate, expand, or build new branch library buildings was approved by 75 percent of Denver's voters. The new 540,000-square-foot central library, designed by Michael Graves and the Denver firm of Klipp Colussy Jenks DuBois, opened in 1995 at 10 West Fourteenth Avenue. Branch improvements were also completed in that year (Denver Public Library 2002a, 1).

The new central library became one of the eight institutions chosen for the 2001 Award of Excellence for Library Architecture, cosponsored by the American Institute of Architects and ALA's Library Administration and Management Association. The awards were presented during the June 2001 ALA conference in San Francisco (Dahlgren 2001, 64–72).

Organization

The library is governed by an eight-member library commission appointed by the mayor (Denver Public Library 2003a, 1). Denver Public Library is comprised of twenty-two branches and the central library and employs a total of 500 staff members. The central library has a staff of 300. Rick J. Ashton is the city librarian. There is a director of library services and five branch cluster managers.

Interview

Rick Ashton, City Librarian, July 13, 2001

Greiner

The history of Colorado, western America, and Native Americans are pre-dominant in the Denver Public Library archives collection. How does the current library philosophy relate historically to the philosophy of John Cotton Dana and other early Denver Public Library administrators?

Rick Ashton

In two ways. One is the legacy of John Cotton Dana and the other is the Western History Collection. John Cotton Dana is one of my heroes. Unusual in the 1890s, Dana promoted the library, started a library newspaper, and was involved in community matters. The "apostle of open stacks" removed barriers between the collection and the citizens. He compared open shelving to clothing stores where people could browse. He established one of the first children's rooms in the country, even cut furniture legs down for small users. A John Cotton Dana aphorism was "The worth of a library is in its use." John Cotton Dana was also revered in the museum world. He was very involved in museum outreach, and that is still an influence in the Denver Public Library. The DPL partners with the Denver Art Museum and the Colorado Historical Society. Dana went from Denver to Springfield, Massachusetts, in 1895 or 1896. In Springfield, he was responsible for both the public library and the museum. This was a professional advancement for Dana. When he moved on to Newark, New Jersey, he had a similar responsibility for the public library and for the museum. The Newark Museum was described as an avante-garde museum.

Malcolm Wyer, city librarian from 1924 to 1951, built up the Western History collection. In the 1930s, regional materials were not likely to be collected. Collectors were still collecting materials about the Pilgrims. The folklore is that Willa Cather came to Denver to do research for the novel *Death Comes for the Archbishop*. She complained that no one was collecting history of the Southwest.

Beginning in the 1930s Wyer pursued books, other published material, newspapers, maps, photographs, graphic materials, and art, all as documentation of the history of the West. This resulted in a deep, broad research collection. Legend has it that he purchased a Remington painting for only $35. Collecting by Wyer and others created a very distinguished public research collection. A recent exhibit of Colorado 1859–60 gold rush materials, for example, revealed the collection's excellence. Of the fifty or so items that we put on display, about fifteen to twenty are unique, only-known copies.

The Western History collection shapes the whole institution, attracts outside attention, and brings customers and financial support from grant makers.

The message this attention sends is that it is important to have "something that makes you famous beyond your boundaries." Every elected official wants national recognition, and beyond. For example, Denver Mayor Wellington Webb presented a special Mayor's Millennium Award to the Denver Public Library in honor of their Hennen top library rating. The effect on the institution as a whole is private financial support, a standing as a "cultural" institution, and fame beyond its local audience. If you are well known outside your local community, it helps you to become better known *within* your community. We operate the Western History and Genealogy collections in a very public, as well as scholarly, fashion. Over the years the library has built up a strong collection linked with genealogy and operated in public library style. We will show materials to a third-grade class, but we are very focused on aggressively building a collection in print material and making it available to the community. Researchers can get more done in three weeks in the Denver Public Library than in three months in another library.

Greiner
   What do you see as unique about the Denver Public Library?

Rick Ashton
   The Western History emphasis is unique, as is the existence of our special research collection in a public library. The value we place on the service-oriented aspect of our institution is unique as well.
   Service orientation is the focus. This was unusual sixteen years ago. [Ashton's sixteenth anniversary at Denver Public Library was on July 15, 2001.]
   About service—that means trying in any way we can to really deliver. We do at a high level. It was not always this way. In the first several months that I was here, the practice was that only one of any book bought for central library circulated. Two copies were shelved side by side in open stacks, but only one could be checked out. When a person asked to borrow the remaining copy, the librarian responded, "You can't check this book out—someone *may want* to use it."
   The key issue is how to match our values to our behaviors. It is not difficult; it is easier to change behaviors than beliefs. We changed behaviors. It is not unusual for a staff member to make a long-distance phone call to help a patron. We have momentum, we built expectations; we could and would do for people. The nineties mission statement is "We find reasons to say yes." This philosophy is internalized by staff, and they are readily socialized into this approach.

Greiner
   Would you give me some background of the library?

Rick Ashton
   The previous director was Henry Shearouse, from 1969 to 1984. When he retired, an acting librarian was hired for over a year. I came in July 1985. The Library had pushed technology in the late 1970s. One of the first large inte-

grated systems—Data Phase—had been installed, but failed. The administration was aggressive but politically unsuccessful about state funding. The environment from the mid-1970s to 1989 was financially negative.

Colorado is like Maryland or Massachusetts. It does not have a state library, in the sense of a building with books and a public service staff. Massachusetts designates Boston Public Library, and Maryland designates Enoch Pratt/Baltimore Public Library, and Colorado designates Denver Public Library as the state resource center library. The key service that the contract between the state and the library covered was an open door to the library for anybody in Colorado. Forty percent of library users did not live in Denver. State politics in the 1970s and state and local budget problems in the 1970s led to a series of budget cuts for the Colorado resource center services. In 1981–1982, Denver Public Library said it would no longer keep its doors open to non-Denver residents. This was an aggressive political move that did not work. Public anger focused on Denver Public Library, not the legislature. In 1984 (before I came to Denver), suburban library directors and county commissioners politically organized the effort to resolve this. Representative Wilma Webb (wife of the present mayor of Denver, Wellington Webb), helped them. Mrs. Webb was a member of the powerful joint budget committee in the legislature, and she pushed an increased appropriation through. I arrived just in time to reopen the doors. Others had done the hard work.

Greiner

What do you perceive as your primary role as the library director? How important is the role of library administrator as politician?

Rick Ashton

The director's job involves internal and external responsibilities. The internal role involves setting overall direction and making everybody feel proud when good things happen at the library. Externally, the director must make connections with the community—the key elements of the community—so the library gets what it needs. An ongoing question is, How can we make it better? I have been here when resources were available—an extremely positive environment.

The external, political role may make the internal role harder. The staff must understand where the director stands as a politician. The library needs other key people who really run things, who can bridge while the director is out in the communities. I do schedule myself for some Sunday duty.

Greiner

How would you describe your management style? Authoritarian, participative, somewhere in between, pragmatic?

Rick Ashton

A little of this and a little of that—more big picture than detailed. I try to stay conceptually focused, trying to release people rather than control them.

I've tried to abolish a bunch of rules. I have specific tenets in place, and I want my staff to make informed judgments. They are informed; they are smart; they can make decisions. Circulation clerks can fix fines. If a staff member's decision doesn't work, we don't give a black mark. We praise rather than criticize. I want staff bragging about what they have done rather than whining about what hasn't happened. One should have a good time in a large public library in a vibrant city. I have to make hard decisions. The mayor can always call me. It is important that I be there at the city council meeting once a month. Here, for example, is a scenario: A member needs a favor. He has a new book published, and I must see that the library buys the book. In order for the library to receive a grant, the city has to pass an ordinance. This process facilitates library awareness; it reminds the council of the library.

Regarding politics—within the city politics of Denver, my role is to *embody* the library, to demonstrate and deliver high performance, team spirit, and good cheer. By building personal credibility and trust, I also build the politicians' trust and support for DPL.

Greiner

What drives the library—technology, patron/customer needs, the political environment, the economy?

Rick Ashton

All of the above. Ideally, interplay between the community's needs and the organization's capability and ambition drives the library. Also, a sense of who we are and what we do outside and inside supplies momentum to the library.

Greiner

What is the design of the organization chart for the DPL? Is it hierarchical or more flattened?

Rick Ashton

It recently became steeper. I originally had eight or ten people reporting to me, now I have four. We have larger spans of responsibility. The purpose of this change is to achieve greater integration and cohesiveness. Driving the reorganization is generational change; many people have retired. We had two key retirements. There were three strong librarian leaders—one of the central library, one of technical services, and one of branch libraries—replaced by a director of library services. All library functions are accountable to one person, like president and provost. In 2001, a director of library services subsumed the positions of director of technical services, director of branch libraries, and director of the central library. The objective of these changes is bigger entities, more critical mass. There are twenty-two branch libraries. Ten branch cluster managers were reduced to five. There are four or five buildings in a region. This way, we can move staff around, concentrate on administrative work. In this consolidated environment, every structure has advantages and disadvantages that are reinforced by the skills and personalities of the key individuals and the overall operating environment.

Greiner

Where do you see the DPL ten years from now in terms of finances, technology, services, and staffing?

Rick Ashton

It's hard to predict that far in advance. In three or four years, I hope we will be healthy financially with larger private and state money, with effective lobbying. Our financial condition will depend on state and national economic directions.

In the technology and services arenas, there are several initiatives that we will attempt to integrate. Your Library in a Changing World is our name for the major change initiatives we have undertaken—Library Without Walls, Destination Library, Young People's Library, and New Immigrants' Library—and the organizational structure and strategies to support them. We must be sure the library will be useful to the community. We're making that effort with Library Without Walls, which is a technology and services initiative; Young People's Library; and more multicultural resources and services. One third of the population is Hispanic. The schools are one half Hispanic. There are many recent immigrants. The library must learn how to connect with these communities. Open doors are insufficient. The library will look different. Staffing will be different; boomers will have a smaller role, and I am not sure how the balance will be struck. In 1960–1980, they had a bigger role.

Greiner

You have had a very successful year—one of seven recipients of the 2001 Award of Excellence for Library Architecture and ranked number one in the nation by Hennen's American Public Library Ratings Index. What were the primary reasons, strategies, and contributors to this success, and what are your plans for next year?

Rick Ashton

Denver Public Library is successful because it concentrates on great service to its community. Every decision, top to bottom, is driven by this one consideration. We build and configure buildings, buy books, design systems, train staff, do publicity, raise public and private money, all for *service* reasons. We try hard to be *useful*. As John Cotton Dana often said, the worth of a library is in its *use*.

Greiner

The Dr. Laura incident must have been handled effectively by the library.

Rick Ashton

Internet filtering was the issue. "Ten Most Dangerous" was Dr. Laura's list of libraries she had been attacking on the radio for not doing Internet filtering. She got this list, I believe, from David Burt, who was visible for a while as the library world's chief advocate for filtering. DPL was on the list of ten.

"Dr. Laura" Schlessinger was making the transition from radio to television. A syndicated program, carried locally on CBS, was taped in late August to air in the middle of September. To launch her national TV show, Dr. Laura sent a fifteen-year-old girl with a hidden camera into the Denver Public Library to videotape explicitly sexual Internet sites. I had a call alerting me about this from Bob Willard at the National Commission on Libraries and Information Sciences (NCLIS). The library immediately went into a damage-control mode with the professional marketing and public relations staff. We focused on our message that we care about kids and families. The Denver Public Library offers unfiltered Internet. We are in the free-speech business. I sent an e-mail to Urban Library Directors and Library Directors in Colorado.

Dr. Laura's folks called DPL. They had made and tested the video with an audience who found it dull. They were reshooting segments and wanted to ambush me. I declined their invitation to participate. The Dr. Laura group would not send me a tape. There were one or two letters to the editor in the local newspaper after the program aired.

The library was awarded the John Cotton Dana Public Relations Award for the effective public relations response to the attempt to target the library as a dangerous place for children. The whole filtering issue is still up in the air. Federal and state legislation may well remove this matter from local library control. The climate of fear evident since September 11 may contribute to this direction.

Information Updates

In 2002 the Denver Public Library retained its status as the number one public library in the United States, among libraries that serve a population greater than 500,000, according to Hennen's American Public Library Rating System, a national index that ranks the nation's libraries according to a variety of measurements (Hennen 2002, 64).

In 2003, Denver Public Library, for the third consecutive year, was designated as number one in the 2003 Hennen Public Library ratings in libraries serving populations of 500,000 or more (Hennen 2003, 46).

The Denver city administration changed in July 2003. John W. Hickenlooper was elected mayor of Denver in June 2003 (The City and County of Denver 2003, 1).

In November 2003 it was reported that the Denver Public Library's budgets have undergone significant changes due to budget shortfalls at the state and city levels. DPL currently receives 93 percent of its fiscal budget from the city. In July 2003 the Denver Public Library Commission approved a recommendation to close libraries throughout the system for one day each week. The library was commended by the library commission president Wesley Brown for its vigilance in these challenging times for managing funding and resources and "providing greater opportunities for the public."

The library commission is exploring the possibility of forming a library district. A survey of Denver voters showed that 69 percent of voters polled would like to see the library district placed on the ballot. In addition to the strong support for a district vote, the poll also showed that "Denver voters overwhelmingly believe the library is important for equal opportunity, free access, and the quality of life." Ashton's response was, "We recognize full well the obligations that come with this acknowledgment. We remain committed to providing our customers with the best possible services and expertise our resources will permit" (Denver Public Library 2003b, 1).

Legacy of Access and Service

John Cotton Dana was the first librarian of the Denver Public Library, which started in a wing of Denver High School in 1889. In 1910 the Carnegie-funded central library opened in downtown Civic Center Park. In 1956 a new central library opened at the corner of Broadway and Fourteenth Avenue.

The library is now housed in a building that is one of eight institutions that received the 2001 Award for Excellence, co-sponsored by the American Institute of Architects and ALA's Library and Management Association. The central library opened in 1995.

Rick Ashton, the city librarian since 1985, identifies John Cotton Dana as one of his heroes, and demonstrates his loyalty to Dana's legacy by the library's making the collection available to the public and providing service. He stresses Dana's maxim that "the worth of a library is in its use." The valuable Western History and Genealogy collections are available to users and operated "in a very public, as well as scholarly fashion" (see Ashton interview, this chapter).

In addition to the 2001 Award for Excellence for the central library building, the Denver Public Library has received the John Cotton Dana Public Relations Award in 2001 for the public relations response toward the attempt by Dr. Laura Schlessinger to target the library as a dangerous place for children. In 2001, 2002, and 2003 the Denver Public Library was designated as the number one public library in the United States among libraries serving a population greater than 500,000 by the Hennen's American Public Library Rating System.

Chronology

June 1889   First Denver Public Library established in a wing of the Denver High School

1910	Andrew Carnegie funded a central library building, located in downtown's Civic Center Park
1913	First four branch libraries opened
1924–1951	Malcolm Wyer served as city librarian and began to develop the acclaimed Western History collection
1940	Denver Public Library's Friends Foundation founded
1956	New central library opened at the corner of Broadway and Fourteenth Avenue to replace the main library in Civic Center Park
1969–1984	Henry Shearouse served as city librarian
1985	Rick J. Ashton became the city librarian
1990	A $91.6 million bond issue to build a new central library and to renovate, expand, or build new branch buildings was approved by 75 percent of Denver voters
1995	New 540,000-square-foot central library opened at West Fourteenth Avenue Parkway
2001	DPL was one of seven recipients of the 2001 Award of Excellence for Library Architecture for the new central library building
2001	DPL ranked number one in the nation in public libraries with populations of 500,000 or more by Hennen's American Public Library Ratings index
2001	DPL awarded the John Cotton Dana Public Relations award for the effective public relations response to the attempt by Dr. Laura Schlessinger's television program to target the library as a dangerous place for children
2002	DPL ranked number one in the nation in public libraries with populations of 500,000 or more for the second consecutive time by Hennen's American Public Library Ratings index
2003	DPL ranked number one in the nation in public libraries with populations of 500,000 or more for the third consecutive time by Hennen's American Public Library Ratings index

References

City and County of Denver. 2003. "Elected Officials." http://www. denvergov.org/jump_elected_officials.asp (accessed November 22, 2003).

Dahlgren, Anders C. 2001. "Solutions in Hand, Planners Earn High Marks from Their Peers." *American Libraries* 32, no. 4 (April): 64–72.

Denver Public Library. 2002a. "DPL History." http://www.denver.lib.co.us/about_us/history.html (accessed September 13, 2002).

Denver Public Library. 2002b. "Mission & Organization." http://www.denver.lib.co.us/about_us/dpl_mission.html (accessed September 21, 2002).

Denver Public Library. 2003a. "DPL: About Us." http://www.denver.lib.co.us/about_us/history.html (accessed October 16, 2003).

Denver Public Library. 2003b. "DPL News, Featured Branch Events." http://www.denver.lib.co.us/dpl/news/hennen.html (accessed November, 14, 2003).

Hennen, Thomas J. 2002. "Great American Public Libraries: The 2002 HAPLR Rankings." *American Libraries* 33, no. 9 (October): 64–68.

Hennen, Thomas J. 2003. "Great American Public Libraries: The 2003 HALPR Rankings." *American Libraries 34,* no. 9 (October): 44–49).

Fort Worth Public Library, Texas: The Public Library—The Great Equalizer

Mission Statement

The Fort Worth Public Library welcomes and supports all people in their enjoyment of reading and recreational materials, and their pursuit of learning and information (Fort Worth Public Library n.d.c).

History and Background

The Fort Worth Public Library Association, with a membership of twenty women who paid a membership fee of $1 each, was established April 2, 1892, at the home of Mrs. Charles (Jennie) Scheuber. Mrs. Scheuber was a charter member of the Woman's Wednesday Club, established in 1889, the nucleus of the Fort Worth Public Library Association. Bylaws were established and a charter was granted to the association from the state of Texas. The group's first challenge was the erection of a building for a public library. Mrs. Sarah Jennings granted a plot of land known as Hyde Park for a library, but the project was virtually halted for five years by the depression of 1893. Men, perceived to be better fund-raisers, were admitted to the association in 1898.

But it was a woman trustee, Mrs. D. B. Keeler, who wrote to Andrew Carnegie and asked that he donate the price of a cigar for the library. This fund-raising technique, asking for a donation as small as the price of a cigar, had already increased the library fund to $11,000. In response to Mrs. Keeler, Andrew Carnegie wrote, "If the City of Fort Worth will furnish a site and agree to maintain a Free Library which would cost not less than $4,000 per year, I shall be glad to provide funds for the building as needed up to fifty thousand dollars" (Kinney 1951, 4).

Mrs. Jennie Scheuber was chosen to be the first librarian of the Fort Worth

Fort Worth Central Library

Carnegie Public Library. She went to the School of Library Economy, Amherst College, July 9 to August 17, 1900, to study. The library opened October 17, 1901, with 6,907 cataloged books (Taylor 1968, 92). The initial aim of the Fort Worth Public Library Association was for a "public library and art gallery." The Fort Worth Museum of Art (now the Modern Art Museum of Fort Worth) was housed in the library. Mrs. Scheuber was the director of the museum from 1910 to 1937, as well as director of the library (Texas State Historical Association 2002, 1).

Involved in a wide range of activities, Jennie Scheuber was a charter member of the Texas Library Association (1902), was elected president of the association in 1906, and was reelected in 1907. She was vice president of the American Federation of Arts from 1910 to 1917; member of the executive committee of the Fort Worth Equal Suffrage Association; delegate to state Democratic Party conventions from 1918 to 1920; and chairman of the Fort Worth Children's Hospital from 1919 to 1943. On June 13, 1928, Jennie Scheuber was honored in a public ceremony and her portrait was given to the museum of art.

Fort Worth is the county seat of Tarrant County. In 1922, the Tarrant County Library started providing library service to the county. The service continued until 1985, when Tarrant County funding of the library ended, and non-resident fees were established. In 1928 an annex was rented to house part of the county library's collection, due to limited space in the Carnegie building and the failure of a bond issue for a larger library. A bond issue was ratified for a new library building on September 3, 1935, and presidential approval for a federal loan and grant was given on August 24, 1937. The Carnegie building closed on December 2, 1937, and the library opened in temporary quarters on December 23 of that year (Fort Worth Public Library 2002, 1, 2).

John Adams Lowe, director of the Rochester Public Library in New York, had been requested by the American Library Association and authorized by the Fort Worth Library Board of Trustees to assist the architect with plans for a new building and to conduct a survey of the Fort Worth Public Library in November 1937. In his report he criticized the "lack of modern library management in the operation of the library, and the librarian's devotion to art interests" (Lowe 1937, 12). Lowe also recommended "that immediate steps be taken to free the Fort Worth Museum of Art, including the Historical Museum, from being "a subsidiary organization" of the library association to develop its own purposes and services through its own independent organization" (Lowe 1937, 37). On March 28, 1938, the library trustees requested that Jennie Scheuber retire from the library effective April 1, 1938 (Taylor 1968, 93). Mrs. Scheuber retired and Helen P. Toombs was appointed acting librarian April 1, 1938.

On June 15, 1939, the library opened in new quarters as Fort Worth Public Library, with Harry N. Peterson of Yonkers, New York, as librarian (Taylor 1968, 94). The Fort Worth Public Library Association's function ended December 17, 1946, with the appointment of the library board of trustees. There was a Fort Worth Board of Trustees prior to 1946, but the Library Association played a prominent role until 1946. Joseph S. Ibbotson, who succeeded Peterson as director in 1948, was instrumental in organizing the Friends of the Library and initiating bookmobile service. He was also responsible for forming the Fort Worth Public Library Staff Association in January 1948 (Kinney 1951, 30, 31).

A new central library opened in 1978 in an underground building. Voter approval for a new central library was secured in 1972, but the funding was delayed until 1975 by litigation and because of loss of funds due to inflation.

In 1992 a new central library expansion project began, and in 1993 the Fort Worth Public Library Foundation was founded. The foundation began a capital improvements campaign to complete the expanded central library. In 1995 exterior expansion of the central library was completed. The interior expansion of the library began in May 1998. The finished expansion of the central library opened on October 22, 1999. The Fort Worth Public Library Foundation sponsored a weekend of festivities and entertainment following the grand opening.

On March 28, 2000, a tornado hit the central library, resulting in over $1 million damage (Fort Worth Public Library 2002a, 1, 2). But the Fort Worth Public Library survived and was repaired and rebuilt. The library is currently moving forward with a master services plan that will enable it to be even more of a presence in the community, and fulfill its mission "to provide the highest quality of user-oriented public library service for all citizens of Fort Worth" (Fort Worth Public Library n.d.c [Mission Statement 2001]). The Centennial celebration for the Fort Worth Library was celebrated in October 2001.

Organization

The Fort Worth Public Library (FWPL) serves a population of 550,000. The library is a general fund department of the city of Fort Worth and is funded from city property tax monies. FWPL gets some money from state and federal government by way of grants. The interlibrary loan program is state-funded, and those monies are channeled to the library through the city. FWPL employs an interlibrary loan manager and three clerks.

People who do not live or own property in Fort Worth must pay for a non-resident library card. Fees for nonresident cards are based on the per capita rate paid by Fort Worth residents for the use of library materials. Nonresident students may purchase a one-year card to be used for school-related items for $30. Out-of-city users may also obtain a card by making a $100 donation to the Fort Worth Public Library, the Friends of the Fort Worth Public Library, Inc., or the Fort Worth Public Library Foundation. A card will be issued for one year to volunteers who have completed a minimum of 100 hours of service to the library. A card valid for a year is available to full-time students who have completed 8 hours of volunteer service.

FWPL belongs to the North Texas Regional Library System, a system of seventy-three libraries. There are ten state library systems in Texas. FWPL has contracts with five libraries: Richland Hills, Watauga, Keller, Haltom City, and Benbrook. Libraries that have contracts with the city have access to the DYNEX integrated circulation system. FWPL and its five partner libraries have an interlocal agreement. Delivery of interlibrary loan materials is provided two or three times weekly.

The Fort Worth Public Library is responsible for delivering library services to meet the educational, informational, cultural, and recreational needs of Fort Worth citizens of all ages. The department is divided into five divisions: administration, automation/support services, central library, branch libraries, and regional libraries.

The library has a strictly advisory board with nine members appointed by the city council. There is no official board of trustees. Dr. Gleniece Robinson became the Fort Worth Public Library's eighth director and its first African American director in March 1999. The expanded central library opened on October 22 of that year.

Interviews

Tessie Hutson, Administrative Assistant to the Library Director, November 10, 2000

Tessie Hutson joined the FWPL staff as administrative secretary to the assistant director and director in March 1985. She was the recipient of the North Texas Regional Library System 2000 Library Employee of the Year Award.

Hutson described the administrative organization, including some background, of the FWPL. Linda Allmand was the library director for sixteen years, prior to Dr. Gleniece Robinson, who became director on March 15, 1999. Linda Allmand retired in February 1998, and Cate Dixon was appointed acting director. Linda Allmand had hired Cate Dixon as assistant director in the fall of 1984.

In addition to the director and assistant director, there are two division heads. Wayne Gray, hired during the summer of 2000, is the administrator for the central library, and Denita Barbour, also hired during the summer of 2000, is the administrator for the branches.

There are two regional units: the East region, where the new Summerglen branch is located, and the Southwest region. The East region, the Southwest region, and the branches outside these regions all report to Denita Barbour.

BOLD (Butler Outreach Library Division) and COOL (Cavile Outreach Opportunity Library) satellite libraries, which started with grant funding from the Texas State Library, are located in housing projects. After two years, the city of Fort Worth has taken over the funding for these very positive facilities and programs. Both libraries support their large minority populations with small collections of reference materials to assist with homework assignments, small popular reading collections, a focus on African American materials, microcomputers and software for all ages, and FWPL reading programs.

Kathy Malone, a former schoolteacher, who also earned a master's in library science, serves as technology trainer for the Fort Worth Public Library. She trains staff in Word and Excel and teaches basic computer skills to senior citizens. The computer company Intel donated computers and some furniture to the library's computer lab. The library uses the DYNEX circulation and cataloging systems.

Hutson described some of the activities in the FWPL. The Summerglen branch, which houses state-of-the-art technology, opened on November 12, 2000. This branch is located in the north of the city, which includes many young families with children.

The library's summer reading program is very active, and the children's librarians are very creative. The mayor and council members are involved. For example, at the end of the summer reading program, the children's librarians and children who participated in the summer reading program go to a city council meeting, where awards are presented by the mayor or a member of the council.

The Carnegie Library of Fort Worth opened October 17, 1901, and as a part of the centennial celebration, the library system worked with the Fort Worth Independent School District to sign up 100,000 new library card holders by giving applications for cards to school libraries.

The library always needs funding. It was a priority for Allmand and continues to be for Robinson to educate city council members about the importance of the library. Because the library is a department of the city of Fort Worth, the library director is a city department head and participates with the city's Human Resources Department in interviews for prospective city department heads.

The Friends of the Fort Worth Public Library and Fort Worth Public Library Foundation are two very active library support organizations. The Friends buy things that are not in the regular budget (for example, a reading rug in the children's room). They give the library funds from the book sale that is held in the Will Rogers Memorial Complex in the Poultry Barn, an endeavor that netted $25,000 in a recent year. The Friends also hosted book and author lunches in the fall and spring at the Ridglea Country Club.

The Fort Worth Public Library Foundation was founded in 1993 and began a capital improvements campaign to finish, furnish, and equip the expanded central library, an underground space that covers two blocks.

Hutson described the cooperation of the library with the two accredited library schools in the area: Texas Woman's University and the University of North Texas. Director Gleniece Robinson serves on the board of advisors of Texas Woman's University. The former director, Linda Allmand, taught as an adjunct at the University of North Texas. One of the faculty members at the University of North Texas, Professor Herman Totten, gives talks to library staff to encourage them to get a professional degree. Both schools are valuable resources for hiring professional library staff.

Linda Allmand served as president of the Texas Library Association, and Gleniece Robinson was the first African American president of the Texas Library Association. Her term ended April 2000.

Dr. Gleniece Robinson, Director of the Fort Worth Public Library, August 30, 2001

Greiner

Would you describe your career progression?

Gleniece Robinson

My first work experience was in a school library in 1967; I worked in the high school library and was enrolled in a one-half-credit library science course. From 1969 to 1973, I experienced library work in an academic library as a student assistant. Subsequently, I worked one year as a university archivist, having been trained at the Georgia State Archives/Emory University (Atlanta, Georgia) and American University/National Archives (Washington, D.C.). Later, I worked as a graduate student assistant at the University of Michigan Library School from 1975 to 1976. For the next almost twenty years, Dallas Public Library became my professional home. In 1976, I began my career as adult librarian at Audelia Road Branch. Audelia Road Branch was then and still is the highest circulating branch in the Dallas system. Little did we know that it had nothing to do with us, the staff, and everything to do with the community support and the value they placed on their neighborhood community center, known as the library. Lillian Bradshaw was the library director. From adult librarian, I was promoted to assistant manager of the Audelia Road Branch and served in that capacity for two years. Having served two years, I realized that my training was inadequate as I had focused my studies in academic librarianship. I now understood the necessity of training in specifically focused library services, therefore, I decided to go back to the University of Michigan and concentrate my studies in public library services. Graduating with a Ph.D. in 1982 with a degree in library and information studies was the outcome of that decision.

I came back to Dallas Public and served as research librarian for one year, then Fine arts assistant manager for two years, and moved to manager of Fine Arts Division for a year and a half, then branch administrator. In my position as branch administrator, I had oversight of administrative responsibilities over eleven branch libraries. My next position was a promotion to assistant director for public service (1994–1999). Responsibilities included managing a staff of over 300, a $15 million budget, the central subject divisions, central circulation, interlibrary loan, and literacy, for a total of thirty-three public service units. I became director of the Fort Worth Public Library in March 1999.

Greiner

Does the present Fort Worth Public Library relate historically to the original Carnegie Public Library that opened in 1901?

Gleniece Robinson

Yes, in some respects. The Modern Art Museum of Fort Worth had its origin in the FWPL. The women who founded the Fort Worth Public Library Association in 1892 envisioned bringing art and culture to Fort Worth.

In a partnership effort described as "enviable," the Fort Worth Public Library Foundation mobilized resources in the private sector to complement financial support from the city of Fort Worth to expand the central library by an additional 50,000 square feet. In October 1999, the FWPL dedicated the expansion, which included a 6,000-square-foot gallery, a youth center, a multimedia center, a grand hall, as well as a state of the art computer lab—the Intel Lab. Also, the present outreach service plan, implemented October 2001, addresses children, seniors, and teenagers in much the same way as outreach was envisioned in the earlier years with the support of bookmobiles and the development of branch libraries.

Greiner

What is unique about the FWPL?

Gleniece Robinson

Uncharacteristic usage is a unique characteristic of FWPL. We just finished a benchmark comparison of selected libraries in Texas (Arlington, Dallas, San Antonio, Houston, Austin, and El Paso). These "index cities" are comparable to Fort Worth and are selected by the city manager as cities to which we should compare our services. Many of the variables of these cities are strikingly different; however, there are enough similarities to which we can compare for best practices.

A. Circulation in Fort Worth was significantly higher than in other libraries.

B. Usage per capita was also higher, as was number of visits, reference questions, and circulation.

A corollary to these findings was the staff workload, which was higher. Circulation per staff member and reference questions per staff member were higher.

Higher usage is attributed to demographics in Fort Worth. Some of the population is on the low end of the economic scale and some on the high end, but the majority is average and very family oriented. The central library is open from noon to 6 P.M. on Sunday. There is an active downtown life. The Fort Worth Public Library Foundation, organized in 1993, has mobilized a phenomenal level of support from the community. People give time and energy to partnerships with the foundation. The foundation raised $5 million from the private sector for the expansion of the central library, as noted above. The Friends of the Library, organized in 1948, have traditionally supported the library through book and author events as well as the annual book sale.

In 1962, the Friends started the book and author luncheons. Last year the luncheons had to move from Ridglea Country Club to Will Rogers Memorial Coliseum in order to accommodate the crowds. This year the first Mystery, Mayhem, and Murder affair will be hosted in the evening. Guest authors are Thomas Cook, Carol Higgins Clark, and Lawrence Block.

The staff is very committed to supporting and providing library service. Kay Granger, former mayor of Fort Worth, who is now a congresswoman in Washington, was in the library recently and told me that when she was mayor and the library's budget was cut, the staff voted to take a week off without pay rather than lose five positions. That act on behalf of staff was phenomenal and speaks volumes about the loyalty of this staff to its users and to each other.

Greiner
How important is the role of library administrator as politician?

Gleniece Robinson
Critical! In many ways there is nothing more important than the role of continuously educating policy makers not only on a local level but on state level as well. I had been president of the Texas Library Association, and I recognized that across this great state of Texas we have an unprecedented problem with the alarming rate of illiteracy. Libraries can and should be a major force of reckoning in the literacy arena. However, to get on the playing field, we must exercise political savvy and learn to wheel and deal in an effort to eradicate illiteracy. It is our game and only we can play it, but only if we have the courage and fortitude to step up to the plate. It is important to develop, nurture, and maintain relationships with politicians all the time, not just during a legislative year. The Texas State Library and Archives Commission, aided by

the Texas Library Association and thousands of community supporters, has been successful in getting the state legislature to provide, for the first time, direct aid to public libraries in the amount of $5.9 million per biennium. This accomplishment was realized because of our political efforts.

The role of librarian, or library director, as politician is critical to the success of libraries in all arenas. We must raise the awareness of public officials about the role and the impact libraries have on the economy. The primary role is to represent the visibility of libraries in such a way that we can receive financial support to more adequately provide the level of services demanded by the public.

Greiner
How would you describe your management style?

Gleniece Robinson
A belief in the power of the people. Whatever the people want, we will get it for them because it is their library. However, the demands of the people are balanced by the professional opinions and integrity of the staff. As librarians, we have a responsibility and an obligation to raise the consciousness of the people through the power of information. We must *never* forget that tenet. My style is "responsive to the people" and flexibility. My style is the same with staff.

I spend most of my time out in the community or in a meeting; only about 25 percent of my time is invested in the day-to-day operations of the library. We have a great staff. I do not micromanage (not much, anyway); the staff is very competent and capable. My goal is to get people to understand that their opinions are just as important as mine. However, I do get the opportunity to make the final decision: the buck does stop here; I am held accountable. I am busy forging partnerships, networking, coordinating, and bringing about happenings that have never occurred at our library before now. An example is hosting in the gallery the finalists who had come to the Van Cliburn competition. More than 200 people attended. This made me realize that the public library is indeed the great equalizer. The art exhibits that we have in the library demonstrate this as well.

Greiner
What drives the library?

Gleniece Robinson
Patron needs. We provide services for the public. Everything else follows. The city council as well as the city manager's office believes as we do; we are a public service institution. The only reason we exist is to serve the people of Fort Worth. Needs of patrons are shaped by political support and the economy. One way we are meeting those needs is to have two regional libraries open seven days a week. This initiative was generated at the council level. This council-initiated action and support is a complement to the library.

Greiner

Where do you see this library ten years from now?

Gleniece Robinson

The answer to that question is in the library's master services plan. This plan is significantly beyond where we are today. We are getting ready to have a master services plan based on input from citizens in a 3–7–10-year plan. We will contract with a planning team to develop a plan for the library. While we have some ideas as to the outcome of the plan, we are anxiously awaiting the input of the community and a defined set of recommendations with costs implications.

The Foundation and Friends went to the city council with $200,000 and urged the city council to invest in its libraries with a $150,000 contribution to a master services plan for the library. It is specified that the master services plan will give some direction to the Foundation and Friends for fund-raising. There is a steering committee with Friends, the Foundation, and at-large community members for complete buy in. The Foundation's long-range planning committee lists the priorities as technology and the collection management. The library supports those initiatives totally.

Master Services Plan Updated Information

On Tuesday, December 18, 2001, during a scheduled council meeting, the Fort Worth City Council named Dubberly Associates, Inc., a research firm based in Atlanta, Georgia, as the consultant to engineer the public library's master services plan, which will get library services on the right track. As the library director, Dr. Gleniece A. Robinson, explained, "Fort Worth Public just concluded its centennial celebration that had earned it the nickname, the Original Search Engine" (Fort Worth Public Library 2001, 2).

On April 8, 2003, Dubberly Associates made a presentation to the city council of the completed Fort Worth Public Library Long Range Services Plan. The final report was presented to the board of trustees and a copy of the document was issued in October 2003 (Fort Worth Public Library n.d.b).

The long-range services plan

- Identifies community needs

- Enables the library to be a more responsive city service

- Determines the most appropriate services for the library to provide

- Helps the library make effective decisions about resource allocation

- Develops supportable requests for operating and capital project funding

- Focuses and assists the activities of the library advisory board, the Friends of the Fort Worth Public Library, Inc., and the Fort Worth Public Library Foundation

- Focuses and supports grant applications and other funding requests

- Supports staff recruitment activities (Fort Worth Public Library n.d., 2)

As a result of input from 3,500 residents who participated in two surveys and twenty opinion-gathering sessions throughout Fort Worth, top service priorities were identified as:

- Current topics and titles

- Lifelong learning

- Information literacy (Fort Worth Public Library n.d.a, 17)

Additional service priorities identified were:

- Local history and genealogy

- Cultural awareness

- General information (Fort Worth Public Library n.d.a, 19)

Greiner
Would you describe the organization chart?

Gleniece Robinson
It has not changed significantly. The chart is rather flat. There is the director, assistant director, and three administrators—one for branches, one for the central library, and one for collection management. That is the top layer. There are managers for fourteen branches and ten public service units and support services. The organization of the library is sometimes underestimated—organization is essential. And libraries are organized to achieve maximum efficiency and effectiveness.

Greiner
Would you explain the ten state library systems?

Gleniece Robinson
There are ten library systems authorized under the Texas State Library Systems Act. There are 73 public library members of our system, the North Texas Regional Library System (NTRLS); it is a consortium of public libraries, similar to the ten regions for school systems in the state of Texas. The benefit is support, in various forms, from the state through the system. It provides funding for equipment, continuing education, staff development, and publicity for the library. System consultants provide free services to its members. Money is channeled through the state and the system to the library. It is helpful to small public libraries. direct aid, mentioned earlier, is separate, and is channeled from the state to a particular library. It can be used for anything a library wants, ex-

cept new construction. In a broader context, direct aid is aimed at providing library services beyond the boundaries of a city's legal jurisdiction.

Greiner

How does the interlibrary loan system work with the city?

Gleniece Robinson

The Interlibrary Loan Grant Program is financed through the state. It is operated as a major resource library, at the Fort Worth Public Library, in the North Texas Regional System. Money comes to the city from the state and then to the library.

Greiner

Are library cards free to all residents of Fort Worth?

Gleniece Robinson

Yes, library cards are free to residents of Fort Worth and to persons who own property in Fort Worth. Also, there are other alternatives available for persons who do not live in Fort Worth to get a free library card, such as a $100 contribution to the Foundation, the Friends, or the library, or volunteering a specified number of hours.

Greiner

Is the Fort Worth Public Library a union operation?

Gleniece Robinson

The FWPL is not a union operation

The Public Library—the Great Equalizer

The twenty women members of the Fort Worth Public Library Association, established in 1892, were determined to see a public library building in their city. One of the members, Mrs. Sarah Jennings, donated a plot of land, known as Hyde Park. The depression of 1893 delayed the project for five years. Men were invited to join the association in 1898. Mrs. D. B. Keeler wrote Andrew Carnegie, and asked for a donation as small as the price of a cigar for the library. Carnegie responded with the offer of a gift of $50,000 for a building if the city would provide a site for the library and agree to maintain the library at a cost of not less than $4,000 a year.

The Carnegie Public Library of Fort Worth opened in 1901. The original plan included an art gallery as a part the public library. The director of the library was also director of the museum. Mrs. Jennie Scheuber was appointed the first librarian and served until she retired at the request of the board of trustees in 1938.

John Adams Lowe in his evaluation of the Fort Worth Public Library in 1937 was critical of the emphasis given to the art museum and encouraged its separation from the library. Frances B. Worden reviewed the history of the Fort Worth Library and Art Museum, "Some early European libraries, such as the British Museum, housed artifacts as well as graphic works, as did the Fort Worth library. It was a good beginning, in spite of its troubles, perhaps more firmly founded because of them. There are no perfect mirrors" (Worden 1971, 36).

A new and larger Fort Worth Public Library opened in 1939. The new central Fort Worth Public Library opened in an underground building in 1978, and an expansion to the central library began in 1993 and was completed in 1999.

A tornado caused over $1 million damage to the library on March 28, 2000. The library, as in the past, survived the disaster, and prevailed to celebrate the centennial for the Fort Worth Public Library in October 2001.

The director, Gleniece Robinson, told me in a telephone interview on August 30, 2001, that the library was moving forward with its 3–7–10-year master services plan based on input from citizens. On April 8, 2003, the completed long-range services plan was presented to the Fort Worth City Council and the approved document was made available to the public October 3, 2003.

Chronology

1889	Woman's Wednesday Club, the nucleus of the Fort Worth Public Library Association, established
1892, April 2	Fort Worth Public Library Association established
1898	Men admitted to the association
1901, October 17	Fort Worth Carnegie Public Library opened with Jennie Scheuber as the first librarian
1910–1937	Jennie Scheuber was director of the Fort Worth Museum of Art, as well as director of the library; the museum was housed within the library
1922	Tarrant County Free Library started providing library service to the county
1928	An annex was rented to house part of the collection, due to limited space in the Carnegie building
1928, June 13	Jennie Scheuber was honored in a public ceremony and her portrait was given to the museum of art
1935, September 3	A bond issue was ratified for a new library building
1936	A total of twenty-four depository stations had been established

1937, August 24	Presidential approval for a federal loan and grant for a library was given
1937, November	John Adams Lowe, director of the Rochester Public Library in New York, was requested by the American Library Association and authorized by the Fort Worth Board of Trustees to assist the architect with plans for a new building and to conduct a survey of the library
1937, December 2	Carnegie building closed
1937, December 23	Library opened in temporary quarters
1938, March 28	The library trustees requested that Jennie Scheuber retire from the library
1938, April 1	Jennie Scheuber retired; Helen P. Toombs appointed acting librarian
1939, June 15	The library opened in new quarters as Fort Worth Public Library with Harry N. Peterson of Yonkers, New York, as librarian
1946, December 17	Library board of trustees appointed and Fort Worth Public Library Association's function ended
1948	Joseph S. Ibbotson succeeded Harry N. Peterson as director of the library and was instrumental in organizing the Friends of the Library and initiating bookmobile service
1948, January	Fort Worth Public Library Staff Association formed
1954	Arless Nixon became director, and branch libraries were considered
1962	The first free-standing branch, Southwest, opened in the Wedgwood area
1964	Wyman Jones became the fifth director; the East branch opened in Meadowbrook
1967	Five additional branches opened
1971	Mabel Fischer became the first female director since Jennie Scheuber
1972	Voter approval for a new central library secured
1975	Funding received for the new library
1978	New central library opened in underground building

1981	Linda Allmand hired as director
1985	Tarrant County funding to provide library service to the county ended, and nonresident fees were established
1986	Library automation project completed, featuring computerized catalog
1992	A new central library expansion project began
1993	The Fort Worth Public Library Foundation founded and began a capital improvements campaign to finish, furnish, and equip the expanded central library
1994	COOL (Cavile Outreach Opportunity Library) opened as the first satellite in a public housing community
1995	Exterior expansion of the central library completed
1996, July	The library's World Wide Web homepage was launched
1997, January 25	BOLD (Butler Outreach Library Division) opened as FWPL's second satellite library located in a public housing community
1998, May	Interior expansion of central library began
1999, March	Dr. Gleniece Robinson became the Fort Worth Public Library's eighth director and first African American director
1999, October 22	Finished expansion of the central library opened
2000, March 28	A tornado hit the central library, resulting in over $1 million damage
2000, November 11	Summerglen branch opened
2001, October 17	Fort Worth Public Library celebrated its 100th birthday
2001, December 18	The Fort Worth City Council awarded a contract to Dubberly Associates, Inc., a research firm based in Atlanta, Georgia, as the consultant to engineer the public library's master services plan for long-range planning (3–7–10-year) and establishing priorities for the library based on input from citizens
2002, May 3	Regional libraries began seven-day-a-week schedule
2003, April 8	Fort Worth Public Library Long Range Services Plan presented to Fort Worth City Council (Fort Worth Public Library n.d.b, 1)

2003, October	Final Report Long-Range Services Plan for the Fort Worth Public Library (Dubberly Associates, Inc.) document available to the public

References

Fort Worth Public Library. n.d.a. "Final Report: Long-Range Services Plan." http://www.fortworthlibrary/org/lrsp_2.htm (accessed November 17, 2003).

Fort Worth Public Library. n.d.b. "Long Range Services Plan Presentation to City Council on April 8." http://www.fortworthlibrary.org/l4sp_apr8.htm (accessed November 10, 2003).

Fort Worth Public Library n.d.c "Welcome to the Fort Worth Public Library," http://www.fortworthlibrary.org/ (accessed May 7, 2004). Last modified May 3, 2004.

Fort Worth Public Library. 2001. "Press Releases." http//www.fortworthlibrary.org/press.htm (accessed December 30, 2001).

Fort Worth Public Library. 2002. "History of the Fort Worth Public Library." http://www.fortworthlibrary.org/history.htm (accessed August 28–30, 2001).

Kinney, Helen Toombs. 1951. *History of Public Library of Fort Worth, Texas*. Local History Room, Fort Worth Public Library. Fort Worth, Texas.

Lowe, John Adams. 1937. *Report of a Survey of the Public Library of Fort Worth for Trustees of Fort Worth Public Library Association, Nov. 4–11, 1937*. Chicago: American Library Association.

Taylor, Robert Noel. 1968. "Jennie Scott Scheuber: An Approach to Librarianship." Local History Room, Fort Worth Public Library. Fort Worth, Texas.

Texas State Historical Association. 2002. "Jennie Scott Scheuber," The Handbook of Texas Online. http://www.tsha.utexas.edu/handbook/online/articles/view/SS/fsc39.html (accessed July 18, 2002).

Worden, Frances B. 1971. The Mirror: A History of the Carnegie Public Library of Fort Worth, Texas, 1901–1939. Master's thesis, Texas Woman's University. Local History Room, Forth Worth Public Library. Fort Worth, Texas.

Section D

Public Libraries in Southern States

Preview

I collected information in April and November 2002 from the Library of Hattiesburg, Petal, and Forrest County in Hattiesburg, Mississippi, and from the DeKalb County Public Library in Decatur, Georgia, in October 2001. Because the library of Hattiesburg, Petal, and Forrest County is located in my home city, I was able to visit numerous times during this research activity to collect information and to attend many special programs. I also traveled to Decatur, Georgia, for an interview with the director of the DeKalb County Public Library and to visit some of the DeKalb County Public Library branches.

I conducted two formal interviews with the director of the Hattiesburg, Petal, and Forrest County Library, one at the beginning of the research process and another for additional information. Access to library minutes, a local history of the library compiled by the Mississippi Library Commission, and a detailed campaign plan to gain citizen approval of a referendum for a new library in 1991 was made available to me.

A spectacular mural, *The Spirit That Builds,* located in the library atrium, exemplifies the spirit of the library and the community that made it possible. The mural celebrates the concept of "people working together towards a common goal." Funding for the new building is the result of concentrated community effort to pass a bond issue. The University of Southern Mississippi faculty and students were involved in the campaign for the new library and are proud of the impressive building. The library building, both outside and inside, is a selling point for Hattiesburg, Mississippi. For example, prospective faculty members for the University of Southern Mississippi's School of Library and Information Science are often given a tour of the library.

During a site visit to the headquarters library of the DeKalb County Public Library in Decatur, Georgia, the director of the DeKalb County Public Library hosted a tour of three of the branch libraries and shared information about the system in an interview in October 2001. He has continued to provide news about the system through the summer of 2003.

The library in Decatur projects a sense of a diverse cultural community and at the same time it is reminiscent of the elegance of the Old South. When I entered the reception area of the administrative offices, my attention was drawn to the formal portrait of the first director of the library, who continued as the chief administrator for thirty-one years. The library board meeting room has similar portraits of the first director's successors.

The diversity of the clientele and of the services provided was evident in the three branches that I visited with the director. DeKalb County Public Library's philosophy of inclusiveness is communicated by administration and staff to library clientele. "Inclusion" and "participation" are terms that best describe the DeKalb County Public Library's management philosophy and behavior.

The Library of Hattiesburg, Petal, and Forrest County, Mississippi: The Power of the People

Mission Statement

The Library's primary mission is to provide information and reading materials to the citizens of Hattiesburg, Petal and Forrest County. The Library's staff and the collection supply accurate and timely information through a variety of formats to support learning for the traditional student and the independent learner. The Library also has a strong commitment to introducing reading to children and young adults. Recognizing the importance of reading in enhancing our lives, the Library provides a current collection of popular reading materials. The Library accepts its challenge to promote reading and to provide materials that meet contemporary society's demand for information and a highly literate population.

History and Background

The Library of Hattiesburg, Petal, and Forrest County, with the main library in Hattiesburg, Mississippi, and a branch in Petal, Mississippi, serves a population of 73,000. The new 54,000-square-foot main library in Hattiesburg opened in March 1996. There are five full time professional staff

The city of Hattiesburg was officially incorporated in 1898–99. In 1916 the library was established with a circulating collection of books at the Firm Lumber Company. Later that year, the library moved to the lounge on the first floor of the Forrest County Courthouse. During World War I, the American Library Association established twelve branch libraries in Hattiesburg to serve soldiers training at Camp Shelby, as well as local citizens.

The first public library building, located on Main Street, was dedicated in May 1930. Ordinance No. 805, adopted and approved on July 12, 1928, provided for the construction, equipment, and operation of the public library of the city of Hattiesburg, Mississippi. B. D. Moore was mayor of the city of Hattiesburg. (City of Hattiesburg n.d., 580–581). A referendum was held on February 19, 1929, for a bond issue of $25,000 for the purchase of First Baptist Church property at the corner of Main and Jackson streets. An alternate site of land, formerly used as a pound and already owned by the city, had been proposed but was not accepted. A new $100,000 library was built on the former church property and opened May 22, 1930 (Mississippi Library Commission 1971, 1). Mayor W. S. Tatum and former mayor B. D. Moore were scheduled as the main speakers (*Hattiesburg American* 1930). Lois Rumph assumed the position of librarian on June 1, 1930. In 1950 the Hattiesburg Library entered into a cooperative agreement with Forrest County.

The historical need for and use of the public library are demonstrated with the following statistics. In 1937, the collection was reported as 14,546; by 1970 it had grown to 87,303. Circulation had increased from 76,347 in 1937 to 214,502 in 1970. The number of patrons had grown from 6,599 to 34,410, and the budget had increased from $6,459 to $130,800 (Mississippi Library Commission 1971, 9).

In the South, public libraries in the pre-1960s were segregated. Libraries serving blacks were separate from the public libraries serving whites. Pamela Pridgen, the current library director, recalled hearing an African American grandmother, who came into the new library with her young grandson, say to him, "When I was your age, I could not have come in this building."

Bobs Tusa, Mississippi archivist at the University of Southern Mississippi, in "How the Civil Rights Movement Came to the Hattiesburg Public Library," described the efforts of volunteers from four national civil rights organizations to encourage and help African Americans in Mississippi register to vote during the summer of 1964, known as Freedom Summer. The Congress of Racial Equality (CORE), the National Association for the Advancement of Colored People (NAACP), the Southern Christian Leadership Conference (SCLC), and the Student Nonviolent Coordinating Committee (SNCC) united in Mississippi as the Council of Federated Organizations (COFO). Volunteers (mostly white) from outside the state joined with local volunteers (mostly black) to teach in the Freedom Schools (Tusa 1998, 56).

One of the white Freedom School teachers, Sandra Adickes, and six of her black students went to the Hattiesburg Public Library and asked for library cards so they could check out books. When the students were refused applications, they sat at tables to read magazines. The police chief arrived at the library and made everyone leave, announcing that the library was being closed. According to Doug McAdam (1988, 276), Hattiesburg Mayor Claude F. Pittman later stated that the library was closed for inventory (McAdam in Tusa 1998, 57). Dr. Adickes, now professor of English at a midwestern university, recently returned to Hattiesburg for a statewide reunion of Freedom Summer volunteers in 1994 (Tusa 1998, 57).

In October 1991, after three failed attempts to gain citizen approval for funding a new public library, an ambitious campaign for the construction of a new main library and a branch library in Petal began. The campaign featured communitywide involvement and a creative and well-executed public relations program. The bond issue passed with a 71 percent majority, and in March 1996 the new library opened ("Support the Next Generation's Library" 1992).

Organization

The library is governed by a board of trustees composed of six members appointed by Forrest County, six appointed by the city of Hattiesburg, and three appointed by the city of Petal. Regular monthly meetings are held. The library director is the chief administrative officer of the library. The director administers and establishes procedures according to the policies established by the board of trustees. Organizational units of the institution are public services, youth services, technical services, and administration.

Pamela Pridgen, director of the library, is a graduate of the School of Library and Information Science at the University of Southern Mississippi. She began her professional career in 1980 as a bookmobile librarian of the Public Library in Hattiesburg. She was then promoted to assistant director with public relations as a main responsibility. In 1983, she became director of the Pine Forrest Regional Library, a five-county system with fifteen branches. Pridgen served there until 1988, when she returned to Hattiesburg Public as director of the library. She remarked that she was interviewed on the basis of being able to build community support and to gain support for the new library and coordinate the building program.

Library Bond Campaign

The level of community support for the library bond was demonstrated in the fall of 1991 during the library bond campaign, which sought approval from the citizens for funding for a new library. The campaign was launched on October 1, 1991, and continued through November 6, 1991, Election Day. This $6 million library bond issue was to fund construction of the new library of Hattiesburg, Petal, and Forrest County. The bond would add 3 mills to the property tax bill or about $18 a year for the average property owner, and would be repaid over a period of fifteen years. There had been three unsuccessful attempts to gain citizen approval for a library bond prior to this. The goal for this campaign was a 60 percent positive vote, which would allow funding for a new main library for Forrest County, a new branch library for Petal, and an automation system.

Hattiesburg serves as the medical, legal, banking, and trade center for surrounding counties. The University of Southern Mississippi had a student population in 1991 of 11,000; William Carey College, 1,000. There were four school districts and three private or parochial schools. The population distribution in 1991 was 72 percent white, 27 percent black, and 1 percent other. There are numerous art groups, civic clubs, and organizations in Hattiesburg.

The program title for the bond campaign was Support the Next Generation's Library—A Bond Campaign to Nov. 5. The first objective was to find registered voters. The strategy was to identify "yes" voters and encourage them to vote, and to provide information to the undecided voters. Public service announcements (PSAs) supporting a new library aired on radio and television: five television PSAs aired 56 times and five radio PSAs aired 686 times over the course of the campaign. Television and radio stations donated production and airtime valued at $10,882.50.

Campaign headquarters was the central point for information and distribution of materials. The target audiences were local businesses and the general public. The library could not use public funds for the campaign. The Bank of Mississippi donated a suite of furnished rooms with separate entrance and parking, as well as copier and office supplies. A banner was erected at headquarters. A member of the Friends of the Library who had office management experience coordinated campaign headquarters activities. A press conference was held on opening day.

The finance committee targeted local businesses and philanthropic individuals. The objective was to recruit committee members, establish a budget for the campaign, raise funds to meet expenses, and acknowledge all donations. The finance committee raised $9,670 in pledges for donations, recruited five committee members, and secured donations from twenty-seven individuals or businesses. The Godwin Group, an advertising agency in Jackson, provided information for a campaign kit and press packet. Their in-kind contribution amounted to $22,350.

Information about the campaign was available at the library, campaign headquarters, schools, businesses, and city hall. Brochures were mailed to undecided voters. Strategies included a telephone canvas, direct mailings, small group meetings and neighborhood coffees, bumper stickers, yard signs, and user surveys. The Friends of the Library funded programs featuring Mississippi authors Richard Ford and John Grisham. The Community Brown Bag Concert Series and Hubfest also highlighted the library bond campaign. Writing letters to the newspaper editors was encouraged. Problems with the existing library building, built in 1930, were identified. A primary concern with the old library was the limited access for people with disabilities.

A four-member speaker's bureau was established. The targets were local educational, civic, cultural, and business groups. The speakers were an attorney and state legislator, a university professor and director of a center for business research and development, a homemaker, and the library director. Members spoke at twenty-five group meetings—PTA, Rotary Club, Historic Neighborhood Association, AARP, and Petal and Hattiesburg Chambers of

Commerce. Forty-five hundred endorsement cards were distributed. The objective was to receive 100 endorsements for the bond from individuals and groups. In fact, 364 individuals and thirty-four groups endorsed the library bond proposal. The Hattiesburg School Board and a state representative were among the supporters. Letters of endorsement from University of Southern Mississippi educators came from the School of Library and Information Science, the Center for Business Development and Research, the College of Education and Psychology, Department of Education Leadership and Research, the School of Nursing, and the dean of the College of Liberal Arts.

The results were: yes votes, 10,614, or seventy-one percent; and no votes, 4,241, or twenty-nine percent. A building questionnaire was distributed in the community seeking input from the residents about what they would like to see included in the new library. The original 1930s building is to remain on the National Register of Historic Places. The library won the John Cotton Dana Award in 1992 for the successful library bond campaign. This comprehensive public relations effort was a grassroots campaign that engendered wide community support, not only for the bond issue but for long-term operation of the library.

Programs and Services

The expanded facilities include a 54,000-square-foot main library and the 7,111-square-foot Petal library, part of a community center complex. Automation includes a computerized card catalog and an automated system that links the main library and Petal branch. User-friendly computer terminals allow requests and next-day mailing for patrons to locations throughout Forrest County. The collection has expanded from 75,600 to 182,500 at the main library and in Petal to 25,000 volumes. Quiet study areas are available, as are meeting rooms for groups of from 4 to 200. The larger meeting rooms have video projector capabilities and an adjacent kitchen. Microcomputer rooms with sixteen user-friendly computer workstations and three rooms with individual computer workstations are available. The reference area includes reference volumes and computer reference tools for information retrieval. There is also a business reference area and an audiovisual area. An art gallery features works by local artists, local students, and traveling exhibits.

The Local History Room houses more than 10,000 volumes about Mississippi and Forrest County, as well as books by and about Mississippi authors. The entrance to the Mississippi Room is a replica of the entrance to the governor's mansion in Jackson. The door handle is the original brass handle from the door to the new capitol building in Jackson built in 1920. The heart pine columns at the entrance to the room are from virgin timber dated circa 1855.

A monumental mural, *The Spirit That Builds,* by artist William Baggett, graces the library's atrium. The scale painting is approximately 10 feet in height by 167 feet in circumference, and took three years to complete. Suspended 30 feet from the floor above the circulation desk, the mural celebrates the concept of "people working together towards a common goal, with an emphasis on collaboration, team spirit and a strong work ethic" within the framework of local history. The artist, William Baggett, is currently a professor in the Art Department at the University of Southern Mississippi and best known for his figurative paintings. Many of the properties ascribed to his paintings are encountered in the works of distinguished southern writers (Library of Hattiesburg, Petal, and Forrest County 1995–2002b, 1). For example, the characters that William Faulkner and Eudora Welty treat with such dignity are simple folk. They have a commitment to one another and a belief in a brighter future. The mural "begins with images of Native Americans and proceeds through the settling of south Mississippi" (Davis 2001, 5).

In 1997, the Library received the Governor's Award for Excellence in the Arts for the community involvement in the design in the new Hattiesburg library building. The award was given by the Mississippi Arts Commission. Pridgen described the library as a light, welcoming place in which you want to spend time. "We used a process that was dependent on community involvement to design a building unique to our community's needs. The result is a building with roots in our history yet projecting to the future."

In the same year, Pamela Pridgen was designated by the Hattiesburg Lions Club as the 1997 Distinguished Citizen of the Year (Bill Strong n.d., 2).

Pridgen added, "In summer 2000, a juried National Small Sculpture Exhibit brought in from all over North America was funded by the Mississippi Arts Key Community Grant. The library partnered with the city of Hattiesburg for the grant. The library has been very successful because of community partnerships we have forged. The community is very responsive and the library works to develop relationships throughout the community."

Pamela Pridgen was awarded the Public Achievement in the Humanities Award by the Mississippi Humanities Council in 2002. The award recognizes the humanities programming the library has offered through the library's cooperation with state humanities groups, educational institutions, and community organizations.

Friends of the Library

The Friends of the Library is a nonprofit charitable organization with the goal of promoting and improving library service. This group of active volunteers had a major impact on the library's ability to serve the community. The Friends were major players in the successful library bond campaign. The annual spring fund-raiser, Buy a Book for the Library, is a significant source of new materials for the library.

The Friends of the Library gave the Sidney Berry Award for meritorious service in a professional manner to the library in 1990. Sidney Berry was the first chairman of the library board of trustees in 1930. The Sidney Berry Award has been given to the previous mayor, Ed Morgan, and also to state Senator Rick Lambert and state Representative Bill Jones, who were instrumental in the passage of the first bond appropriation for state support of public library buildings in 1994. The Berry Award was given to Bill and Melinda Gates in 1999.

The library has twenty-five docents trained for tours, with knowledge of architectural and art features. The strengths of individual docents are matched with interests of different groups.

Exhibits that have been in the library include: Free at Last—The Abolition of Slavery from the Gilder Lehrman Institute in New York City; The Great Experiment: George Washington and the American Republic from the Huntington Library in Los Angeles; Produce for Victory: The Home Front During World War II from the Smithsonian; and Faulkner's World from the Center for the Study of Southern Culture in Oxford, Mississippi. There is a retail gift shop for traveling exhibits.

In the fall of 2002, the library was selected as one of four libraries nationally to host an evening with Michael Blake, author of the novel *Dances with Wolves*. Over 500 people attended.

The exhibition Forever Free: Abraham Lincoln's Journey to Emancipation was on display November 13, 2003, to January 9, 2004, at the Hattiesburg, Petal, and Forrest County Library. "Organized by the Huntington Library, San Marino, California, and the Gilder Lehrman Institute of American History, New York City, in cooperation with the American Library Association (ALA), this traveling exhibition was made possible through a major grant from the National Endowment for the Humanities (NEH) (Library of Hattiesburg, Petal, and Forrest County 2003, 1). Friends of the Library contributed local support.

Special library services include the Library Book Club, which meets monthly for an informal discussion of an assigned book. A Lunch with Books program features local authors and book signings by authors. The library provides a collection of materials designed for adults seeking to improve their reading skills or learn to read, and provides space for the Hattiesburg Education Literacy Project (HELP) volunteer tutoring program. Literacy materials, which include books and books on tape, are designated with an ANR classification (adult new reader) and are located in the literacy support area of the main library. The library offers a free books-by-mail service for users who cannot come to the library. Users can phone in requests and receive books in a zippered bag with return postage included. The talking book service provides sound recordings to people with visual impairments. This service is provided free by the Library of Congress through the Mississippi Library Commission's Service for the Handicapped. Service is also provided to residents of area nursing homes through deposit collections and biweekly visits. The library is currently conducting a pilot program, providing service to users in outlying areas through biweekly visits to community centers, where users may check out, or request items and enjoy programs for children. The South Forrest Recreation Center is the pilot center for this program, with expansion of the program planned (Library of Hattiesburg, Petal, and Forrest County 1995–2002a, 1).

The library is now a Cooperating Collection of the Foundation Center, providing print and online information for grant writers. The first workshop was held in January 2002, and representatives of forty-eight agencies attended.

Interview

Pamela Pridgen, Director of the Library of Hattiesburg, Petal, and Forrest County

Greiner
Does the present library relate historically to the founding library?

Pamela Pridgen
The original library, built in 1930, was considered a state-of-the-art facility. When we were planning the present library we felt the responsibility to maintain that high standard of library service for our community. Both buildings are landmarks. Like the founding library, the present library provides the traditional library services of information, popular materials, and services to children for our community. In addition, the present library offers a wide range of electronic resources and services.

When the original library was built, library service was segregated. Today, the library's board of trustees, staff, and users are as diverse as our community.

Greiner
What is unique about this library?

Pamela Pridgen
The most obvious answer is *The Spirit that Builds,* the library's monumental-scale painting by artist William Baggett. It is a masterpiece. When people enter the library, their eyes are naturally drawn up to the mural and they stand there gazing in wonder. The mural also demonstrates what is truly remarkable about the library: the sense of community that is alive at the library. The mural project was funded through the generosity of local patrons. The board of trustees and staff work to involve the library as a partner throughout the community, and consequently the library enjoys a wide perspective of public awareness and support.

Greiner
What do you see as your primary role as library director?

Pamela Pridgen
My primary role is representing the library to the community and integrating it into the fullness of all aspects of community life. The aim is to bring

the library outside and make the library a part of the community. We emphasize networking and partnering. To be successful, you must have a building, resources and materials, and people.

Greiner

What do you see as your political role? What is the political role of the library administrator?

Pamela Pridgen

Service is based on how the library is funded, and as a result the resources of a library are based on the political astuteness of the library manager.

We have the opportunity and responsibility to continue to move the libraries forward with newly elected mayors in Hattiesburg and Petal, as well as new councilmen and aldermen in both cities. The faces of local government have changed completely. I put together a packet of materials along with letters of congratulation for the winners. I offered to meet with the new administration and discuss the library and its mission. All of the new people are on the mailing lists for Hattiesburg and Petal—they get announcements of the activities of each of the libraries. During the campaign, we watch the media and other forms of communication. Who were the key supporters for the candidates? Then you can identify library supporters who are in each camp. Regardless of who is elected, a library supporter can speak to that winning candidate. The newly elected person would not be unknown. I try hard to be politically active but not be partisan. The library is a visual institution, and a lot of people want to make announcements here, or to shoot ads here. When that happens, we call the other party or independent candidate and offer them the same opportunity.

Greiner

How would you describe your management style?

Pamela Pridgen

Between 75 and 80 percent is participative. I am a team manager. But the remaining 20 to 25 percent is the responsibility of the administrator. Someone has to be responsible—this is where the buck stops. It is rare that we do not come to consensus as a management team. When there is disagreement, it has more often been between two staff members, but there have been disagreements between me as administrator and a librarian or me as administrator and staff. The aim is to make decisions that all can support, find ground that all can support and work toward. Within the team there is a wide range of management styles. We have to find common ground; there has to be consistency in how situations are handled, regardless of section, department, or branch.

I make a conscious effort to notice the good things people do and thank people for them. People work harder and are more creative in a positive atmosphere. I also try to minimize the mistakes. There is a management school of thought that says to look at what you do well and use that as a model for future success. "Appreciative Inquiry" is new, and basically proposes, "Take your successes and use them as a pattern for your future."

Greiner

What drives the library—technology, patron needs, the political environment, the economy?

Pamela Pridgen

All of these elements. The primary driving factor is patron needs. Patron needs must be balanced against what the community views as the library mission. Economic policy is also a factor. The need for and use of technology has to be balanced. Technology allows the library to do more. We must launch technology against the latest best seller against the budget.

The library interacts positively with the board of trustees. We have a procedure when a new board member joins. There is an orientation session which includes a description of the role of the library in the community, the role of the board, and the role of the library administration. Administrative staff bring to each board meeting policy recommendations and also long-range planning issues. They report on daily operations, usage patterns, and expenditures. We make a clear distinction: When we ask for recommendations, it is from the librarians' standpoint, but decisions should be based on the needs of this community. The Board needs to come to agreement. The library has a cardinal rule that no board member shall be surprised. When the library is contacted about an issue that will be publicly addressed, everyone—the mayor and all board members—is contacted by senior management staff. In this informative way, the board is protected.

The library board and library administration worked together to form the library's Internet policy. The library administration brought examples of Internet policies to the board. Using local community standards, the board made the decision to filter Internet content. The library is heavily used by children and families. There is no area where children are not regularly found. It is against the law in Mississippi to display pornography where children are regularly in attendance.

Because of the overall economic outlook, the library's future looks good. There is a progressive government in Hattiesburg that perceives the library as a community asset. The library was the first stop on the tour of the Mississippi League of Mayors.

Greiner

What is the library's relationship with the School of Library and Information Science at the University of Southern Mississippi?

Pamela Pridgen

I have been president of the advisory council to the school. I was local president of the local Beta Phi Mu chapter. I teach as an adjunct. I have taught Public Library Management, Fundraising/Grant Writing, Creative Programming, and The Library Building Process.

I am a constant advocate for the school, and I make recommendations for curriculum from the practical perspective of the library administrator who hires and continues to train library and information science graduates. I strongly recommend practicum experiences for students, and many of the school students enroll in and complete practicums in the library. I suggest a practicum early in the program. This enables a student to answer the question, "Do I want to be in a public library?" On the other hand, the student should have all of the basic core courses or related courses before doing the practicum. My strongest criticism is the lack of appreciation for the need for public service. The students have a strong professional interest, but it is not balanced with the service attitude.

The Hattiesburg library is one of three training centers in Mississippi for the Gates Foundation. The library is fortunate to have a high level of community financial support. This allows more opportunities and affords the library the responsibility to extend opportunities to the community. One of the reasons that the library applied to be a Gates training center was that the library has the staff and facility to support a training center. Hattiesburg is a good geographical location. The lab, with eleven computers, is open during library hours and in constant use. This allows the library to provide training opportunities for library users; 2000 software and support is provided for three years by the Gates Foundation.

In return for the Gates support, the Library served as a computer training hub. The Gates Foundation brought its own trainers. Sean Farrell, the assistant librarian, went to the training center in Seattle, and has done training on the Magnolia Network, an online database service, for state libraries. Two students from the School of Library and Information Science served as trainers. The Gates trainers from the school provided technical assistance and training to public librarians participating in Gates Foundation–supported activities in Mississippi. A professor at the school was assigned the responsibility of supervising the students.

I was on the committee, along with a member of the Mississippi Library Commission, a faculty member of the school, and the director of the school, to choose a recipient for the Gates Scholarship. The student received a full graduate scholarship to the school and completed an internship at the Library of Hattiesburg, Petal, and Forrest County.

The Power of the People

The first circulating collection of books was established in 1916 in the Firm Lumber Company, and later that year moved to the Forrest County Courthouse. The American Library Association established branch libraries in Hattiesburg to serve soldiers serving at Camp Shelby during World War I. The libraries also served local citizens. The first public library building opened in May 1930.

Public libraries pre-1960s were segregated, with libraries serving blacks separate from those serving whites. This history is depicted in the giant mural that dominates the entrance to the library. The artist, Baggett, acknowledged segregation by painting two separate classrooms in an early period of the time span the mural encompasses. "The mural ends with present-day students, black and white, studying together while a librarian and a young person look to the future" (Davis 2001, 5). The artist celebrates progress and the prevailing spirit of community. Pridgen said, "Today the library's board of trustees, staff, and users are as diverse as our community."

Pamela Pridgen is a graduate of the School of Library and Information Science at the University of Southern Mississippi. She serves on the advisory board to the school and as an adjunct faculty member. The public library management, programming, and grant writing courses that she teaches are informative, demanding, and very popular with students.

The new Hattiesburg library is a source of pride for citizens of the city of Hattiesburg. Pamela Pridgen, director of the Library of Hattiesburg, Petal, and Forrest County since 1988 demonstrates a management style that gets things done. She said in our interview that she was hired to gain support for a new library and coordinate the building program. That goal was achieved with broad community support for a magnificent new library that opened in March 1996.

Chronology

1898–99	City of Hattiesburg officially incorporated
1916	Library with a circulation of books established at the Firm Lumber Company
1917, 1918	During World War I, American Library Association established twelve branch libraries in Hattiesburg to serve soldiers training at Camp Shelby, as well as local citizens
1928, July 12	Ordinance adopted and approved that provided for construction, equipment, and operation of the Public Library of the City of Hattiesburg
1929, February 19	Referendum for a bond issue of $25,000 for purchase of First Baptist Church property at the corner of Main and Jackson streets
1930, May 22	New $100,000 public library building located on former church property opened
1950	The Hattiesburg Library entered into a cooperative agreement with Forrest County

1964, Summer	Volunteers from four national civil rights organizations: the Congress of Racial Equality (CORE), the National Association for the Advancement of Colored People (NAACP), the Southern Christian Leadership Conference (SCLC), and the Student Nonviolent Coordinating Committee (SNCC) united in Mississippi as the Council of Federated Organizations (COFO) to teach in the Freedom Schools
1988	Pamela Pridgen became director of the Library of Hattiesburg, Petal, and Forrest County
1991, October 1	Library bond campaign launched to support a new library
1991, November 6	Bond issue to fund a new library approved by 71 percent majority
1992	Library won John Cotton Dana Award for the successful library bond campaign
1994	Reunion of Freedom Summer volunteers
1996, March	New main library opened
1997	Mississippi Arts Commission designated the library as recipient of the Governor's Award for Excellence in the Arts for the community involvement in the design of the new Hattiesburg library building
1997	Pamela Pridgen designated by the Hattiesburg Lions Club as the 1997 Distinguished Citizen of the Year
2002	Pamela Pridgen awarded the Public Achievement in the Humanities Award by the Mississippi Humanities Council

References

Bill Strong's Eclectic Mississippi Photo Tour. n.d. "New Hattiesburg Library." http://www.phototour.com/echtml/library.html (accessed October 20, 2003).

City of Hattiesburg. n.d. Municipal Minute Book "J." Hattiesburg, Mississippi.

Davis, Kathy. 2001. "Murals in Mississippi Libraries." *Mississippi Libraries* 65, no. 1 (Spring). http://www.misslib.org/publications/ml/spr01/murals.htm.

Hattiesburg American (Hattiesburg, Mississippi). 1930. May 21.

Library of Hattiesburg, Petal, and Forrest County. 1995–2002a. "Special Library Services." http://www.hpfc.lib.ms.us/special.html (accessed November 22, 2002).

Library of Hattiesburg, Petal, and Forrest County. 1995–2002b. "Welcome to the Library." http://www.hpfc.lib.ms.us/introduc.html (accessed November 22, 2002).

Library of Hattiesburg, Petal, and Forrest County. 2003. "Forever Free: Abraham Lincoln's Journey to Emancipation." http://www.hpfc.lib. ms.us/lincoln/desc.html (accessed November 5, 2003).

McAdam, Doug. 1988. *Freedom Summer.* New York: Oxford University Press.

Mississippi Library Commission. 1971. *History of the Hattiesburg Forrest Co. Public Library.* Compiled under the direction of the Mississippi Library Commission Jackson, Mississippi.

"Support the Next Generation's Library—A Bond Campaign." 1992. Scrapbook submitted to the John Cotton Dana Public Relations Awards Contest.

Tusa, Bobs. 1998. "How the Civil Rights Movement Came to the Hattiesburg Public Library." *Mississippi Libraries* 62, no. 3 (Fall): 56–57.

10

DeKalb County Public Library, Georgia: A Proud Past, A Bright Future

Vision Statement

We envision a DeKalb County where every person has the opportunity to reach his or her own full potential in an economically strong community which values family, diversity, and cooperation.

Mission Statement

DeKalb County Public Library is a place to grow. The library enlightens and enriches the people of DeKalb County by providing responsive, dynamic services that meet the changing informational needs of a diverse population. Through a trained, service-oriented staff, partnerships, and ready access to both print and electronic resources, the library is committed to superior service that promotes a strong, literate DeKalb community and enhances the quality of life.

History and Background

In 1907 the first public library service in DeKalb County began when a small library opened in Lithonia. The Decatur Library was founded in 1925 to serve a large and rural county. In 1925 a group of prominent Decatur citizens planned a library for their city, and a year later, in 1926, the Decatur Public Library opened on the second floor of the Decatur Building and Loan Association. The library was relocated to the second floor of the Decatur City Hall when it was built in 1927. The main library building was constructed in 1950 at 215 Sycamore Street.

The Decatur DeKalb Library became a regional system when the neigh-

Decatur Public Library, DeKalb County

boring Rockdale County Library joined in 1951. In 1952 the main library was renamed the Decatur DeKalb Library. Newton County Library joined the system in 1953. In 1962 the Decatur DeKalb Library was renamed the DeKalb Library System. In 1989 the DeKalb County Public Library withdrew from the three-county system and established a single county system. The Maude M. Burrus library was named the Decatur Library (DeKalb County Public Library n.d.b. 1).

Maude Burrus was appointed as the first director of the Decatur Public Library in 1930, and she served in that capacity until her retirement in 1961. On February 23, 1965, the name of the Decatur DeKalb Library was officially changed to the Maude M. Burrus Library in appreciation of her many years of faithful service.

The portrait of Maude Burrus is the focal point of the reception area in the administrative offices of the DeKalb County Public Library in Decatur, Georgia. Portraits of Louise Trotti (1961–1981), the successor to Maude Burrus, and Barbara Loar (1982–1991), Trotti's successor, hang in the library boardroom. Burrus and Trotti are revered in this community by people who knew them, and Loar continues to be a high-profile local presence working on behalf of literacy and senior services. A portrait of Donna Mancini (1991–1995), Loar's successor and predecessor to the current director, Darro Willey, is displayed in the reception area of the administrative offices.

Darro Willey joined the DeKalb County Public Library in 1995 from the Broward County Public Library, where he was deputy director. In addition to serving as DeKalb County Public Library's director, he has provided planning consultant services to a number of library systems throughout the southeast United States since 1985.

Organization

Legally, DeKalb County Public Library (DCPL) is a state-chartered government organization governed by a board of trustees. DCPL also operates as a department of DeKalb County, Georgia (DeKalb County Public Library n.d.d, 1).

The DeKalb County Public Library serves a population of 665,865. Circulation, according to the library's fiscal year 2002 statistics, as of June 30, 2002, was 2,972,687. The library has one central library and twenty-two branch libraries, consisting of four area libraries, ten community libraries, six neighborhood libraries and two homework centers. The central library is in Decatur, Georgia (DeKalb County Public Library 2002).

Director Willey gave me a tour of three of the branch libraries: Wesley Chapel–William C. Brown, Covington, and Chamblee. The Wesley Chapel Library was established in 1990, and renamed the Wesley Chapel–William C. Brown Library in 1992 for the longtime chair of the library board of trustees. William C. Brown was the first African American to serve on the library board, from 1976 to 1990, and chair from 1978 until 1990 (DeKalb County Public Library n.d.e, 1). The Covington branch is the audiovisual library for the system. The Chamblee Library, one of the four area libraries, has a multilanguage collection in Spanish, Chinese, Vietnamese, and Korean.

Interview

Darro Willey, Director, October 15, 2001

Greiner

Would you describe your library career?

Darro Willey

In my public library career, my first position was in a library of approximately 4,000 square feet. I was the only professional librarian. It was soon after library school, and one of those situations where you feel more as if you are playing at being a librarian. It was probably the most fun I have had in my career, since I knew just enough to be dangerous, and didn't realize how little I did know.

When I went to library school, I was awarded a scholarship from what was then known as Kansas State Teacher's College. I remember when I was looking for a program, someone—actually the dean of a media specialist program—recommended Kansas State Teacher's College as the best Master of Library Science program in the country. When I asked why, he replied, "It is the cheapest." It was his opinion that in library science degree programs you didn't learn all that much. He felt that you learn more in the actual job situation. I understand his philosophy. Practically, things change so quickly in library and information science due to the constant improvement of technology that what you've learned in library school probably may not be all that relevant soon after you've finished. You end up replacing this information with new knowledge at a rapid pace.

The principles or theories and learning research methodologies are probably the most valuable lessons I learned in library school. I believe the portion of research that is important is not the actual research itself, but how one learns to organize information. This has helped me in terms of developing reports, organizing projects, reviewing people, and advising staff on how to organize a project. The organization and presentation of information is important. In other words, a good degree program should teach you how to think, more than what to think.

Greiner

How does the present library relate historically to the founding library?

Darro Willey

How we operate is probably more participative than in the past—not probably, *is* more participative. Sometimes a library operation becomes a "personal expression of the director." This can be debilitating. Building a consensus of the entire library staff and community will ultimately yield a more effective organization. An organization should ideally adopt a shared, or community-based, culture. In other words, it should not come out of the mind of one or two people. Sometimes I think of myself as a team leader rather than a manager. Usually, when I first meet with a staff committee, I might give a general direction to help with the vision of what we will want or need to do. I usually try to convey this message without expressing it as "what I want done." I prefer to pass along responsibility by giving other people the necessary tools. This allows the staff members to participate, even though the final responsibility is still mine. In only a few instances I believe I will need to ask staff to carefully reexamine a committee decision.

You asked about my management style. It is largely situational, based on and determined by each situation. I use my previous experience to play different roles in different situations, depending upon what is required at the time.

Greiner

What do you see as unique about the DeKalb County Public Library?

Darro Willey

All libraries have some degree of uniqueness. They strive to achieve different things. In this library, perhaps our most "unique" quality is our culture of participation in decision making. I also believe we are very successful with our community. There are times when we receive national attention for various programs, which is all very well and good, but that is not why we do what we do. We really care about the people in the community—what they want, think, and need. We do not think of ourselves as a government agency, like the post office, but more like schools and churches think of themselves. We do not necessarily beat our own drum, saying, "Hey, look at us and how good we are," but our staff and many of our customers believe there is not a better library system around. What *we* think about it is what drives us. There is an energy within the system that I believe translates into a really strong community ethic. The community *is* what gives us our drive.

We have a core of outstanding people that stay within the library system. In any one year, 20 percent of our staff might change. People come and go, but there remains a core there that provides a strong organizational ethic, and an ethic boils down to the service provided to the community. This ethic depends on the community. Our community is also unique in Georgia because of its considerable diversity. No one social or ethnic group has an overwhelming presence, and this is a real strength because it is a community that is tolerant of differences. It makes it a real pleasure to work here.

Greiner

How important is the role of library administrator as a politician?

Darro Willey

Not as a politician per se, but as one who works in particular political circles, the political role is the second most important portion of the job, after an overall community relations role. Obviously political and community issues are intertwined. To create a vision that everyone can share, one must be a highly visible person in the community. I know each of our legislators personally. I meet and speak often with them at community events as well as during office visits, so they know me, and know I am also involved in the political arena. Our current library board chair is also the executive director of Stone Mountain Park, a major state-supported recreational facility. The vice chair of the board recently ran for superior court judge and is very involved in politics. Two city commissioners, a state legislator, a county school board member, and a member of the Georgia Arts Council are all on our library board. So you will see, these people are all connected with other agencies active in the political arena. To summarize, the role of the library director as a politically involved figure cannot be overemphasized. More than any other department head within the county organization, you will see me at the same kinds of events at which you will see legislators and politicians.

Greiner

How would you describe your management style—as more authoritarian, participative, somewhere in between, or pragmatic?

Darro Willey

Participative management guides most of what we do. The library board strongly takes the view that they should deal only in policy. That view translates on down the hierarchy to the staff. The board leaves management issues entirely to the director, and I as the director try to leave the running of the library to the staff. Although I am actively involved in both policy and operational issues, "Sometimes I sits and thinks and sometimes I just sits." Things must be left to just happen to a certain extent. Sometimes directing people who are participating is like herding cats. They go where they are going to go, and sometimes you just have to accept that. It is not because we have willful personalities; it's just the nature of the process. If you want to let a process develop, you can't expect to constantly control it. Also, I try not to burden people with endless requests for reports and information, which impacts the amount of time they can devote to their duties. If I have a particular need for information, I will ask for a particular report, but I do not ask for information that I may or may not use in some specific manner. That is not a good use of time—the staff's or mine.

The administrative staff is fairly lean. Most of our administrative services are on the front line. We spend a great deal of our administrative energy supporting those people on the front line. I believe a certain amount of hierarchy is necessary, to allow adequate delegating of responsibility. Overly flat organizations can tend to concentrate power at the top, other than the way of the flat organization. Middle managers are ultimately where you have your success in an organization.

In DeKalb County, there are only two county departments that operate with some degree of independence from the county administration: the library and the health department. The library is legally a separate unit of administration. The county budget even uses the term "payment to other governments" in listing the library line item. I answer directly to the library board. The library board hires and terminates the library director. The library board has its own purchasing operation separate from the county. We pretty much run our own information technology (IT) operation. Personnel operations are directly overseen by the county, and our salaries are paid by the county, but we also hire approximately seventy part-time merit-exempt employees that the library pays directly. They are not part of the county staff, but they are employed by the library board. This partial separation from the county processes has made us very nimble. We have a very short decision-making process. This is also true for many other library systems in Georgia, particularly the multicounty regional library systems in Georgia which also operate as separate units of administration. One thing our library board cannot do is function as a taxing authority. The library board annually develops a budget request that is submitted to the county administration in September. The board of county commissioners determines what level of funding will be provided to the library board by the end of February. The library board then sets the following fiscal year's budget based on what we receive from the county and the state. The library budget year conforms to the state fiscal year (beginning in July) which is six months off from the county fiscal year. Once we know the sum of money that has been authorized, it is totally within the library board's discretion as to how the money is spent.

At the DeKalb County Public Library the assistant director doubles as the head of public services, besides overseeing day-to-day operations. I believe the assistant director is a critical position within the organization, when analyzing the success of an organization. In our case, much of our effectiveness is due to our assistant director, Magda Sossa. I believe that the assistant director should take care of the inside library activities so that the library director can concentrate on the overall community picture, budgetary matters, and political issues. Some library directors have tried to flatten the organization, eliminating the assistant director position, leaving several major department heads reporting directly to the library director. I think this tends to involve the library director in more of the day-to-day activities of the library and can reduce the amount of time he or she can devote to community issues. If an organization follows this model, it may be more of a matter of how the person personally prefers to operate, but I do not believe it is as effective as when the library director is out working more with the community, letting the assistant director take care of the day-to-day details. It is like Mr. Outside and Ms. Inside in our particular case. This type of management probably comes more from my background as a deputy director than anything else. I had the chance to see how things operate from that perspective. I believe that experience has made me a more effective director because I understand the kinds of issues that must be dealt with by an assistant director on a day-to-day basis. The politician role, as I mentioned earlier, is paramount for a library director.

Greiner

You aren't seen in the library very much, right?

Darro Willey

On the contrary, you will often see me in our libraries. I do some director workdays where I go out to the different libraries. It is important for the director to be seen by the public in the library. The staff also needs to see you. In a way, the library staff is another community for me to relate to. I have a schedule where I try to get out to each branch several times a year. I will occasionally have workdays where I work at every branch in the system at one time or another, even if it is for only two or three hours. This is a little dangerous because I probably learn more than I should about how things really operate. Then I can make life miserable for people.

Greiner

What drives the library—technology, patron needs, the political environment, the economy?

Darro Willey

Patron need drives the library ultimately. Technology is a means to providing services. The political environment and the economy affect the ability of the library to provide services. Economically, we project difficult times in the next couple of years.

Greiner

I was thinking in terms of the customers' needs, you must have the technology . . .

Darro Willey

Yes, you must have the technology. New technological options change how you provide services and add considerable complexity to the service mix. Libraries are much more complex now than they ever were before, which raises the whole issue of training. Technology does in fact also drive the library. Political environment and the economy obviously drive the library one way or the other. As I mentioned earlier, we expect some very difficult times in the next two years. I am expecting a staff freeze next week. Nevertheless, patron needs are the basic driving influence.

[**Updated Information, November 5, 2003**

Darro Willey responded to my question regarding the anticipated staff freeze.

"The county's personnel freeze went into effect on October 19, 2001. It remains in effect, but it has not substantially affected us. The freeze doesn't prevent us from hiring staff. It only requires us to send in specific justification for filling a vacancy to the executive assistant (this is the top nonelected position in DeKalb County government—a county manager, per se). The freeze announcement said that the executive assistant may approve exceptions on a case-by-case basis, and he has been very supportive, approving the filling of all of our vacancies over the past two years. Until recently, to keep with the spirit and intent of the freeze we have tried to leave about seven or eight positions vacant at any one time on a floating basis, a level that allows us to maintain business as usual. The only major effect has been that we have tended to hold up forwarding exception requests until we have cumulated at least five or six vacancies that we want to fill, in order to avoid sending requests too often. More recently we ceased trying to keep several floating positions vacant, and now we have only four positions that are vacant out of 227 merit positions. So as you can see, the freeze has not been onerous" (D. Willey, e-mail message to author, November 5, 2003).]

Greiner

Where do you see this library ten years from now in terms of finances, technology, services, staffing?

Darro Willey

When you see how much libraries have changed in the past ten years, it is difficult to predict conditions ten years from now, but there will be still be books and buildings. There will be new ways of accessing information that we do not know of right now. There will be some new training challenges for staff—new learning opportunities. But we will need more building space. Ten years from now, my wish for DeKalb County Public Library is additional space for programming activities. I see the library of the future becoming much more involved in programming, becoming a community destination. There aren't as many places as there used to be, I believe, for the community to come together.

One more paramount duty of the director is the development of the resources necessary to support the operation. Obviously, it is the duty of the library board as well, but the library director plays a leadership role in this, as well as dealing with ongoing financial issues. How successful you are in developing these resources is often considered a measure of your abilities, but success may well depend upon matters beyond a library director's control. A director might be fortunate to work with a mayor or administrator who suddenly decides he or she loves libraries, and the library does great. The director will seem like a wizard. Whereas, another director working in an organization or setting that is not as supportive might achieve more modest gains, but those gains might be all the more impressive for having been achieved in a less nurturing environment. Sometimes things are beyond your control.

Regardless of the scope of program improvements, I believe the important thing is to maintain constant forward motion. Even if measured progress is less than desired, continual positive change adds to the entire culture of the environment. In the past five years at the DeKalb County Public Library, there has not been any one year where the library has leaped forward. However, every year something positive has been achieved, so that in five years we have increased our staff by approximately 10 percent, with no real new facilities. Increasing staff size is easier when adding new facilities, because everyone knows you need new staff to run new libraries. Doing so without new facilities, even though just a little bit here and there is a less noticeable, is perhaps a more notable achievement. It creates the perception that in the organization and community there is constant forward movement, which is very positive.

Greiner
I agree that it is important to always give that impression of forward motion.

Darro Willey
Right—both for the community and for your own organization. In other words, success breeds success. Generally, libraries will do better when they concentrate on successes, rather than focusing excessively on how bad things are, and how much improvement is needed. There is a time and a place for everything. Obviously, at times you bring out the negative issues, but by and large, people want to be identified with success. It is for this reason that we try to focus on the library's achievements when we work with our library foundation in the community. People tend not to give their support to ineffective or static organizations.

A Proud Past, A Bright Future

Library service began in DeKalb County in 1907 in a small library in Lithonia. The Decatur Library was founded in 1925, and in 1926 the library opened on the second floor of the Decatur Building and Loan Association.

Maude M. Burrus was appointed as the first librarian in 1930 and served until 1961.

The main building at 215 Sycamore Street was constructed in 1950. In 1951 the Decatur DeKalb Library became a regional system and included the Rockdale County Library, and in 1953 the Newton County Library joined the system. In 1962 the system was renamed the DeKalb Library System, and in 1965 the library was named in honor of Maude M. Burrus.

In 1989 the DeKalb County Public Library withdrew from the three-county DeKalb-Rockdale-Newton regional system and established a single-county system.

Darro Willey became director of the DeKalb County Public Library in November 1995. In our interview, he shared a philosophy that emphasized consensus building with library staff and community. He identified "situational" management as appropriate in most cases, and a "culture of participation in decision making" as a unique characteristic of the DeKalb County Public Library. The library serves a diverse community where "no one social or ethnic group has an overwhelming presence. . . . It is a community that is tolerant of differences."

Willey identified the overall community relations role as the most important part of his job. He said it was important to know and be involved in the state, county, and city political arenas. Willey said that the assistant director plays a critical role and should take care of the inside library activities while the director concentrates on the overall community picture, budgetary matters, and political issues. The driving force for the library is patron needs, and technology is a means of providing service to address those needs.

In projecting the future, Willey said that there would still be books and buildings, and there would be more new ways of accessing information. He projected that the library would become a community destination, a place for the community to come together. This expectation was expressed in several librarian interviews in this study. Willey strongly recommended "the impression of forward motion for the community and for your own organization. . . . Success breeds success."

Chronology

1907	First library service began in DeKalb County in a small library in Lithonia
1925	Decatur Library founded
1926	Decatur Public Library opened on the second floor of the Decatur Building and Loan Association
1927	Decatur City Hall was built and the library was located on the second floor

1930	Maude M. Burris appointed the first director of the Decatur Public Library
1940	Bookmobile service officially began
1950	Main library building at 215 Sycamore Street constructed
1951	Decatur DeKalb Library became a regional system and included the neighboring Rockdale County Library
1953	Newton County Library joined the system
1961	Maude Burris retired and Louise Trotti appointed as her successor (DeKalb County Public Library n.d.c, 1)
1965	Decatur DeKalb Library named the Maude M. Burrus Library (DeKalb County Public Library n.d.b, 1)
1982	Barbara Loar appointed as successor to Louise Trotti after she retired in 1981
1983–1985	Committee of system staff and trustees cooperated to develop long-range plan, Strategies for the Future, focusing on the next five years
1985–1995	DeKalb County Library System facilities development plan developed
1986	Bond issue approved to build and stock new libraries and renovate and expand existing branches
1989	DeKalb County Public Library withdrew from the three-county DeKalb-Rockdale-Newton Regional System and established a single-county system.
1989	Maude M. Burris Library renamed the Decatur Library
1990	Wesley Chapel Library branch established
1991	Donna Mancini appointed as successor to Barbara Loar
1992	Wesley Chapel Library branch renamed the Wesley Chapel–William C. Brown Library
1995	Donna Mancini resigned as director to become director of Nashville and Davidson County Library
1995, November	Darro Willey, deputy director of the Broward County Library System in Fort Lauderdale, Florida, became director of the DeKalb County Public Library
1997	DCPL designated by the Library of Congress to host the Georgia Center for the Book

1998   Library foundation created to receive gifts and requests on behalf of the library (DeKalb County Public Library n.d.c, 1)

References

DeKalb County Public Library n.d.a. "Decatur History." http://www.dekalb.public.lib.ga.us/about/decahist.htm (accessed October 21, 2003).

DeKalb County Public Library. n.d.b. "Decatur History." http://www.dekalb.public.lib.ga.us/aboutdecahist.htm (accessed November 22, 2002).

DeKalb County Public Library. n.d.c. "History of DCPL." http://www.dekalb.public.lib.ga.us/about/dcplhist.htm (accessed October 21, 2003).

DeKalb County Public Library. n.d.d. "Library Board of Trustees." http://www.dekalb.public.lib.ga.us/about/board.htm (accessed October 21, 2003).

DeKalb County Public Library. n.d.e. "William C. Brown Biography." http://www.dekalb.public.lib.ga.us/branches/wcbrown.htm (accessed November 22, 2002).

DeKalb County Public Library. 2002. "Statistics." http://www.dekalb.public.lib.ga.us/sitemap.htm (accessed November 22, 2002).

Part III

Closing

11

The Public Library: A Tradition of Service, A Future of Performance

Advancing Public Libraries Through Community Service and Political Astuteness

After conducting interviews and research in public libraries in Great Britain and the United States, I identified similarities and differences regarding the libraries' development, organizational structures, and current philosophies. A commonality among all of the libraries was the commitment to service to their community of library users. Library administrators agreed on the library's role in the community. It should be "a gathering place," "a community destination," and the library should be "at the table as a community center."

The library administrators also expressed that it was essential that the library become a part of community life, and be relevant to the community. The consensus was that the director must empower staff in the branches and encourage them to develop services that are responsive to the special needs of their communities.

Political Role

Regarding the political role of the library administrator, Rick Ashton, the Denver city librarian, said that the administrator's political role makes the internal role harder, and that the staff must understand where the administator stands as a politician. "Within the city politics of Denver, my role is to *embody* the library, to demonstrate and deliver high performance, team spirit, and good cheer. By building personal credibility and trust, I also build the politicians' trust and support for DPL."

Adie Scott, the head of Croydon Libraries, identified her political responsibility as promoting the message of the changing and developing role of the libraries. Councillors, she asserted, must be informed of customers' requirements and of key issues and developments in the library.

Dorothy Miller, the Dunfermline librarian, was mindful of the central government as the primary funding source. Fife Councillor David Arnott emphasized, "A good librarian must be politically aware."

Pamela Pridgen, the Hattiesburg library director, echoed the statements of the British librarians: "Service is based on how the library is funded, and as a result the resources of a library are based on the political astuteness of the library manager."

On a slightly different note, Susan Hildreth, the San Francisco city librarian, said, "I don't see myself as a politician, but my job is a political one. I need to communicate well with all elected officials, making sure that they know the value of the library. I need to be politically sensitive as many of the service and facility issues that we are involved with can become politicized."

Taking a stronger position, Neel Parikh, the Pierce County Library System director, cited politician as the largest and most important role of the director. Everything involves political awareness, she noted, along with the ability to position the library and work effectively with leaders and decision makers. It cannot be done by the director alone. The staff's understanding of local issues and their credibility are important for developing good political relations.

Recommendations from San Diego's former and current directors, William Sannwald and Anna Tatar respectively, were to develop Friends groups and a strong relationship with the library commission. The more library advocates that can be recruited, the better, they noted, because politicians listen to an outsider more than to staff. Communication is critical.

The DeKalb County Public Library director does not see himself as a politician per se, but as one who works in particular political circles, with the political role holding the second most important position in the job, after an overall community relations role. He sees political and community issues as intertwined. Noting that the director must be highly visible in the community, he stated that the role of the library director as a politically involved figure cannot be overemphasized.

Management Styles

There was also consensus among the respondents about their management styles. The overall response was the participative approach, with the final, hard decisions in the hands of the administrators. The directors emphasized giving credit to hard-working and knowledgeable staffs. Achieving objectives through people was a common philosophy.

Two of the administrators stated that they encouraged staff to use their own judgment to make recommendations and choices. They wanted the staff to take appropriate responsibility for decision making. If a staff member made a wrong decision, no black marks would be put in his or her file.

The director of the Library of Hattiesburg, Petal, and Forrest County referred to a relatively new management strategy, "appreciative inquiry," which proposes to managers, "Take your successes and use them as a pattern for the future." Another approach was to be consistent and to balance the demands of the patrons with the professional opinions of the librarians, and the integrity of the staff. It was noted as important to have a responsive and flexible style with both the community and the staff.

Responding to patron needs was unanimously cited as the driving force of the library. Other driving forces mentioned were the possibilities of technology, the political environment, and the economy. One administrator observed that the national political environment had been driving libraries within the lifelong learning agenda for the past five years. Technology was generally identified as a method of delivery of services to meet patron needs.

British and American librarians agreed that traditional sources of funding would have to be supplemented by partnerships and by bids for competitive funding sources. In Great Britain, such sources as the New Opportunities Fund and the Heritage Lottery Fund have contributed, while in the United States, fund-raising by library foundations and Friends groups have historically supported public libraries.

Although there was a great deal of consensus among libraries, I saw three areas of differences between British and American libraries. They are organizational structure and governance, sources of funds, and the issue of censorship. Public library administrators in England and Scotland have a more complex route through the political hierarchy than their counterparts in the United States.

Organizational Structures and Funding Sources

A variety of public library organizational structures exist in the United States. In the libraries in this study, Pierce County Library System is a public library district; five libraries are city departments—Chicago Public Library, Fort Worth Public Library, San Diego Public Library, Denver Public Library, and San Francisco Public Library; DeKalb County Public Library is a county library; and the Library of Hattiesburg, Petal, and Forrest County is a city–county library. Chicago, San Francisco, and Pierce County are union operations.

The central government is the major funding source for libraries in Great Britain. The New Opportunities Fund (NOF) was established as a lottery distributor by the National Lottery Act of 1998. One of the programs, with an allocation of 20 million pounds, is designated to provide training for public library staff. The goal of the training "is to equip public library staff with the skills, knowledge and confidence to use ICT effectively in their day-to-day work and to use the new technology to benefit the users of public libraries" (New Opportunities Fund 1998, 3). Croydon Libraries and the Dunfermline Carnegie Library reported the advantages of this plan. They were also encouraged that politicians would better understand the educational and informational role of the public library.

In contrast, local property taxes provide the major funding for public libraries in the United States, federal and state funds on average make up only 15 to 20 percent of library resources. Federal money, in the form of grants, is channeled through the state library agencies.

Taxing structures for public libraries that are city departments vary. The San Francisco Public Library receives a share of tax collected, not additional tax above what is required for other services.

The Chicago Public Library is a home-rule entity. Separate bonds do not require a public referendum, but a city council vote. The first library bond passed in 1997 (48 to 2), and helped get the building projects going. In 1999, an $800 million bond passed the city council 49 to 1 to be used for new police stations, new fire stations, more new libraries, and some park improvements.

The DeKalb County Public Library and the health department operate with some degree of independence from the county administration. The library is legally a separate unit of administration. The county budget uses the term "payment to other governments" in listing the library line item. The DeKalb County Public Library director answers directly to the library board, and the board hires and terminates the library director. The library board has its own purchasing operation separate from the county's. Personnel operations are overseen by the county, and salaries are paid by the county. The library also hires and pays part-time merit-exempt employees.

In Washington, the Pierce County Library System is a junior taxing district funded from a separate tax levy. The system was established as a public library district in 1946. It resulted from an approval vote by the citizens of the unincorporated areas of Pierce County. Cities or towns can vote to annex, and they can vote to de-annex the system. The state law provides for an organized property tax structure, based on a millage rate.

Censorship and Other Issues

Another area where differences can be observed is around the issue of censorship. There are differences between Great Britain and the United States, and in the United States among individual libraries that adhere to "community standards." Accessibility to Internet sites and filtering Internet sites is a point of controversy in U.S. public libraries. The Children's Internet Protection Act (CIPA) allows the Federal Communications Commission (FCC) and the Institute of Museum and Library Services (IMLS) to withhold funding from public libraries that do not install filters on their computers (American Library Association 2002, 1). The American Library Association challenged the constitutionality of the CIPA and the lower court ruled in favor of the American Library Association. This ruling was appealed to the Supreme Court, and on June 23, 2003, the Supreme Court handed down its decision upholding the constitutionality of the Children's Internet Protection Act ("Supreme Court Upholds CIPA" 2003, 12).

In contrast, access to Internet sites did not seem to be a problem in Great Britain. Computer terminals were situated so that inappropriate sites would not be viewed. W. C. Berwick Sayers, chief librarian of Croydon Libraries in 1915, expressed a philosophy that continues into the present in public libraries in Great Britain, "If it is in print, you can get it at the public library" (Sayers 1947, 4). That philosophy also seems to apply to Internet sites in libraries in Great Britain.

Another interesting dissimilarity between Great Britain and United States libraries involved author royalties. The Public Lending Right Act, approved in the United Kingdom March 22, 1979, allows British authors to receive payment for the free lending of their books in public libraries (Parker 1999, 3). The Public Lending Right exists in Canada, the United Kingdom, Australia, and Germany, but not the United States.

It is worth noting that Andrew Carnegie extended his library philanthropy to public libraries in Great Britain and the United States. Five of the ten libraries in this study, Dunfermline, San Francisco, Fort Worth, Denver, and San Diego, received funding to establish their libraries from Andrew Carnegie.

The Future

Library administrators were cautiously optimistic as they discussed projected changes over the next ten years. A shift from government funding to monies from trusts and charitable organizations was predicted. Community support in the form of Friends of the Library organizations and other volunteers will play a major part in the success of libraries. State and national economic directions will affect the direction of library finances. Diversity among users will require expanded multicultural resources and services.

There is emphasis on information technology in all of the libraries and the role that it will play in providing services to the community. But one is reminded of the words of Chris Batt, when he was borough libraries and museum officer for Croydon Libraries, Museum and Arts, that information technology "cannot replace motivated staff, it cannot cover up bad management, it certainly cannot work without a clear vision of how services should progress into the future" (Batt 1994, iii).

Closing

Service to the public was obviously the priority in every library that I visited. Governing, funding, or organizational structures varied between Great Britain and the United States, and differed within the countries. Creative strategies, astute political behaviors, and a management style that worked in a particular community environment were requirements for success. Public library administrators made the right choices, and exemplary service to the people is the commitment in their libraries.

The mission of libraries today, although they may differ in wording and tone, remains much the same in spirit. James Baldwin's statement reprinted from *Library Journal* in Bob Usherwood's *Public Library as Public Knowledge* is a reminder of the opportunity and responsibility for public libraries:

"I went to the 135th Street library at least three or four times a week, and I read everything there. I read every single book in that library. I read books like they were some weird kind of food. I was looking in books for a bigger world than the world in which I lived" (Baldwin 1964, in Usherwood 1989 148). The libraries that will serve tomorrow's public will do just that—offer a "bigger world."

References

American Library Association. 2002. U.S. Supreme Court Arguments on CIPA Expected in Late Winter or Early Spring. http://www.ala.org/news/v814/cipa.html (accessed January 12, 2003).

Baldwin, James. 1964. "The Library's War on Poverty." *Library Journal* (September 15): 3375. Reprinted in *The Public Library as Public Knowledge*, by Bob Usherwood. London: Library Association Publishing, 1989.

Batt, Chris. 1994. *Information Technology in Public Libraries*. London: Library Association Publishing.

New Opportunities Fund. 1998. *ICT Training for Public Library Staff*, 3.

Parker, Jim. 1999. Introduction in *Whose Loan Is It Anyway?* Essays in Celebration of PLR's Twentieth Anniversary 2003. Registrar of Public Lending Right.

Sayers, W. C. Berwick. 1947. "The Province and Purpose of the Public Library." Croydon Public Libraries. Croydon, UK.

"Supreme Court Upholds CIPA." *American Libraries* 34, no. 7 (August 2003): 12–17.

Appendix: Timelines

Great Britain

Libraries Established Under the Museums Act of 1845

1847   Canterbury (Kelly 1977, 10)

1848   Warrington, first municipal rate-supported free library (Kelly 1977, 10)

1849   Salford (Kelly 1977, 11)

1850   Public Libraries Act of 1850, the first public library act. Major proponents were members of Parliament William Ewart and Joseph Brotherton, and a librarian, Edward Edwards (Kelly 1977, 3)

1851   Winchester, first public library to open under the act of 1850 (Kelly 1977, 41)

1852   Manchester, first major library, opened September 2 under the 1850 act. Edward Edwards appointed first librarian (Kelly 1977, 41)

1852   Liverpool, second major civic library, opened October 18 (Kelly 1977, 44)

1861   Birmingham, third major civic library, opened (Kelly 1977, 47)

1866   Library act removed the population limit for establishment of a library (Kelly 1977, 21)

1867   Free Libraries Act (Kelly 1977, 110)

1870   Leeds, last of four big civic libraries, established (Kelly 1977, 49)

1868–1886   Second phase of public library development; majority were in centers of industry and commerce; London still lagged behind (Kelly 1977, 24)

1870   Education Act (Kelly 1977, 19)

1875   Public Health Act (Kelly 1977, 3)

1877   Library Association of the United Kingdom established in October (Kelly 1977, 100)

1878   Reading rooms opened on Sundays in Manchester (Kelly 1977, 43)

1880   Dunfermline Town Council adopted the Free Libraries Act of 1867 (Murison 1971, 66)

1883   Dunfermline Public Library, Andrew Carnegie's first gift of a library to the town of his birth, opened (Kelly 1977, 116)

1887   Total of 125 libraries opened before 1887 (Kelly 1977, 32)

1888   Croydon Council adopted the Public Libraries Act of 1850 (Roberts 1985)

1890   Croydon Library opened in two shop premises, 104 and 106 North End (Roberts 1985)

1891   Elementary education made free (Education Resources 2002, 1)

1892   Public Libraries Act of 1892 simplified the confusion of terminology regarding library authorities (Kelly 1977, 110–111)

1893   The library association began to try to meet the needs of training and started offering summer schools, classes, and correspondence courses; Library Assistants' Association (founded in 1895) also helped arrange meetings and study circles (Kelly 1977, 205)

1896   The Croydon Library moved to new premises in the new town hall in Katharine Street (Roberts 1985)

1896   The Croydon Lending Library was opened, one of the first libraries in the country to allow readers to choose books from the shelves (Roberts 1985)

1898   L. Stanley Jast appointed chief librarian of Croydon Libraries; during his tenure (1898–1915) Croydon Libraries expanded in size and range of activities (Roberts 1985)

1898   Jast established telephone links between Croydon Central Library and the branches (Roberts 1985)

1899   Library association began publishing its own journal, *The Library Association Record* (Kelly 1977, 102)

1905–1915 Stanley Jast was president of the library association (Roberts 1985)

1919 The first full-time school of librarianship was established at University College, London, with the help of a five-year grant from the Carnegie Trust (Kelly 1977, 206)

1920 The original Dunfermline Public Library building extended, funded by the Carnegie Dunfermline Trust (see Neale interview, chapter 1)

1920 In Croydon, the children's library opened, the first in the country, and the first to have a woman in charge, Edith G. Hayler (Hayler 1928)

1927 Croydon's children's librarian, Edith G. Hayler, visited children's libraries in the United States and Canada (Hayler 1928)

1933 "Croydon had the largest library system in the South of England with a bookstock of 278,000 and an annual issue in 1932/3 of 2,142,106" ("Croydon Public Libraries Facts of 1933–34")

1974 Local government reorganization in Scotland ended town councils; Dunfermline and surrounding areas became Dunfermline District (see Neale interview, chapter 1)

1978 The first committee meeting of the staff association (CPLSA) of Croydon Libraries was held (Roberts 1985)

1979 The Public Lending Right Act, which by law allows authors to receive payment for the free lending of their works, was approved in Great Britain (Parker 1999, 3)

1983 The Code of Professional Conduct was approved by library association council and the annual general meeting in accordance with the library association's bylaw 45(a) (Library Association 1998, 1)

1993 New Croydon Central Library was formally opened November 5 during National Library Week by Heritage Secretary Peter Brooke (Broad Brief for Croydon Suppliers 1993)

1996 Local government in Scotland reorganized again; Dunfermline District and two other adjoining districts combined under one authority, Fife Council (see Neale interview, chapter 1)

1998 The New Opportunities Fund (NOF) was established as a lottery distributor by the National Lottery Act (New Opportunities Fund, 3)

United States

1731	Benjamin Franklin and fifty of his friends formed the Library Company of Philadelphia (subscription library) (Sager 1984, 11)
1803	Caleb Bingham bequeathed 150 books suitable for children to Salisbury, Connecticut, to establish the first children's library in the United States (American Library Association 1997, 1)
1833	Peterborough Town Library established in Peterborough, New Hampshire (Sager 1984, 11–12)
1849	New Hampshire Act of 1849 provided for the establishment of public libraries (Sager 1984, 12)
1851	Massachussetts Act of 1851, an act to authorize cities and towns to establish and maintain public libraries (Shera 1965, insert between pages 192 and 193)
1854	The reading room of the Boston Public Library opened (Shera 1949, 157)
1871–1872	English book donation; after the great Chicago fire, October 8, 1871, citizens of England presented a "free library to Chicago" which led to citizen approval of the Illinois Library Act (Chicago Public Library 2000, 1)
1872	Illinois Library Act approved (Chicago Public Library 2000, 1)
1873	Chicago Public Library opened in January (Chicago Public Library 2000, 1)
1876	American Library Association founded in Philadelphia (American Library Association 1997, 1)
1876	The *Library Journal* was established
1879	San Francisco Public Library opened (Ferguson 1985, 3–4)
1880	California State Legislature approved an act to establish free public libraries and reading rooms; the act gave cities the authority to levy taxes for this purpose (Breed 1983, 179)
1882	Caroline Hewins introduced children's storytelling to U.S. public libraries at the Hartford, Connecticut, public library (American Library Association 1997, 1)
1882	City of San Diego first levied a tax for library support (Breed 1983, 179)

1882	San Diego Public Library opened on the second floor of the Commercial Bank and included a small reading room for ladies (Breed 1983, 179)
1882	The citizens of Baltimore approved the acceptance of a gift from Enoch Pratt, a New England merchant, of funding for a central library, branches in four quarters of the city, and an endowment, a gift to his adopted home worth $1,145,833 (Enoch Pratt Free Library 2002, 1,2)
1884	The first library school authorized by Columbia University (Bobinski 1969, 8)
1886	Andrew Carnegie first donation of library to Allegheny, Pennsylvania (Bobinski 1969, 13)
1889	Denver Public Library opened (Denver Public Library 2002, 1)
1889	Los Angeles Public Library was considered a municipal agency, although it still charged subscription fees to its users (Sager 1984, 12)
1890	Carnegie gift to Johnstown, Pennsylvania (Bobinski 1969, 78)
1890	Carnegie gift of a main building and eight branches to Pittsburgh, Pennsylvania (Bobinski 1969, 13)
1892	Carnegie gift of a library building to Fairfield, Iowa (Bobinski 1969, 13)
1895	Carnegie gift of a library building to Braddock, Pennsylvania (Bobinski 1969, 77)
1895	New York Public Library formed from a combination of all of New York's libraries (Sager 1984, 12)
1896	Carnegie gift of a library building to Homestead, Pennsylvania (Bobinski 1969, 13)
1896	New Orleans Public Library founded (Sager 1984, 12)
1896	The monthly journal *Public Libraries* began publication (Bobinski 1969, 8)
1899	San Diego was the recipient of Andrew Carnegie's first gift to any library west of the Mississippi (Breed 1983, 179)
1901	Fort Worth Carnegie Public Library opened (Taylor 1968, 92)
1902	San Diego Public Library, as a result of Carnegie's gift, opened April 23 (Breed 1983, 179)

1906   Earthquake destroyed San Francisco city hall, the main library, and two of the six branches opened before the earthquake ("San Francisco Public Library" n.d., 7)

1916   The city of Hattiesburg Public Library established (Library of Hattiesburg, Petal, and Forrest County Library 1995–2002b, 1)

1917   New San Francisco main library opened (Wiley 1996, 10)

1917   The first American library union is formed at the New York Public Library (American Library Association 1977, 1)

1926   Carnegie Corporation announces a $4 million grant program to improve library education (American Library Association 1977, 1)

1930   The DeKalb Public Library opened with Maude Burrus as director (DeKalb County Public Library n.d., 1)

1935   A bond issue was ratified on September 3 for a new Fort Worth library building (Fort Worth Public Library 2002, 1, 2)

1937   Presidential approval for a federal loan and grant was given to Fort Worth on August 24 (Fort Worth Public Library 2002, 1, 2)

1937   Carnegie Building (Fort Worth) closed December 2 and the library moved to temporary headquarters (Fort Worth Public Library 2002, 1, 2)

1939   Library opened in new quarters as Fort Worth Public Library on June 15 (Taylor 1968, 94)

1939   Library Bill of Rights is adopted (American Library Association 1997, 1)

1946   Pierce County Library System in Washington established as a public library district (Pierce County Library System 2001)

1948   Fort Worth Public Library Staff Association (FWPLSA) formed in January (Kinney 1951, 30, 31)

1950   *Public Library Inquiry* overall report published (Bobinski 1969, 199)

1952   The San Diego Carnegie Building demolished (Breed 1983, 180)

1954   New central San Diego Public Library opened June 28 (Breed 1983, 180)

1978   New central Fort Worth Public Library opened in an underground building (Fort Worth Public Library 2002, 1, 2)

1996   The new Library of Hattiesburg, Petal, and Forrest County opened (Library of Hattiesburg, Petal, and Forrest County 1995–2002b, 1)

1997   The Bill and Melinda Gates Foundation joined with public libraries to improve access to technology; by the end of 2003, the foundation will have fulfilled its commitment of $250 million to install 40,000 computers in 10,000 libraries (Bill and Melinda Gates Foundation 2002, 2)

1999   Expansion on the Fort Worth Central Library began in 1993 and was completed in 1999 (Fort Worth Public Library 2002, 1, 2)

2000   A tornado caused over $1 million of damage to the Fort Worth Central Library (Fort Worth Public Library 2002, 1, 2)

2001   The centennial of the Fort Worth Central Library celebrated in October; the library had been repaired and rebuilt after the tornado in 2000 (Fort Worth Public Library 2002, 1, 2)

References

American Library Association. 1997. "About ALA." http://www.ala.org/pio/alaid.html (accessed February 2, 2003).

Bill and Melinda Gates Foundation. 2002. "Connections—Progress in Libraries." http://gatesfoundation.org/libraries/relatedinfo/connections/connectionsvol11.htm (accessed January 23, 2003).

Bobinski, George S. 1969. *Carnegie Libraries: Their History and Impact on American Public Library Development.* Chicago: American Library Association.

Breed, Clara. 1983. *Turning the Pages: San Diego Public Library History 1882–1982.* Kingsport, TN: Kingsport Press.

"Broad Brief for Croydon Suppliers." 1993. *Library Association Record Trade Supplement* 9 (December).

Chicago Public Library. 2000. "A Free Public Library for Chicago." In "History of the Chicago Public Library: Windows on Our Past." http://www.chipublib.org/003cpl/003cpl.html (accessed November 15, 2001).

"Croydon Public Libraries Facts of 1933–1934." Local Studies and Archives, Croydon Central Library, Croydon, UK.

DeKalb County Public Library. n.d. "Decatur History." http://www.dekalb.public.lib.ga.us/about/dcplhist.htm (accessed November 22, 2002).

Denver Public Library. 2002. "DPL History." http://www.denver.lib.co.us/about_us/history.html (accessed October 16, 2003).

Education Resources. 2002. "Key Dates in Education: Great Britain 1100–1899." http://www.netcentral.co.uk/steveb/dates/education.htm (accessed February 2, 2003).

Enoch Pratt Free Library. 2002. "Enoch Pratt's Legacy: A History of the Enoch Pratt Free Library, Every Person's Favorite Library." http://www.pratt.lib.md.us/info/history (accessed February 2, 2003).

Ferguson, Jane. 1985. "Revised History of the San Francisco Public Library." San Francisco History Center, San Francisco Public Library, San Francisco, CA, January 9.

Fort Worth Public Library. 2002. "History of the Fort Worth Public Library." http://www.fortworthlibrary.org/history.htm (accessed August 30, 2001).

Hayler, Ethel G. 1928. "A Report to the Croydon Public Libraries Committee on a Personal Visit to America, August and September, 1927." Children's Central Library, Town Hall, Croydon, UK.

Kelly, Thomas. 1977. *A History of Public Libraries in Great Britain, 1845–1975.* London: Library Association.

Kinney, Helen Toombs. 1951. "History of Public Library of Fort Worth, Texas." Local History Room, Fort Worth Public Library, Fort Worth, Texas.

Library Association. 1998. "The Library Association's Code of Professional Conduct." http://www.la-hq.org.uk/directory/about/conduct.html (accessed January 29, 2003).

Library of Hattiesburg, Petal, and Forrest County. 1995–2002b. "Welcome to the Library." http://www.hpfc.lib.ms.us/introduc.html (accessed November 22, 2002).

Murison, W.J. 1971. *The Public Library: Its Origins, Purpose, and Significance.* London: Harrap & Co.

New Opportunities Fund. *ICT Training for Public Library Staff,* 3.

Parker, Jim. 1999. Introduction in "Whose Loan Is It Anyway?" in *Essays in Celebration of PLR's Twentieth Anniversary.* Registrar of Public Lending Right.

Pierce County Library System. 2001. *Overview.* March.

Roberts, Richard. 1985. "Croydon Public Libraries—A Brief History." Local Studies and Archives, Croydon Central Library, Croydon, UK.

Sager, Donald. 1984. *Managing the Public Library.* White Plains, NY, and London: Knowledge Industry Publications.

"San Francisco Public Library." n.d. San Francisco History Center, San Francisco Public Library, San Francisco, CA.

Shera, Jesse E. 1965. *Foundations of the Public Library.* North Haven, CT. The Shoe String Press (Orig. pub. 1949.)

Taylor, Robert Noel. 1968. "Jennie Schott Scheuber: An Approach to Librarianship." Local History Room, Fort Worth Public Library, Fort Worth, Texas.

Wiley, Peter Booth. 1996. *A Free Library in This City.* San Francisco: Weldon Owen.

Selected Bibliography and Guide to Online Sources

American Library Association. 1997. "About ALA." http//www.ala.org/ pio/alaid.html (accessed February 2, 2003).

American Library Association. 2002. http://www.ala.org/news/v814/cipa. htm (accessed January 12, 2003).

Audit Scotland. 2001. "Annual Report 2000–2001." http://www.audit-scot-land.gov.uk/annualreport/index.htm (accessed November 7, 2002).

Baldwin, James. 1964. "The Library's War on Poverty." *Library Journal* (September 15): 3375. Reprinted in *The Public Library as Public Knowledge*, by Bob Usherwood. London: Library Association Publishing, 1989.

Batt, Chris. 1994. *Information Technology in Public Libraries*. London: Library Association Publishing.

Batt, Chris. 1996. *The Public Library and the Learning Society*. Local Studies and Archives, Croydon Central Library, Croydon, UK.

Berry, John N. 2002. "More Successful Than Begging." *Library Journal* 127, no. 11 (June 15): 8.

Bill and Melinda Gates Foundation. 2002. "Connections—Progress in Libraries." http://gatesfoundation.org/libraries/relatedinfo/connections/ connectionsvol11.htm (accessed January 23, 2003).

Bill Strong's Eclectic Mississippi Photo Tour, n.d. "New Hattiesburg Library." http://www.phototour.com/echtml/library.html (accessed October 20, 2003).

215

Bobinski, George S. 1969. *Carnegie Libraries: Their History and Impact on American Public Library Development*. Chicago: American Library Association.

Brawner, Lee B. 1993. "The People's Choice: Public Library Districts." *Library Journal* 118, no. 1 (January): 59–62.

Breed, Clara E. 1983. *Turning the Pages: San Diego Public Library History 1882–1982*. Kingsport, TN: Kingsport Press.

"Broad Brief for Croydon Suppliers." 1993. *Library Association Record Trade Supplement* 9 (December).

Carnegie, Andrew. 1920. *Autobiography of Andrew Carnegie*. Boston and New York: Houghton Mifflin.

Chicago Public Library. 2000a. "Appendix: The Librarians." In "History of the Chicago Public Library: Windows on Our Past." http://www.chipublib.org/003cpl/003cpl.html (accessed November 15, 2001).

Chicago Public Library. 2000b. "Early Development of the Chicago Public Library." In "History of the Chicago Public Library: Windows on Our Past." http://www.chipublib.org/003cpl/003cpl.html (accessed November 15, 2001).

Chicago Public Library. 2000c. "A Free Public Library for Chicago." In "History of the Chicago Public Library: Windows on Our Past." http://www.chipublib.org/003cpl/003cpl.html (accessed November 15, 2001).

Chicago Public Library. 2000d. "A New Central Library." In "History of the Chicago Public Library: Windows on Our Past." http://www.chipublib.org/003cpl/003cpl.html (accessed November 15, 2001).

Chicago Public Library. 2000e. "A New Kind of Library: Looking Toward the 21st Century." In "History of the Chicago Public Library: Windows on Our Past." http://www.chipublib.org/003cpl/003.html (accessed November 15, 2001).

Chicago Public Library. 2000f. "Serving the Neighborhoods." In "History of the Chicago Public Library: Windows on Our Past." http://www.chipublib.org/003cpl/003cpl.html (accessed November 15, 2001).

Chicago Public Library. 2000g. "Serving the Neighborhoods." In History of the Chicago Public Library: Windows on Our Past." http://www.chipublib.org/003cpl/cpl125/neighborhoods.html (accessed October 10, 2003).

Chicago Public Library. 2002. "Chicago Public Library Mission." http://www.chipublib.org/003cpl/003cpl.html. (accessed November 15, 2001).

Chicago Public Library. 2003. "This Month at CPL What's New?" http://www.chipublib.org/003cpl/003whatsnew.html (accessed October 15, 2003).

City and County of Denver. 2003. "Elected Officials." http://www.denvergov.org/jump_elected_officials.asp. (accessed November 22, 2003).

City of Hattiesburg. n.d. Municipal Minute Book "J." Hattiesburg, Mississippi.

City of San Diego. n.d. "Library Building Projects; New Main Library." http://www.sannet.gov/public-library/about-the-library/newmain.shtml (accessed October 12, 2003).

City of San Diego. 2001. Manager's Report. San Diego, CA (February 22).

City of San Diego. 2002. "San Diego Public Library Mission Statement." http://www.sannet.gov/public-library/about-the-library/mission.shtml (accessed June 30, 2002).

Convention of Scottish Local Authorities (COSLA). 1995. *Standards for the Public Library Services in Scotland.* Cited in Audit Scotland, "Annual Report 2000–2001" (2001).

Croydon Council. 1999. *Croydon Libraries News* 3 (September). http://www.croydon.gov.uk/ledept/libraries/cr-libnews.3.htm (accessed July 7, 2002).

Croydon Council. 2000. *Croydon Libraries News* 5 (March). http://www.croydon.gov.uk/LEDept/libraries/cr-libnews5.htm (accessed March 6, 2001).

Croydon Council. 2001a. "Annual Library Plan 2001." London: Croydon Council. http://www.croydon.gov.uk/LEDept/libraries/cr-libs.htm (accessed December 8, 2001).

Croydon Council. 2001b. "Annual Library Plan 2001 Consultation. London: Croydon Council. http://www.croydon.gov.uk/LEDept/libraries/cr-libs.htm (accessed December 8, 2001).

Croydon Council. 2001c. *Croydon Libraries News* 9 (April). http://www.croydon.gov.uk/ledept/libraries/cr-libnews9.htm (accessed July 7, 2002).

Croydon Council. 2002a. "Annual Library Plan, 2002." London: Croydon Council. http://www.croydon.gov.uk/LEDept/libraries/Annual_Library_plan_2002.htm (accessed November 13, 2002).

Croydon Council. 2002b. Croydon Online. http://www.croydononline.org (accessed July 9, 2002).

Croydon Council. 2002c. "Library Developments." http://www.croydon. gov.uk/LEDept/libraries/cr-libs.htm (accessed October 21, 2002).

Croydon Council DCMS (Department of Culture, Media and Sport). 2001. "Appraisal of Annual Library Plans and Approach to the Public Library Standards—2001: Report on Outcomes and Issues." London: Croydon Council. http://www.culture.gov.uk/heritage/index.html (accessed November 28, 2001).

"Croydon Public Libraries Facts of 1933–34." (Local Studies and Archives, Croydon Central Library, Croydon, UK.

Dahlgren, Anders C. 2001. "Solutions in Hand, Planners Earn High Marks from Their Peers." *American Libraries* 32, no. 4 (April): 64–72).

Davis, Kathy. 2001. "Murals in Mississippi Libraries." *Mississippi Libraries* 65, no. 1 (Spring). http://www.misslib.org/publications/ml/spr01/murals.htm.

DeKalb County Public Library. n.d.a "Decatur History." http://www. dekalb.public.lib.ga.us/about/decahist.htm (accessed October 21, 2003).

DeKalb County Public Library. n.d.b. "Decatur History." http://www. dekalb.public.lib.ga.us/about/dcplhist.htm (accessed November 22, 2002).

DeKalb County Public Library. n.d.c. "History of DCPL." http://www. dekalb.public.lib.ga.us/about/dcplhist.htm (accessed October 21, 2003).

DeKalb County Public Library. n.d.d. "Library Board of Trustees." http:// www.dekalb.public.lib.ga.us/about/board.htm (accessed October 21, 2003).

DeKalb County Public Library. n.d.e. "William C. Brown Biography." http://www.dekalb.public.lib.ga.us/branches/wcbrown.htm (accessed November 22, 2002).

DeKalb County Public Library. 2002. "Statistics." http://www.dekalb.public.lib.ga.us/about/stats.htm (accessed November 22, 2002).

Denver Public Library. 2002a. "DPL History." http://www.denver.lib.co. us/about_us/history.html accessed September 13, 2002).

Denver Public Library. 2002b. "Mission & Organization." http://www .denver.lib.co.us/about_us/dpl_mission.html (accessed September 21, 2002).

Denver Public Library. 2003a. "DPL: About Us." http://www.denver.lib.co .us/about_history.html (accessed October 16, 2003).

Denver Public Library. 2003b. "DPL News, Featured Branch Events." http://www.denver.lib.co.us/dpl/news/hennen.html (accessed November 14, 2003).

Education Resources. 2002. "Key Dates in Education: Great Britain 1100–1899. http://www.netcentral.co.uk/steveb/dates/education.htm (accessed February 2, 2003).

Enoch Pratt Free Library. 2002. "Enoch Pratt's Legacy: A History of Enoch Pratt Free Library. Every Person's Favorite Library." http:// www.pratt.lib.md.us/info/history (accessed February 2, 2003).

Ferguson, Jane. 1985. "Revised History of the San Francisco Public Library." San Francisco History Center, San Francisco Public Library, San Francisco, CA, January 9.

Fort Worth Public Library. n.d.a "Long-Range Services Plan." http://www. fortworthlibrary/org/lrsp_2.htm (accessed November 17, 2003).

Fort Worth Public Library. n.d.b. "Long Range Services Plan Presentation to City Council on April 8." http://www.fortworthlibrary.org/14_apr8. htm (accessed November 10, 2003).

Fort Worth Public Library. 2001. "Press Releases." http://www/fortworth-library.org/press.htm (accessed December 30, 2001).

Fort Worth Public Library. 2002. "History of the Fort Worth Public Library." http://www.fortworthlibrary.org/history.htm (accessed August 30, 2001).

Greiner, Joy. 1998. "Collection Development in the Information Age: Great Britain's Public Libraries." In *Public Library Collection Development in the Information Age*, ed. Annabel K. Stephens, 73–89. Binghamton, NY: Haworth Press.

Hattiesburg American (Hattiesburg, Mississippi). 1930. May 21.

Hayler, Ethel G. 1928. "A Report to the Croydon Public Libraries Committee on a Personal Visit to America, August and September, 1927." Children's Library, Croydon Central Library, Town Hall, Croydon, UK.

Hennen, Thomas J. 2002. "Great American Public Libraries: The 2002 HAPLR Rankings." *American Libraries* 33, no. 9 (October): 64–68.

Hennen, Thomas J. 2003. "Great American Public Libraries: The 2003 HAPLR Rankings." *American Libraries* 34, no. 9 (October): 44–49.

Kelly, Thomas. 1977. *A History of Public Libraries in Great Britain, 1845–1975.* London: Library Association.

Kinney, Helen Toombs. 1951. "History of Public Library of Fort Worth, Texas." Local History Room, Fort Worth Public Library, Fort Worth, Texas.

Library Association. 1998. "The Library Association's Code of Professional Conduct." http://www.la-hq.org.uk/directory/about/conduct. html (accessed January 29, 2003).

Library of Hattiesburg, Petal, and Forrest County. 1995–2002a. "Special Library Services." http://www.hpfc.lib.ms.us/special.html (accessed November 22, 2002).

Library of Hattiesburg, Petal, and Forrest County. 1995–2002b. "Welcome to the Library." http://www.hpfc.lib.ms.us/introduc.html (accessed November 22, 2002).

Library of Hattiesburg, Petal, and Forest County. 2003. "Forever Free: Abraham Lincoln's Journey to Emancipation." http://www.hpfc.lib. ms.us/lincoln/desc.html (accessed November 5, 2003).

Local Government etc. (Scotland) Act 1994. 1994. http://www.hmso.gov. uk/acts/acts1994/Ukpga_19940039_en_1.htm (accessed October 23, 2003).

Lowe, John Adams. 1937. *Report of a Survey of the Public Library of Fort Worth for Trustees of Fort Worth Public Library Association, Nov. 4–11, 1937.* Chicago: American Library Association.

McAdam, Doug. 1988. *Freedom Summer.* New York: Oxford University Press.

McCook, Kathleen de la Pena. 2000. *A Place at the Table.* Chicago and London: American Library Association.

Mailer, Norman. 1968. *Miami and the Siege of Chicago.* New York: Signet Books.

Mississippi Library Commission. 1971. *History of the Hattiesburg Forrest Co. Public Library.* Compiled under the direction of the Mississippi Library Commission, Jackson, Mississippi.

Munford, W. A. 1968. *Penny Rate.* London: Library Association.

Murison, W. J. 1971. *The Public Library: Its Origins, Purpose, and Significance.* London: Harrap & Co.

New Opportunities Fund. 1998. *ICT Training for Public Library Staff,* 3

News (Croydon, UK). 1997. February 28, 13.

Parikh, Neel. 2001. "Grants Awarded for New Projects." Pierce County Library System. July 23.

Parker, Jim. 1999. Introduction in *Whose Loan Is It Anyway?* Registrar of Public Lending Right.

PCLS Administration. 2001. "Board Meeting Minutes." February 14. http://www.pcl.lib.wa.us/BoardMinutes/BMFeb_14_2001.htm (accessed November 10, 2003).

People's Network. 2002. http://www.peoplesnetwork.gov.uk (accessed December 8, 2001).

Pierce County Library System. n.d. "About the Pierce County Library Foundation." http://www.pcl.lib.wa.us/foundation/about.html (accessed November 15, 2003).

Pierce County Library System. 2001. *Overview*. March.

Pierce County Library System. 2002a. "Pierce County Library System Administration." http://www.pcl.lib.wa.us/pcl_info.htm (accessed September 14–19, 2002).

Pierce County Library System. 2002b. "PCLS Administration: A Short History of our Library System." http://www.pcl.lib.wa.us/pclhistory. htm (accessed September 19, 2002).

Roberts, Richard. 1985. "Croydon Public Libraries—A Brief History." Local Studies and Archives, Croydon Central Library, Croydon, UK.

R. R. Bowker. 2001–2002. *American Library Directory*. 54th ed., Vol. 1. New Providence, NJ: R. R. Bowler.

Sager, Donald. 1984. *Managing the Public Library*. White Plains, NY, and London: Knowledge Industry Publications.

"San Francisco Public Library." n.d. San Francisco History Center, San Francisco Public Library, San Francisco, CA.

San Francisco Public Library. 2001. "News Release: Paul Underwood Appointed San Francisco Deputy City Librarian." News Release Archives, November 13. http://sfpl4.sfpl.org/news/news_releases. html (accessed November 15, 2001).

Sayers, W. C. Berwick. 1947. "The Province and Purpose of the Public Library." Croydon Public Libraries. Croydon, UK.

Shera, Jesse E. 1965. *Foundations of the Public Library*. North Haven, CT: Shoe String Press. (Orig. pub. 1949.)

Support the Next Generation's Library—A Bond Campaign. 1992. Scrapbook submitted to the John Cotton Dana Public Relations Awards Contest.

"Supreme Court Upholds CIPA." 2003, *American Libraries* 34, no. 7 (August): 12–16.

Tacoma Rotary #8. 2001. Tacoma, Washington. (February).

Taylor, Robert Noel. 1968. "Jennie Scott Scheuber: An Approach to Librarianship." Local History Room, Fort Worth Public Library. Fort Worth, Texas.

Texas State Historical Association. 2002. "Jennie Scott Scheuber." The Handbook of Texas Online. http://www.tsha.utexas.edu/handbook/online/articles/view/SS/fsc39.html (accessed July 18, 2002).

Tusa, Bobs. 1998. "How the Civil Rights Movement Came to the Hattiesburg Public Library." *Mississippi Libraries* 62, no. 3 (Fall): 56–57.

Wiley, Peter Booth. 1996. *A Free Library in This City*. San Francisco: Weldon Owen.

Worden, Frances B. 1971. "The Mirror: A History of the Carnegie Public Library of Fort Worth, Texas. 1901–1939." Master's thesis, Texas Woman's University, Local History Room, Fort Worth Public Library, Fort Worth, Texas.

Index

About the Author

JOY M. GREINER is an associate professor in the School of Library and Information Science at the University of Southern Mississippi. She was director of the school from 1991 to 1999. She received a Ph.D. in library science from Florida State University. Her publications include *Research Issues in Public Librarianship, Trends for the Future* (Greenwood Press, 1994). Other publications include articles in *Library Trends, Public Libraries, The Acquisitions Librarian,* and *Advances in Library Administration and Organization.* She is a former public library administrator and has served as a consultant in the public library field.

Recent Titles in
The Libraries Unlimited Library Management Collection
Formerly entitled Greenwood Library Management Collection